MATILDA

MATILDA

EMPRESS
QUEEN
WARRIOR

CATHERINE HANLEY

YALE UNIVERSITY PRESS
NEW HAVEN AND LONDON

For information about this and other Yale University Press publications, please contact:
U.S. Office: sales.press@yale.edu   yalebooks.com
Europe Office: sales@yaleup.co.uk   yalebooks.co.uk

Set in Adobe Caslon Pro by IDSUK (DataConnection) Ltd
Printed in Great Britain by Bell & Bain Ltd, Glasgow

Library of Congress Control Number: 2018962168

ISBN 978-0-300-22725-3

A catalogue record for this book is available from the British Library.

10 9 8 7 6 5 4 3 2

For James

CONTENTS

MAPS AND TABLES

Maps

Genealogical tables

ILLUSTRATIONS

ACKNOWLEDGEMENTS

AS EVER I AM GREATLY indebted to a number of friends and colleagues for their assistance and encouragement, and it is a pleasure to thank them here.

Heather McCallum and Rachael Lonsdale at Yale were enthusiastic from the start about a new book on Matilda, as was my agent Kate Hordern, who has been a tower of strength throughout; they have all helped me to navigate my way along a lengthy path. Marika Lysandrou has been a rock throughout the latter stages of the publication process, and her help with the intricacies of the plate section was much appreciated.

Helen Castor, whose own book *She-Wolves: The Women Who Ruled England before Elizabeth* (along with its associated TV series) shines a spotlight on Matilda, was kind enough to read and comment on large swathes of draft text, particularly those that related to issues of gender and to Matilda's relationship with her half-brother Robert of Gloucester; I am extremely grateful for her time and insight.

Susan Brock, my former colleague, now supposedly 'retired', read through the draft book in its entirety and was as always both indefatigable and insightful; the end result is much the better for her ideas and attention to detail.

My thanks also go to Levi Roach, an expert on medieval Germany and the Salians, who read Chapter 1 and picked me up on numerous points of detail to do with the Investiture Controversy and the (emphatically not, at this time, Holy Roman) Empire; to Sophie Harwood, a PhD researcher

ACKNOWLEDGEMENTS

working on medieval women at war, who was kind enough to share thoughts, references and the latest thinking on the subject; to Andrew Buck, a specialist on the crusades, who supplied much useful information on the Crusader states and on Melisende of Jerusalem in particular; to Minji Lee, a PhD researcher working on medieval women, for her translation of passages from the *Draco Normannicus*; and to Dean Irwin, who located and drew to my attention the poem 'He Never Smiled Again', which is mentioned in Chapter 2. Any errors or inaccuracies that remain in the book are of course my own; please feel free to send me tweets written entirely in capital letters.

The sourcing of images for the plate section was made considerably easier thanks to the advice and generous contributions of a number of people and institutions: I would particularly like to thank Oliver Creighton, James Lancaster, Jon Mann, the 'Anarchy? War and Status in Twelfth-Century Landscapes of Conflict' project of the Centre for Medieval Studies at the University of Exeter, the Friends of Reading Abbey, the British Library, the Parker Library, Roxburghe Estates and all those who upload their images to the Pixabay photo-sharing website along with permission to reproduce them.

On a personal level I would like to express my love and gratitude to my three wonderful children, for whom the arrival in the post of replica swords and spearheads no longer comes as any surprise; and to my long-suffering husband James, who works in a field about as far removed from medieval studies as it is possible to get. This one, finally, is for you.

xii

Map 1 England in the twelfth century

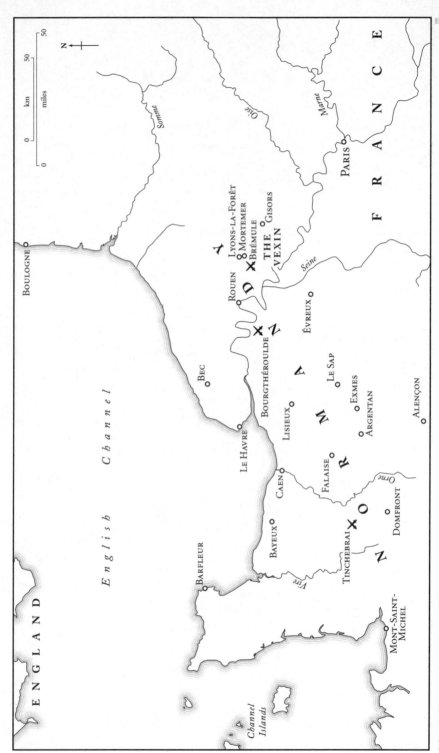

Map 2 Normandy in the twelfth century

The Anglo-Norman kings and queens of England

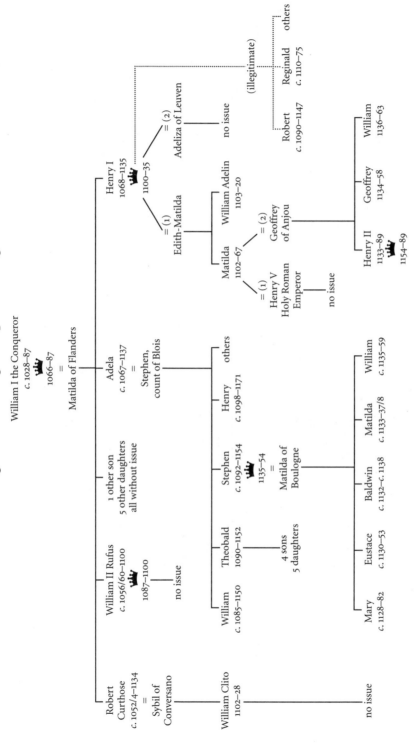

Table 1 The Anglo-Norman kings and queens of England

The Anglo-Saxon and Scottish royal line

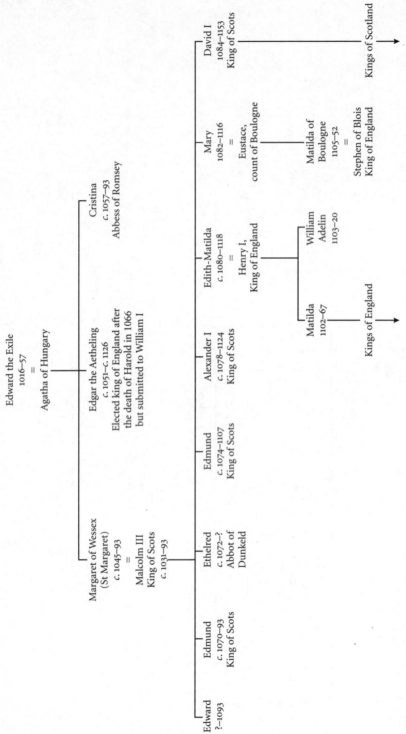

Table 2 The Anglo-Saxon and Scottish royal line

The house of Anjou

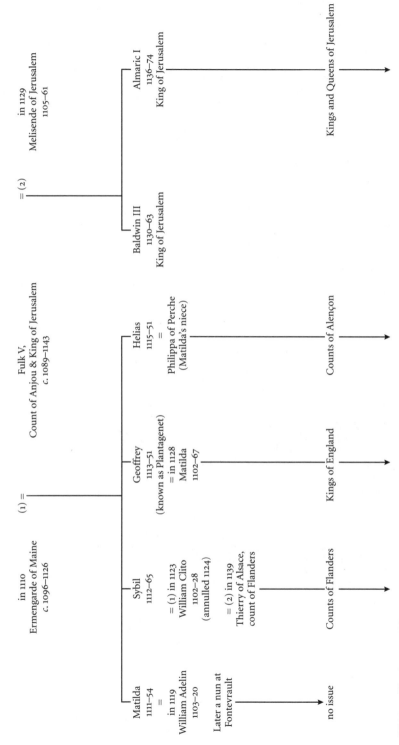

Table 3 The house of Anjou

INTRODUCTION

Great by birth, greater by marriage, greatest in her offspring
Here lies the daughter, wife and mother of Henry.

S O READS THE EPITAPH INSCRIBED on the tomb of Matilda: queen, empress and one of the most remarkable individuals of the Middle Ages. These words were commissioned by her son, Henry II, king of England, and they reflect his desire to honour her memory while making sure that his own importance was foregrounded. But the rather patronising description of Matilda as a daughter, wife and mother commits the all-too-common error of defining a woman only by the men around her: Matilda was indeed all of these things, but she was also a leader, a ruler, a strategist and an able military general in her own right.

Despite the odds being stacked against any woman assuming the throne, England and Great Britain have been subject to a number of illustrious queens regnant over the centuries. All of them owe a great debt to the woman who came first, who fought for her rights, and who proved that royal power could be both held and transmitted in the female line. The kings, too, should be grateful: since Matilda fought to put her son on the throne, every subsequent monarch of England or Britain has been directly descended from her. Were it not for her efforts to overturn the status quo, the mighty Plantagenet dynasty would never have occupied the throne of England, and neither would the Tudors, the Stuarts or any of the later houses.

Matilda's story is therefore an important one, but it has rarely been told. There are a number of reasons for this. The first is that, compared with a modern subject, the available contemporary evidence on her life is meagre. We do not really know what she looked like, for example, which is a considerable disadvantage when attempting to envisage or depict her. There are very few contemporary images or even descriptions of Matilda's physical appearance, apart from the occasional conventional epithet noting that she was 'noble' or 'beautiful'. Nor do we have much insight into her private thoughts or views; one of the greatest frustrations for the biographer of a twelfth-century individual is the lack of personal correspondence or diaries. Only a very few of Matilda's letters have survived – dating from the later stages of her life (although these do give a flavour of her character and style, as we shall see) – which means that her own voice is noticeably almost absent from the story.

All of the above might well apply to any twelfth-century figure, but in Matilda's case the situation is compounded by her being a woman. She lived at a time when daughters were thought to be of lesser value than sons, and many noble (even royal) families did not bother to record their births with any care. Indeed, in some cases noble women or girls of this period are simply known to us as 'the daughter of' a male magnate, without even a reference to their own names. This, of course, is not the case with Matilda, but it is a reflection of the fact that women were deemed to be of lesser importance, that they held fewer public roles and are therefore vastly less likely than men to appear in official documents such as charters and grants. Women also feature less frequently in the chronicles of the period, and when they do they are seen through the invariably male (and often clerical) eye of the writer. This is a point to which we will return later.

Given the above constraints, the writing of a biography of Matilda requires a fair amount of detective work – we must examine those charters and grants, and read (between the lines of) those chronicles, to extrapolate what information we may. We can also, of course, stand on the shoulders of earlier scholars and their research. In Matilda's case the ground-breaking work is the 1991 biography *The Empress Matilda: Queen Consort, Queen Mother and Lady of the English* by the late Marjorie Chibnall. Our book does not seek to replace Professor Chibnall's work, but rather to contribute to an ongoing debate by providing a new and different interpretation of Matilda's character and actions, taking advantage of the large amount of scholarship that has been published on the twelfth century and on twelfth-century sources since 1991.

The present volume aims to bring Matilda's story to a new and different type of audience. Chibnall's *The Empress Matilda* is a work of outstanding scholarship, but it is one intended for academics and therefore it assumes a great deal of prior knowledge in the reader. What we are aiming for here is to inform those who are perhaps less familiar with the subject about Matilda's life and times in an accessible – and hopefully engaging – way. This was a process that began with the work of Helen Castor in 2010; Matilda appears as one of six short case studies in her influential and enjoyable *She-Wolves: The Women Who Ruled England before Elizabeth*.

With the notable exceptions of Chibnall's biography and Castor's case study, the number of works written on Matilda pales into insignificance when compared with those that feature her rival Stephen, her father Henry I, her son Henry II or her grandsons Richard I and John; in biography, as in her epitaph, she is drowned out by her male relatives. However, she is mentioned in passing in many of these works, so with judicious reading we can use them to some effect.

The fact that historians have managed to gather sufficient contemporary evidence about Matilda's male peers to write so much about them shows that there is information about the period available if one looks for it, so scarcity of resources does not entirely explain why Matilda has been the subject of so little scholarly attention – she is, for example, the subject of fewer biographies than some medieval queens consort. We are led to the conclusion that she has somehow been considered less interesting than her peers, or that her pivotal importance in the history of England and Normandy has not been adequately recognised. Our dual ambition here, then, is to fill a gap in the story of the kingdom and the duchy, and to bring into the spotlight the woman who was at the centre of their events for two decades.

In order to build a picture of Matilda and her world we will need to make use of a range of contemporary sources of different types. As noted above, there is little surviving personal documentation relating to her, so what remains falls into one of two principal categories: the factual details that can be extrapolated from charters, grants and official records; and the writings and views of other people.

The first type of evidence can give us valuable information on where Matilda was at various points in her life, what she was doing, and who else was there; charters generally include a place, a date and a list of witnesses, meaning that they can act as useful anchor points. However, this skeleton outline of her whereabouts is not enough to form anything like a complete picture. In order to fill in the gaps around these points and build a more coherent narrative of the whole of her life, we must look to the chroniclers of the age who wrote more extended texts detailing both history (or, at least, history as they saw it) and current events. These chronicles, of course, have to be used with caution: each author had his – and in this book all the works we rely on most heavily were written by men – own purposes and prejudices. It will be useful, therefore, to have an idea before we start of who they were and what their points of view might have been. In approximate chronological order, the chronicles we will use most frequently are the following.

The *Anglo-Saxon Chronicle* exists in several versions, one of which is the Peterborough manuscript, sometimes referred to as a separate work, the *Peterborough Chronicle*. Along with the others it covers the period before Matilda's birth, and the early part of her life, but it is the only version to carry on after 1122; its two continuations encompass the years 1122–31 and 1132–54. Its main focus during these years, perhaps unsurprisingly, is events in the Peterborough region, but it does also touch on national events and personalities without being particularly partisan.

The Jersey-born Norman writer Wace was the author of a number of works, but the one that will concern us here is his *Roman de Rou* (literally *The Story of Rollo*, Rollo being the first Norse ruler of Normandy, but more often translated as *The History of the Norman People*), which deals with the Norman Conquest of England and its aftermath, including the struggles between the sons of William the Conqueror for the throne of England and the duchy of Normandy. The work ends with the events of 1106, at which point Wace directs his readers to the lengthy *Chronique des ducs de Normandie* (*Chronicle of the Dukes of Normandy*) of his fellow Norman Benoît de Sainte-Maure. Benoît's work covers much of the same ground but then continues on to 1135; he also writes in a different style to Wace, adding some more personal touches to his narrative.

The German chronicles that we will rely on most heavily for Matilda's time in the Empire have been the subject of different authorial attributions and mis-attributions over the years. However, recent scholarship has identified them as five distinct works: the anonymous *Kaiserchronik* (*Imperial Chronicle*) and the works of Frutolf of Michelsberg and Ekkehard of Aura, plus their two subsequent continuations by anonymous authors. A sixth German chronicle is the more clearly defined and slightly later work of Otto of Freising, who was both bishop of Freising and nephew to Matilda's first husband Emperor Henry.

Over in England, the abbey at Worcester was the home of the impressively named *Chronicon ex chronicis* (*Chronicle of Chronicles*), written by the monks Florence and John of Worcester. The exact attribution of different sections is unclear: it was once thought that Florence wrote up until 1118 and John thereafter, but it is also possible that John did the bulk of the writing throughout, based on materials collected earlier by Florence. Regardless of the exact authorship of different sections, the chronicle is an ambitious attempt at a universal history: it begins with nothing less than the creation of the world. It ends, rather more prosaically, in 1141.

One of the greatest chroniclers of the twelfth century was Orderic Vitalis. Unusually, we are quite well informed about him: he was born in England in 1075, the son of a Norman father and an English mother, and was sent across to Normandy at the age of ten to become a monk at the Benedictine abbey of Saint-Évroul. His mother tongue was English, and he notes in his work that he could not speak French when he arrived, and that nobody could pronounce his name. However, he went on to settle there and remained a monk of Saint-Évroul for the rest of his life. Orderic's monumental thirteen-volume *Historia ecclesiastica* (*Ecclesiastical History*) comprises much more than the name implies, including as it does an account of the history of Normandy, the Norman Conquest of England and the reigns of William I, William II and Henry I; Orderic started to write about Stephen's reign and Matilda's actions during it, but he died in 1141 while the turmoil was at its height.

For further information on the war in England following Matilda's invasion, we are primarily dependent on three chroniclers: Henry of Huntingdon, William of Malmesbury and the anonymous author of a text called the *Gesta Stephani* or *Deeds of Stephen*. Henry was the archdeacon of Huntingdon (and not to be confused with Henry, earl of Huntingdon, whom we will meet later), and his *Historia Anglorum* (*The History of the English People*) covers the period 1000–1154, ending with the coronation of Henry II. In the passages dealing with earlier years – which are based on his reading of previous works – he can be terse, but once he reaches the events of his own lifetime he becomes more descriptive. He also includes an extraordinary section in which he muses on the nature of time, noting in 1135 that a millennium has passed since the Incarnation, and speaking directly ('I, who will already be dust by your time') to anyone who might be reading his book in the year 2135.

William of Malmesbury and the *Deeds of Stephen* provide the most detailed accounts of the war in England, and they are a useful study in contrast. The latter work, as the name implies, is an account of King Stephen's reign from 1135 to 1154; it is sympathetic to him and markedly hostile to Matilda. William's *Gesta regum Anglorum* (*Chronicle of the Kings of England*) starts in AD 449 and initially ended in 1120, though he later revised it and added a section up to and including 1127. The work is dedicated to his patron Robert, earl of Gloucester and Matilda's half-brother. William later wrote a second, shorter, chronicle, the *Historia novella* (*New History* or *History of Current Events*), an account of contemporary events that he was still writing at the time of his death in 1143. It too is dedicated to Robert, and William makes little attempt to disguise his appreciation of the earl and, by extension, the sister whose cause Robert espoused. William is, however, careful throughout his work to make a distinction between those events he has seen with his own eyes and those he has only heard about.

For the period after Matilda left England for the last time and settled in Normandy we rely on two Norman chroniclers, both of whom knew her personally. Robert de Torigni was a monk and then prior of the abbey of Bec and later abbot of Mont-Saint-Michel (he is sometimes known as Robert de Monte for this reason). Bec benefited from Matilda's patronage and generosity and was a very influential foundation, providing Canterbury with several of its most scholarly archbishops over the years. Being based at such a hub was useful for a chronicler, and Robert was extremely well informed on current affairs. He began writing in 1150, covering events from 1100 onwards (relying on Henry of Huntingdon for content dating from the earlier years), and carried on in some depth until the 1170s; he continued to make sporadic additions to his text up until his death in 1186.

A younger contemporary of Robert at Bec was a monk named Stephen; he was probably based at Bec's subsidiary house at Notre-Dame-du-Pré in Rouen (where Matilda took up residence after she left England for Normandy in 1148) as he is generally known as Stephen of Rouen. He began his text, the *Draco Normannicus* (generally translated in its metaphorical sense as the *Norman Standard* rather than more literally as the *Norman Dragon*) in 1167; it is a rhetorical work that is an unusual mix of chronicle and epic, including both contemporary events and Arthurian legend, and it is sympathetic to Matilda.

We will occasionally refer to other chroniclers and works, where they offer additional information about specific events; where this is the case we will introduce them as we go along. Further details of the various editions and translations of all these primary sources may be found in the note on sources and the bibliography at the end of this book.

Much scholarly analysis of these chronicles has been carried out in the past thirty years or so, and this enables us to examine their depictions of Matilda in greater context. Some of the work on individual chronicles includes (but is not limited to) that of T.J.H. McCarthy on the German texts; Charity Urbanski on Benoît de Sainte-Maure; Elizabeth Kuhl on Stephen of Rouen; and Rodney Thomson and Kirsten Fenton on William of Malmesbury. Valuable studies on chronicles more generally have also appeared, including Michael Clanchy's *From Memory to Written Record* and Chris Given-Wilson's *Chronicles: The Writing of History in Medieval England*. The seminal text remains Antonia Gransden's earlier *Historical Writing in England*; Michael Staunton's recent *The Historians of Angevin England* (published after work on the present volume was complete) will be a valuable addition to the field.

During the last two decades there has been an upsurge in interest in the field of queenship studies, which is greatly to the benefit of our book. The role of medieval queens has traditionally been given much less attention than that of kings, due in part to the fact that most medieval historians of the nineteenth and early twentieth centuries were male and that – to generalise – they saw the functions of women in the Middle Ages as being of even less interest than those of women in their own time. But medieval queens consort held more power and influence than they were often given credit for, as we shall see in our analysis of Matilda's time in the Empire, and as is also illustrated by the careers of Matilda of Boulogne and Eleanor of Aquitaine (the queens of Stephen and Henry II respectively). A burgeoning group of predominantly – but not exclusively – female historians has spearheaded the development of the field; further details of a selection of the many volumes available that have influenced us here may be found in the note on sources at the end of the book.

There are, of course, many other secondary sources that can tell us much about the times, if not necessarily the life, of Matilda. The archaeological record has hitherto been neglected in many studies of the period, but happily this is now being rectified; a recent study by Oliver Creighton and Duncan Wright, published just as work on the present volume was almost complete, will be of particular interest to future scholars. Among the many other comprehensive studies on the twelfth century in England and Normandy, of the warfare of the period and of the conflict in England in general are those of Robert Bartlett, David Bates, Jim Bradbury, Marjorie Chibnall, John Gillingham, Judith Green and Edmund King; we hope that this study of Matilda may contribute in a small way to the sum of knowledge about the period.

All of the works noted above, along with others focusing on everything from the Investiture Controversy to coinage to childbirth, may be found in the bibliography.

Before we move on to the main text of our book, it might be useful to add a few practical notes on terminology, as twelfth-century names, titles and currencies can be both inconsistent and confusing.

Let us begin with the basic question of our protagonist's name, which will remain 'Matilda' throughout. She has often been referred to, especially in earlier works, as 'Maud', but this diminutive only serves to highlight the first of many double standards to which she was – and continues to be – subjected. Ostensibly the reasoning behind it is to differentiate her from all the other Matildas who were around at the time, and it is true that there were a large number of them. However, although Matilda spent her life surrounded by men called William and Henry, who outnumber the Matildas, suggestions that they be referred to as Bill or Harry to avoid confusion are conspicuously lacking. Equally, although the point could be raised that 'Maud' is merely a rendition of the Anglo-Norman 'Mehaut' rather than the Latin 'Mathildis', again it is noticeable that it is only she who is called by this name; neither Matilda of Flanders nor Matilda of Boulogne (the queens consort of William the Conqueror and Stephen) is referred to by this shortened form. With all this in mind, we will accord Matilda the courtesy of using her full and proper name.

In order to disambiguate the many Henrys, Williams, Matildas and others as we go along, we will use various titles and epithets. Some are mildly anachronistic: for example, Matilda's first husband was not properly 'Emperor Henry' until he was crowned in Rome, being a mere king up until that point, but, as we will be using 'King Henry' for Matilda's father, we will refer to him thus throughout. Similarly, Matilda's brother William Adelin and her cousin William Clito were not really known by their soubriquets until they approached manhood, but we will use them from birth to avoid any confusion.

Continuing with the theme of names, French and German forenames will be Anglicised where a suitable form exists (so we have Henry rather than Henri or Heinrich; Frederick rather than Friedrich; Stephen rather than Étienne, and so on), while more unusual names or those without a direct equivalent (Waleran, Frutolf, Louis) will be rendered in the most commonly accepted English form. The prefix *de* will be retained (rather than amending to 'of') where it forms part of what might be recognised as a surname; 'of' will be used to refer to places or titles – as in 'Robert de Beaumont, earl of Leicester' or the abbreviated 'Robert of Leicester' – and it will also be used for monks and chroniclers who are known by the locations of their monasteries, such as William of Malmesbury or Ekkehard of Aura. Popes will be known by the versions of their names most commonly used in English (Innocent, Celestine, and so on), as will place names. The realm that was later known as the Holy Roman Empire was in the twelfth century referred to simply as 'the Empire', so we will follow this convention.

On the subject of titles, most (such as king, queen, abbot, bishop) are self-explanatory and were the same in different jurisdictions; the exception is that we will use 'earl' for the holder of English counties and 'count' for the holders of French or Norman ones, even though they were equivalent ranks, to highlight the fact that the same individuals could hold multiple titles on both sides of the Channel.

A title often given to the period of civil war in England that forms a primary focus of this book is 'the Anarchy'. This term is not contemporary

– it was first used in the nineteenth century – and its continuing use is contentious in modern scholarship. It is not the purpose of this book to enter into detailed debate on this point, so we will simply avoid using the expression.

Sums of money are given at various points in our narrative. In England, Normandy, France and the Empire the basic unit of currency was the penny (*denarius*), twelve of which made a shilling (*solidus*). Coins were made of silver; gold and bronze were not used in western Europe at this time. In the Empire the basic unit of accounting was the mark, which comprised 12 shillings or 144 pennies. However, due to the wide variety of mints across the Empire's great distances and the consequent range of quality and weight of the coinage, individual coins might only have been accepted locally; accounting on a wider basis tended to be done by weight of silver coin rather than number. This led to the introduction of a new measure of accounting, the pound, which literally meant a pound in weight of pennies.

In England the mints were more tightly controlled – and we will learn of Henry I's efforts to keep them so – so a penny was worth a penny throughout the land. Twelve pennies made one shilling, and twenty shillings one pound, but a mark here was thirteen shillings and four pence, or two thirds of a pound. To complicate matters further, an Angevin pound, as used in Anjou or Normandy, was worth considerably less than an English pound sterling – only around a quarter as much throughout the period of Matilda's lifetime. To avoid confusion, where we mention pounds we will generally mean sterling, and will note instances of Angevin currency as such. No attempt has been made to give modern equivalents of sums of money; instead, such amounts are put into contemporary context by means of comparison with wages or comments on purchasing power.

Using all of the sources detailed earlier in this introduction, this book will adopt a fairly simple chronological structure, starting with Matilda's childhood and ending with her death. This may seem obvious, but such a structure is by no means universal either in biographies or in more general queenship studies. The former are sometimes arranged thematically, while the latter often analyse queenship as a sort of composite phenomenon, with examples drawn together from different periods to show what queens could or could not do in various circumstances. However, the chronological approach is more logical here because the opportunities available to Matilda, and her actions in pursuit of them, differed markedly over time. This allows us to depict and analyse events affecting her in the order in which they occurred, and thus build upon her previous experiences.

At some points, particularly in Chapter 2, we will also step back in order to provide context on the contemporary relationships between allied and rival kings and kingdoms, on the English and Norman situations, and on the background to the succession crisis and the other potential claimants to England's throne. In this way we will get a clearer overall picture and will be able to gain a better understanding of Matilda, her character and her actions.

Matilda's early upbringing, her political and strategic training, and her role as consort in the Empire comprise a period of her life that has been more overlooked than any other: she often appears quite suddenly in histories of the era as a grown woman arriving from Germany, with little indication of what she did there or how this period of her life influenced her development. These years are important because the formative experiences of her childhood and youth in the Empire would have a great bearing on her subsequent actions, particularly once she was designated by her father Henry I as his heir. These years will be the early focus of our story.

As we will see, matters did not turn out to be straightforward, and Matilda's cousin Stephen seized the throne after the death of her father Henry I. Matilda eventually launched an invasion of England, and the central part of our book will detail how her campaign was planned and executed, and how the war was waged in practice. We will concentrate to a much greater extent than has previously been the case on her role as military and political leader, and not just as a woman surrounded and supposedly controlled by men. However, that does not mean that we will view her with an uncritical eye: her mistakes will be analysed along with her successes, and her weaknesses will be investigated along with her strengths.

The vitriol poured out upon Matilda by contemporary chroniclers initially led to simplistic conclusions being drawn about her supposed arrogance and haughtiness causing her to lose her chance of the English throne. A close analysis of these writings in the context of the twelfth century, when also compared and contrasted with the way in which other female rulers (or would-be rulers) and consorts were portrayed, will demonstrate that this view needs to be nuanced.

Matilda often fades from her own story after 1142, and particularly so once her son Henry grew up and took over the armed part of the conflict, but she continued to work behind the scenes and was one of his most valued advisors and deputies, as we will see. This is a book about Matilda, not one about Henry: while we will cover the early part of his career, she will remain the primary protagonist in her own story. We will conclude with an analysis of her actions and their consequences, both in the short and long term, and demonstrate why she deserves to be called warrior, as well as queen and empress.

≥ CHAPTER ONE ≤

THE CHILD EMPRESS

O N A COLD FEBRUARY DAY in the year 1110, a young girl stood looking out over the English Channel. The sky and the sea were no doubt grey, the coastal wind sharp and biting; perhaps she pulled her cloak more tightly around her as she considered the perilous winter journey ahead, across the waves to a strange and distant land. She would undertake the voyage despite the dangers, for she had no choice. She was Matilda, daughter of Henry I, king of England, and she was on her way to meet the man who would be her husband, the Emperor Henry V, to whom she had been betrothed the previous summer. She would be his consort, his queen and empress, the mother of his sons; a glittering future awaited if she could reach out and grasp its opportunities. A new life as a married woman beckoned.

Matilda was eight years old.

Matilda's life until this day had been an unremarkable one for the daughter of a twelfth-century king. She was born in early February 1102, probably at what is now Sutton Courtenay in Oxfordshire, the first child of her parents' marriage; a child whose importance subsequently declined following the birth of a brother some eighteen months later. She survived the perils of infancy, and received her early education at the hands of her mother, Queen Edith-Matilda, who was known to be intelligent, cultured and deeply pious; Edith-Matilda's own mother had been Saint Margaret of Scotland, and she herself had been brought up in a convent before leaving it to marry the king.

13

Royal children like Matilda were expected to undertake both academic studies and a practical education. The former applied to both boys and girls and included not only literacy but also strong religious and moral components; the latter differed according to sex, with boys training in the arts of war, combat and governance, and girls learning how to administer a household and estates which might be of great size, as well as receiving a basic political grounding. A queen consort, which was the future role mapped out for Matilda, was expected to play an active part in supporting her husband in the governance of his realm, so even from her earliest years Matilda was more familiar with politics than with domestic tasks.

Henry I and his queen had only two children, probably ceasing their marital relations after the birth of the all-important son and heir, William, in 1103. As the pair were at this point around thirty-five and twenty-three, and had already produced two children within three years of marriage, it seems unlikely there was any other reason for the lack of further offspring: William of Malmesbury notes in his text that the queen was 'content with having borne a child of either sex'. Given the high rates of child mortality in the early twelfth century this was a risky strategy, and many couples would have persevered until they had two or three sons, just to be on the safe side, but this does not appear to have been the case here. Edith-Matilda's well-known and quite extreme religious devotion perhaps inclined her to a more ascetic and chaste life, and Henry was said to have been revolted by her practice of, as William of Malmesbury puts it, 'washing the feet of the diseased [lepers], handling their ulcers dripping with corruption, and pressing their hands for a long time together to her lips'. But whatever the reason, Edith-Matilda produced no more children.

The same could not be said of Henry, however: over the course of his lifetime he fathered at least twenty illegitimate children, whom he acknowledged and brought to court, later bestowing lands or advantageous marriages upon them. His household in the first decade of the 1100s was therefore a bustling place full of young people. As a child Matilda would have come into contact with her half-brothers, including the king's eldest sons Robert and Richard fitzRoy, a decade or so older than her, as well as her many half-sisters, who, confusingly, included no fewer than three who were also called Matilda (later to become, in order of birth, countess of Perche, duchess of Brittany and abbess of Montvilliers). Henry I's nephews Theobald and

14

Stephen of Blois, the two middle sons of his sister Adela, were in the royal household, as was a boy named Brian fitzCount, illegitimate son of Alan Fergant of Brittany. Also at court was Queen Edith-Matilda's youngest brother David; as the sixth son of Malcolm Canmore, king of Scots, he initially had few expectations in his home country, but he would eventually succeed to the throne there in 1124 after the successive childless deaths of all his brothers. He was fond of his little niece, and would be one of Matilda's firmest supporters in future years.

It was made clear to Matilda during her early childhood in the royal household that she should expect one day to be sent away from home to make a matrimonial alliance that would be advantageous to her father. This was her duty as a king's daughter. But she was perhaps surprised by quite how far she would have to go – and quite how soon – when a delegation from Emperor Henry V arrived to see Henry I while he was in Normandy in the spring of 1109.

The Empire (not yet, as noted in the introduction, the 'Holy Roman' Empire) was a large and powerful realm which, in the early twelfth century, comprised the lands that are now Germany, the Netherlands, Luxembourg, Switzerland, Austria, the Czech Republic and the northern half of Italy, as well as parts of Belgium, eastern France, western Poland and Slovenia; its total population was then around six to seven million people. It combined the kingdoms of Italy and Germany, crowns which were often conferred individually upon the heir to the Empire. Henry V had been crowned king of Germany by his father, Henry IV, as long ago as 1099; in the intervening decade he had succeeded to the imperial throne, although he had not yet been crowned emperor in Rome. As we shall see, he was in conflict with the pope and with some of his own followers, and was short of money; the best way to generate cash in a hurry was to find a royal bride who would come with a rich dowry, so Emperor Henry dispatched his envoys to King Henry, also sending a letter to Queen Edith-Matilda asking for her support in the matter.

The proposed match was attractive to Henry I of England. He had been on the throne for nine years but his status could still be classed as questionable – he was only the second generation of the new Norman dynasty, and he was actually William the Conqueror's youngest son: his older brother Robert Curthose was still living, and had a son of his own,

William Clito (we will learn more about both men in Chapter 2). Thanks to careful financial management Henry was well off, and he was also entitled to levy a 'relief', a kind of one-off tax, from his nobles in order to provide a dowry for his eldest daughter. Uniting his house to that of the emperor would be expensive but it would mean gaining both a connection to a prestigious and well-established dynasty and an ally against the French king, Louis VI, whose lands lay in between their own and who was regarded by both Henrys with suspicion.

The marriage arrangement thus seemed suitable to all parties. Henry I wrote a letter in March 1109 to Anselm, archbishop of Canterbury, in which he noted that the business between him and the emperor had been resolved 'for the honour of God, our own, that of Holy Church and of the Christian people'. Henry then returned from Normandy to England, and imperial envoys (whom the chronicler Henry of Huntingdon described as 'remarkable for their massive physique and magnificent apparel') also made their way across the Channel; the agreement was finalised and the contracts confirmed at the king's Whitsun court in June 1109. Matilda would marry the emperor and would take with her a dowry of 10,000 marks. This was a huge sum: the same amount for which Robert Curthose had pawned the entire duchy of Normandy to his brother William Rufus a dozen years previously, or the equivalent of the daily wage of some 200,000 mercenaries.

At no point in the process was Matilda consulted, and nobody raised the question of the fifteen-year age gap between her and her future husband, both of these situations being seen as completely normal in the context of royal marriage. However, the arrangement did give Matilda a new and improved status that was demonstrated almost immediately: at a council in Nottingham on 17 October of the same year, the seven-year-old was not only present among the royals and nobles, but was one of the witnesses to a charter creating the ecclesiastical see of Ely, being listed as *Mathildis sponsa regis Romanorum*, 'the promised bride of the king of the Romans'. Matilda was now the holder of authority – admittedly by proxy, but authority nonetheless. This was an experience from which she could learn.

The travel arrangements were made during the autumn and winter, and Matilda faced the ship and the sea in February 1110. If she wept, then none of the contemporary observers noted it. They were concerned with the big picture, the high politics of kings and kingdoms; the fate of one small girl did not interest them outside of her role as part of the deal. 'This year before Lent the king sent his daughter with manifold treasures over the sea, and gave her to the emperor,' says the *Peterborough Chronicle*, laconically, while Henry of Huntingdon is more interested in the financial aspects of the transaction: 'the king taxed every hide of land in England three shillings for his daughter's marriage'.

However many times she had been told about the plans for her future, however accustomed to the idea she might have become, it must still have been a very difficult moment for a little girl, saying farewell (perhaps forever) to her father, six-year-old brother and particularly the mother who had cared for and educated her. Despite her exalted rank, Matilda was power-less. Her future life and happiness would depend entirely on a man she had not met and had not chosen, and from whom there would be no escape if things went wrong; she would be in an unfamiliar place surrounded by strangers speaking a foreign language. This was an experience, as those in the twenty-first century now understand more clearly, that could mark a child for life. But the situation was unavoidable, so she would need to behave with the dignity befitting her status. As Matilda looked out at the cold, grey sea, perhaps she reiterated to herself the future which awaited: she would be empress and one of the most powerful women in Europe. Or maybe she reminded herself of her lineage: she was, after all, not only the daughter of King Henry I and the granddaughter of the great Conqueror himself, but also descended from both the Celtic kings of Scotland and the ancient Anglo-Saxon English royal line. Crying for her mother was not an option.

And so, just a couple of weeks after her eighth birthday, Matilda stepped on board the ship and sailed away from her family and her home. The next time she would set foot in England, the circumstances would be very different.

The journey across the Channel was accomplished safely. Although it is unlikely that Matilda had been to the Continent before (Queen Edith-Matilda preferred to stay at the royal palace of Westminster rather than accompany her husband on his visits to Normandy), the trade route was well established, and the Conquest had resulted in kings needing to navi-gate the Channel relatively frequently: William the Conqueror made the crossing seventeen times in the twenty-one years he ruled England, and Henry I had been back and forth multiple times as he sought to take and hold his brother's duchy of Normandy while retaining a grip on his own kingdom of England. But the journey, as all were to learn to their cost a decade later, was still fraught with dangers, so Matilda's entourage no doubt gave thanks to God when they landed in Boulogne.

Matilda then set out for Liège along with her retinue. The group ('a noble rich company', according to Benoît de Sainte-Maure) was made up of a mixture of familiar and unfamiliar faces: men from her father's court who had been sent to accompany her, and envoys of the emperor tasked with bringing his bride safely to him. Presumably the party also included some female companions for the little girl, but if so, none of the chroniclers mentions it. Travelling was a slow business in the early twelfth century, particularly for a large group: a fast and lone messenger on horseback might expect to cover up to 30 miles a day at that time of year, but as the royal party was numerous, accompanied by servants and encumbered with baggage and carts, they would be lucky to make half that. Matilda herself is likely to have been carried in a litter or in a covered wagon, rather than riding on horseback in the chilly weather; although this would have been made as secure and sheltered as possible with cushions and furs and with drapes to keep out the worst of the wind, it would still have been uncomfortable as it jolted along on the rutted roads.

The laborious journey provided Matilda with ample opportunity to examine her surroundings as she peered out at the freezing countryside. This western edge of the Empire was superficially not too different from England: fields of arable crops centred on small villages or hamlets located near springs or streams. More than 90 per cent of the people lived on the land, with the rest dwelling in the occasional urban settlement; men, women and children who toiled at agriculture and trade, and whose lives were very far removed indeed from the style of the imperial court. There were also several much larger conurbations in the region, and it was towards one of these that Matilda was headed. She would have seen the great city of Liège long before she reached it, the towers of the huge cathedral looming in the winter sky, surrounded by numerous smaller churches and wreathed in the smoke from hundreds of household fireplaces. It was a fitting location for the emperor to meet his new bride, a major intellectual and ecclesiastical centre, a bustling metropolis by the standards of the day, with its churches and schools. Henry V had been knighted there in 1101.

It was after her arrival, stiff and cold from the rigours of winter travel, that Matilda met her husband-to-be for the first time. Twenty-three years old, he must have seemed ancient to her – although the fifteen-year age difference was not as great as it might have been, given the medieval royal marriage market. At around 5 feet 11 inches in height, he was tall for the time, and while we do not know exactly what he looked like, there seems to be agreement among contemporaries that he was reasonably good-looking, although not considered handsome. He was an intimidating figure, the holder of a daunting amount of authority across half of Europe; he was used to having his orders obeyed without question, and had already proved himself to be ruthless in the pursuit of power. But on this occasion he evidently made an effort not to overawe his little bride, and he welcomed Matilda to his court in a manner which Henry of Huntingdon describes as 'fitting'.

Emperor Henry's major problem, in 1110, was his quarrel with the papacy, part of an ongoing conflict now known as the Investiture Controversy. This has been the subject of much attention from historians and we will not examine it in great depth here; in brief, as part of a wider disagreement over bishops, Henry's father Emperor Henry IV had argued with Pope Gregory VII, as long ago as the 1070s, on the question of who had the right to control their appointment, or 'investiture'. If a lay ruler appointed a bishop, the bishop was then obliged to support him not only spiritually, but also materially, and the secular and ecclesiastic responsibilities of both prelates and princes had become more and more interdependent over the years. The pope, unsurprisingly, insisted that bishops should only be invested by the church, as to allow secular rulers to do so implied a lessening of the church's authority. The argument escalated: in 1076 Henry IV renounced his obedience to the pope and called on him to abdicate; in retaliation, Pope Gregory proclaimed Henry's deposition and excommunication, a sentence he repeated in 1080 after a temporary reconciliation.

Civil war in the Empire resulted, with some of the nobles unwilling to serve an excommunicate emperor. The future Henry V was crowned king of Germany in 1099 (an honour often bestowed on heirs to the Empire, as noted above), and initially swore to take no part in governing during his father's lifetime. However, he reneged on this promise and revolted in 1104, proclaiming his support for the pope's position and overthrowing his father. Henry IV died the following year, still excommunicate: his body lay in an unconsecrated side chapel at Speyer Cathedral for years before his burial was officially sanctioned, eventually taking place in August 1111. Henry V was now in possession of the Empire. However, he soon realised that he was denying himself precious resources by not appointing bishops himself, so he reverted to his father's position and supported lay investiture. By 1110 he was deep in conflict with Pope Paschal II; he wanted to mount an expedition to Italy to settle the question (and to have the imperial crown set on his head, a coronation which would only be valid if performed in Rome and by the pope) but he lacked the funds to do so. Thus he was satisfied at having realised his goal of alliance with England, and he welcomed both Matilda and her money to his court.

Matilda, meanwhile, had hardly settled in to the emperor's household when she was obliged to perform her first official act: interceding publicly on behalf of Godfrey, count of Leuven and duke of Lower Lotharingia, who for reasons now unknown had fallen into disgrace. The intercessory role of queens consort at this time was well established: they were a channel through which supplicants could hope to reach the ears of the king, who would listen to a sympathetic intermediary; and they were also a means by which those same kings could save face. If a harsh punishment was pronounced which the king subsequently decided not to impose to its fullest extent, his wife could be persuaded to plead for the unfortunates, thus allowing the king leeway to grant leniency out of respect for his queen. Matilda's name occurs sporadically on charters throughout Henry's reign as the intercessor who obtained clemency from him on behalf of various petitioners.

On this occasion Matilda performed her part well – we may choose to imagine a small but intensely dignified child stepping forward to speak in public, the focus of all eyes, enunciating her words carefully before a court full of adults – and Duke Godfrey and his family had cause to be grateful to her. Godfrey's eldest child was a daughter of about Matilda's own age, Adeliza of Leuven. There is no way of knowing whether they met at this point, but Adeliza was later to play a significant role in Matilda's life.

The royal household next moved to Utrecht for Easter, and the formal betrothal – in person rather than by proxy – took place on that holy day. Emperor Henry assigned Matilda's dower (lands which would be hers for financial support if he died before her; a *dower* was distinct from a *dowry*, which was the lands or goods a woman brought to the marriage which were then controlled by her husband). There would be no actual wedding at this point as Matilda was too young: the official canonical age at which girls could be married was twelve, and the emperor, already embroiled in disagreements with the church, would not want to risk any whispers about the validity of his union.

Matilda must have been feeling a little overwhelmed by events, not least because one of the emperor's first acts upon her arrival had been to dismiss all her attendants from home as he wanted her to become as German as possible. Orderic Vitalis claims that these attendants had volunteered to accompany her in order to try and gain favours, lands and wealth from Henry V, but that the emperor 'took precautions against being subjected to the pretensions of overbearing aliens' and sent them away, albeit with gifts. Matilda therefore had to accustom herself to new attendants, but she was generally made welcome at the royal court. Nobody had any particular reason to dislike her, either personally or politically: she had, after all, brought an enormous dowry which would help Henry achieve his political aims. Her extreme youth was also on her side – even those who for any reason might not be predisposed to like her could hardly see an eight-year-old girl as a threat. The *Kaiserchronik* says that she was a 'maiden of noble manners, charming and beautiful of face, and was held in distinction and glory in the Roman empire as well as in the English kingdom. Her forebears on both sides came from a long line of magnificent nobility and royal stock; the mark of future goodness radiated abundantly in her words and deeds to such an extent that all wished her to become the mother of an heir to the Roman empire.'

After Easter the royal party travelled along the Rhine through Cologne, Speyer and Worms before reaching Mainz, where Matilda was crowned queen of the Germans on 25 July 1110. It was the feast of Saint James, an auspicious day for the emperor: one of the treasures of the royal chapel was the saint's preserved hand, a holy relic. The coronation was a solemn and holy event, marking Matilda out as one of God's anointed as she became queen consort. The archbishopric of Mainz was at that time vacant, so the archbishop of Cologne anointed and crowned the little girl as she was held ('reverently', according to Benoît de Sainte-Maure) in the arms of Bruno, archbishop of Trier, one of the emperor's closest advisors. The crown was heavy and several sizes too big, but Matilda was now irrevocably a queen, with all the dignity and authority that implied. She would have plenty of time to grow into the role.

After the conclusion of the solemnities and the attendant festivities it was time for work. In Henry's case this meant planning and starting on an expedition to Rome to settle matters with the pope; thanks to the substantial dowry that Matilda had brought with her, he could now afford to raise and equip a force to accompany him. Orderic Vitalis, Otto of Freising and the French abbot and chronicler Suger of Saint-Denis all give a figure of 30,000 knights in his host, which – even allowing for medieval chroniclers' well-known tendency to inflate troop numbers – indicates an exceptionally large army for the time.

For Matilda, work meant concentrating for a few years on her education. She travelled to Trier, where Archbishop Bruno acted as her guardian and took personal charge of her instruction. Many of her lessons were linguistic, as she had to learn not one but two new languages: Latin was the dominant written language throughout western Europe, but the spoken language at her husband's court, used for day-to-day communication, was the dialect we now call Middle High German. But while she worked hard on her grammar, Matilda also had much to learn about the Empire and its politics. Benoît de Sainte-Maure notes that the emperor desired 'that she should be nobly brought up and honourably served, and should learn the language and customs and laws of the country, and all that an empress ought to know, now, in the time of her youth'. The implication is clearly that Henry wanted an empress who would be a helpmeet in his day-to-day life, who understood something of politics and governance – not a passive wife whose only role would be as mother to his children. Given the age difference between them, it was also surely at the back of Henry's mind that Matilda might at some point in the future be left as a widow who needed to act (as other empresses had done before her) as regent for a young son, in which case she would need a thorough grounding in the ways of the Empire.

While Matilda was busy studying in the comfortable environs of Trier, Henry arrived in Rome in February 1111. He failed to reach an agreement with Pope Paschal on the question of investiture, and Paschal refused to crown him; Henry responded by kidnapping the pope and a number of his cardinals and holding them captive for two months. The *Kaiserchronik* plays down the incident, saying that Henry 'took the lord pope with him and treated him as honourably as possible', but as the avowed intention of this text is 'to serve the honour both of the Roman empire and the German kingdom', we may choose to interpret this sceptically. It would appear that Paschal's confinement was both genuine and uncomfortable, for he made a string of concessions that would otherwise seem unlikely. In order to secure his release, he conceded the right of investiture, promised not to excommunicate Henry, and agreed to his imperial coronation. Henry was crowned emperor by the pope on 13 April 1111. His immediate aim achieved, he then set out on the road back to Germany.

By Christmas 1113 Matilda was almost twelve years old and was a different and more assured child from the one who had arrived in Germany three and a half years earlier. She was proficient in the German language, in addition to her mother tongue of Anglo-Norman French; she could read Latin; and she was familiar with the political situation in the Empire. She had her own personal household and had become accustomed to being addressed and treated with the respect and deference due to a queen and empress. She was also approaching the accepted canonical age of marriage, and so the next big step in her life and career was to be her wedding to Emperor Henry, who, by now in his late twenties, was unwilling to delay any further the process of providing an heir. The ceremony took place in the cathedral at Worms on 7 January 1114, the feast of the Epiphany. Otto of Freising deals with the event briefly, noting that they 'celebrated the wedding magnificently with royal pomp', but the *Kaiserchronik* describes the scene in more detail:

> Such a multitude of archbishops, bishops, dukes, counts, abbots and provosts as well as the most erudite clerics assembled for this wedding that no old man of the times could remember or in any way testify to having seen or even heard of such a multitude of so many of the nobles coming together in one place. At this wedding there were assembled five archbishops, thirty bishops and five dukes ... the number of counts, abbots and provosts could not be guessed by anyone present, be he ever so wise.

Even Emperor Henry, whom nobody could accuse of being jolly in the normal course of events, softened enough to distribute presents: 'No chronicler of the emperor could describe in writing the gifts that many kings and innumerable nobles sent to the lord emperor on the occasion of his wedding, or those that the emperor distributed to the innumerable multitude of jesters and play-actors as well as to many different types of people – to such an extent that none of his chamberlains could keep track of who received and who gave.'

Henry's harshness of character would henceforth become a more immediate concern for Matilda; as his wife she now left her schoolbooks behind and embarked upon her public life at his side. We can assume that the marriage was consummated not long – and possibly even immediately – after the wedding, twelve being considered a reasonable age for a royal bride. Although Henry was keen for an heir Matilda was in some respects fortunate that she did not conceive straight away; although her standing would thereby have been increased, her health and even her life would have been at considerable risk. But despite the lack of a pregnancy we can put together some fragments of information to discern that Matilda made a success of the early stages of her marriage. Orderic Vitalis tells us that 'the emperor loved his noble wife deeply', and we see glimpses of her acting at his side. As the years went by the continuing lack of a child must have become more and more problematic for Henry, but he made no moves to set his wife aside, as other kings had done before and would do later. Their partnership proved effective, and in her position as consort the German people would come to know the empress as *die gute Methilt*, 'the good Matilda'.

Meanwhile, Pope Paschal had recovered from his imprisonment at Henry's hands and had reconsidered his position, confirming that his earlier concessions had been made under duress. In April 1115 the emperor was excommunicated, the sentence being pronounced in Germany by the same archbishop of Cologne who had anointed Matilda at her coronation five years previously. If the conflict were ever to be resolved, Henry would need to return to Rome.

Events took a further turn in July of the same year with the death of Matilda, countess of the province of Canossa in northern Italy. At the time of her death in her late sixties, Countess Matilda was a woman exceptional in her era, who had for many years ruled a large collection of lands across what is now Lombardy, Emilia-Romagna and Tuscany. She had inherited them on the death of her only brother in 1055, and ruled them in her own right, despite being twice married. Frutolf of Michelsberg calls her 'the most powerful

24

woman in the kingdom of Italy', and Ekkehard of Aura adds that 'without doubt nobody in our times was as rich and famous as she'. Countess Matilda had supported Pope Gregory VII in his conflict with Emperor Henry IV, not only politically and financially, but also by leading her armies from the front and riding into battle in person carrying her late father's sword. Her impregnable mountaintop fortress of Canossa was where Henry IV had suffered his humiliation of January 1077, when he visited the pope there in an attempt at reconciliation. Frutolf of Michelsberg tells of his penance, noting that the emperor 'remained outside the gate of the castle for three days, putting aside all trappings of royalty, with bare feet and dressed in woollen clothes'.

Separated from her second husband (whom she had married when she was in her mid-forties and he was seventeen) and with no children, Matilda had previously willed her lands to the papacy but had changed her mind after determined efforts at negotiation by Henry V, which included him appointing her as his 'vice-queen' in Italy; she later named Henry heir to her considerable holdings. Now that they had fallen into his hands at her death, it was imperative that Henry travel to Italy if he were to maximise his gains while pressing for further advantage over the pope. The arrangements took some time to make, and the date of departure was set for February 1116. This time Matilda, now fourteen years old and his wedded and crowned queen, would accompany him across the Alps.

Henry, Matilda and the imperial forces set out from Augsburg with an army smaller than the one Henry had taken with him in 1111, but strong enough to show that he intended to demonstrate his authority in Italy as well as claim the lands left to him by Matilda of Canossa. They reached the Brenner Pass at the beginning of March; this was the lowest of the eight major passes through the Alps, and had been in use for hundreds of years – Matilda's covered wagon travelled on an ancient Roman road, which must have made the experience marginally more comfortable for her. The scenery and terrain were completely alien to a girl who had lived her life in the south of England and the flat western part of the Empire; it is not difficult to picture her gazing up in awe at the silent snow-covered peaks as the imperial party, strung out along the road for miles, made its laborious way through the mountains.

Once on the other side of the Alps, the rigours of travel were lessened considerably as the emperor and his queen were treated to opulence on a grand scale in Italy. They stayed in the luxurious palace of the doge of Venice on 11 and 12 March, then moved on to Padua and Mantua. Henry managed his affairs as they travelled, meeting vassals and working to re-establish his authority after his five-year absence from Italy. He acted generously, wooing towns and citizens by granting rights and privileges, and this – coupled with the implicit threat of force represented by the accompanying troops – meant that they were made welcome and encountered no problems on their journey. Matilda was able to observe her husband's tactics at close quarters, thereby continuing her political education.

When they reached Canossa Henry and Matilda were welcomed by the local vassals and treated to a rendition of a new poem that had been written for the occasion, 'On the Coming of the Emperor and Queen'. Much was made of the new young queen sharing a name with the late, forceful countess. The imperial couple settled into their new lands, and while she remained there Matilda must surely have heard many tales about the extraordinary life of her namesake, and the way in which she, a woman, had successfully ruled in her own right and fought on her own behalf.

Emperor Henry was in no particular hurry to get to Rome. He remained in northern Italy together with Matilda, 'attending to the business of the kingdom', according to Ekkehard of Aura; he sent envoys to the holy city on his behalf, to act as mediators and to try to persuade the pope to reconsider the sentence of excommunication. It was not until a year after his arrival, and now supported by northern Italian allies including the extravagantly named Ptolemy, count of Tusculum, that Henry moved on Rome. With Matilda at his side he reached it in March 1117. The grandeur of the imperial city must have impressed itself on her as she travelled through the streets, the ancient stone buildings vying with the impressive modern palaces in splendour. As the emperor's wife and queen she was the most important woman in the most important city in Europe, and she could look forward to meeting the pope, God's chosen representative on earth.

But Pope Paschal had seen the imperial entourage coming and had withdrawn from the city – evidently he was not able to forget or forgive his kidnapping and incarceration of six years earlier. So when Easter arrived, the traditional time for the emperor (if he was in Rome) to wear his imperial crown in a solemn procession, the highest-ranking clergyman Henry could find to perform the ceremonial coronation was Maurice, the archbishop of Braga. The archbishop obliged, and he repeated the coronation on the feast of Pentecost on 13 May, with Matilda beside the emperor as she was crowned queen of the Romans. She was declared empress, though officially this coronation could only be carried out by the pope. In Henry V's later charters she still therefore appears under the title 'queen', but being declared empress, crowned in the holy city of Rome and being the spouse of the emperor were enough justification for English and Norman writers to use the title 'empress' when referring to her from then on. Matilda enjoyed riding through the streets wearing her crown, amid the acclamation of the people, and she was understandably happy to claim the imperial title; she – and her father and later also her son – used it for the rest of her life.

After the Pentecost ceremonies in Rome the couple returned to northern Italy in order to escape the summer heat and the danger of disease it posed to the city, and there they stayed for a further year while Henry consolidated his position in the lands he had inherited from Matilda of Canossa. He also married his illegitimate daughter Bertha – probably born before his marriage to Matilda – to the son and namesake of Ptolemy of Tusculum, in order to strengthen links in the region. In January 1118, during their sojourn in Canossa, Pope Paschal died. Being, unusually, on the Italian side of the Alps at a time of papal election, Henry V made an attempt to intervene in order to have his supporter the archbishop of Braga named as Gregory VIII; however, this came to nothing. Paschal was succeeded by Gelasius II and the putative antipope was later captured and imprisoned until his death in 1137.

Henry had now been away from Germany for over two years, and unrest there meant he could not prolong his absence any further; he set out on the return journey in the summer of 1118, leaving Matilda as his regent in Italy. This was a moment of crucial importance. Now sixteen years old, Matilda had been watching power at work all her life: first at a distance as a child at her father's court, then a little more closely as the young queen of Germany, and then intimately as she accompanied her husband on his travels. Now she had the chance to put her learning into practice. She was, of course, exercising authority on behalf of her husband, which made it much easier for imperial vassals to accept the rule of a young woman, but nevertheless the experience must have been a solitary one as she sat alone at the head of various meetings and hearings. And any feelings of loneliness caused by her husband's absence were compounded when the news reached her (probably in the summer of 1118) that her mother, Queen Edith-Matilda, had died at the beginning of May. The queen had been much loved in England; describing her passing in a long eulogy, William of Malmesbury notes that 'she was singularly holy, a rival of her mother's piety . . . she addressed clerks kindly, gave to them liberally . . . her generosity became universally known . . . she was snatched away from her country, to the great loss of her people'. Benoît de Sainte-Maure adds that 'there was not a wiser woman in all the world'. Matilda had, of course, not seen her mother since that fateful day of her departure in February 1110, but as she had spent most of her life in the queen's household up until that point, she must have retained some fond memories. The death of her parent was a reminder that she was growing up.

Given that this was such a pivotal period in Matilda's life, it is unfortunate that contemporary details about her time as regent in Italy are almost entirely lacking. One document that does survive details a legal case at Castrocaro, a commune about 40 miles south-east of Bologna and a week's journey from Canossa, where she presided over a dispute between an abbey and a bishop who both claimed rights over a local church. Matilda gave her judgement in favour of the abbey, and pronounced an imperial prohibition on anyone who might challenge her ruling. The document was written by Matilda's clerk and witnessed by Philip, the imperial chancellor for Italy; it is an illustrative example of how Matilda spent her time and the decisions she had to make. One thing we do not know, frustratingly, is whether she felt pressured and overawed at being the sole arbiter and ultimate decision-maker, and longed to have the emperor back by her side, or whether in fact she revelled in the experience of being in charge. The latter is probably more likely.

Administratively speaking, having the emperor in Germany and the empress acting on his behalf in Italy worked well. Personally and dynastically, however, it was less than ideal as it precluded the possibility of producing an heir. The imperial throne would later be held by election, and even at this point heirs needed to be recognised and acclaimed, but in practice Henry V was the fourth direct descendant of his Salian line to sit upon it, and he would no doubt prefer to have a son 'elected' to follow him rather than a rival; he also had no surviving brothers so the dynasty would end with him if he continued to be childless. It was therefore unacceptable to waste Matilda's fertile years, so after a year of exercising authority in Italy she returned to Germany in the autumn of 1119. We do not know the exact dates of her travel, but her name on a charter places her back at Henry's side in Lotharingia in November of that year. We can tell from the dates and locations of other charters that she then travelled with him, but still no pregnancy resulted. Matilda was now seventeen, so the excuse of extreme youth was wearing thin.

The usual custom in a childless marriage was to blame the wife for being 'barren', and in this case the accusation seemed logical: although Matilda would later go on to have three sons with her second husband, nobody could have predicted that in Germany in 1119, and she remained the childless wife of a man who had already fathered at least one child, the daughter whom he had recently given in marriage in Italy. There is no mention in contemporary texts of Matilda experiencing stillbirth or miscarriage, although these were such common occurrences that they might well have gone unremarked, so we cannot be sure whether she endured them or whether she simply did not become pregnant during her marriage to Henry. Either way, no child resulted. It is perhaps a little surprising that there is not more blame attached to Matilda in the imperial chronicles. There are two plausible reasons for this: firstly, that she was, as noted earlier, very popular in Germany and so perhaps the chroniclers did not want to criticise her too strongly; and, secondly, that there was a prevalent thought that the couple's childlessness was a punishment from God for Henry's rebellion against his father.

In December 1120 news reached Germany of the disaster of the *White Ship*, which had sunk in the Channel off Barfleur on 25 November with the loss of some three hundred souls. We will explore this tragedy and its implications more fully in Chapter 2, but in brief, those who died included many of the heirs to great estates in England and Normandy, among them Matilda's brother and the heir to the English throne, William Adelin. We have no direct witness accounts of Matilda's reaction to the news, but we can guess that she was perhaps less personally affected by his loss than she had been by that of her mother; William had been six years old when Matilda left England, and she had not seen him since. And at first it did not really seem as though the disaster would make a great deal of difference to her life in Germany; there was still every hope that she and Emperor Henry would have a son, and that she would remain in the Empire as consort and perhaps regent for the rest of her life. There existed a potential situation whereby an Anglo-Norman–Imperial conglomeration of lands might be created, which would be ruled by their descendants, but this possibility became more remote when King Henry I took the most direct course of action to secure another heir: in the midst of his grief he married again within weeks of the disaster, in January 1121. His new queen was Adeliza of Leuven, on behalf of whose father Matilda had interceded when she had first arrived in Liège a decade before. As King Henry had until recently still been producing illegitimate children with other women, and his new wife was half his age, it was likely they would produce a son or two within the next few years who would secure the English succession. Matilda's future, meanwhile, lay with her husband in the Empire.

The Empire remained the scene of conflict. The Investiture Controversy had not yet been resolved; Henry's excommunication was still in force, despite the deaths of both Paschal II and his successor Gelasius II since the last imperial expedition to Rome. It was time to deal with the situation, the cause of unrest throughout Germany and Italy, once and for all. Otto of Freising notes that the emperor assembled a council, 'seeing that his kingdom was falling away from him on account of the ban of excommuni-cation, and fearing the lot of his father' (that is, being overthrown), and it is not difficult to imagine that Henry did not want to spend the rest of his reign stamping out rebellions in various far-flung parts of his realm. Given his potentially precarious situation, Henry was at last willing to make concessions, and the Controversy was brought to an end in September 1122 by an agreement known as the Concordat of Worms. The anonymous continuation of Frutolf of Michelsberg's chronicle observes 'how prudently, how eagerly and with how much concern the assembly of all the nobles struggled for peace and concord'. The emperor finally renounced investiture with ring and crozier (the symbols of spiritual office) and agreed to the free election by members of the church of bishops and imperial abbots. In return the pope, now Callixtus II, would allow these elections to take place in the presence of the emperor, who would invest the new incumbents with a sceptre (a more neutral symbol) as a sign of the temporal aspects of their appointment. Henry formally renounced his support for the antipope Gregory VIII, and his excommunication was lifted. 'Everyone departed with infinite joy', concludes the account in the continuation to Frutolf's chronicle, with some relief.

Finally at peace with the church, Henry could now concentrate on more secular matters. Earlier that same year, 1122, Matilda had attempted to travel to England to visit her father, her first return journey since leaving her homeland twelve years earlier. By now there were some warning signs that King Henry's succession plans were not proceeding as intended: he had been married to his new wife Adeliza for over a year, and she travelled everywhere with him, but she had not become pregnant. King Henry was now in his mid-fifties, and hopes of another legitimate son were receding; even if one were to make an appearance, it was likely that he would accede to the throne of England – as well as to the duchy of Normandy – while still a minor, a dangerous situation all round. It would have been interesting to know what father and daughter planned to talk about, but the visit never happened. In order to reach the coast and take ship for England, Matilda would have to travel through lands held by the count of Flanders, Charles the Good. Flanders was a border region between the Empire and France, and Charles was a vassal of the French king as well as the emperor; he refused to allow Matilda safe passage. It was not wise to attempt to cross his lands without such a guarantee, and it was also not the right time to start a war with France about it, so there was no alternative but to postpone the visit.

Matilda was naturally not pleased by this turn of events, but she had been made to wait. However, once the Investiture Controversy was finally over, Emperor Henry had the leisure to turn his attention to the matter. In late 1122 and early 1123 he engaged in a struggle to gain control of Utrecht from the bishop there, to give the Empire an important link with the North Sea coast and direct communication with England – a clear corridor where the French king held no sway. Although Matilda had not visited England since her departure in 1110, and had not seen her family in person in all that time, the emperor and King Henry corresponded frequently. An English chronicler, Eadmer of Canterbury, notes that an envoy from Henry I reached the emperor while he was in Rome in 1117 and spent a week in his company; and according to Orderic Vitalis one of the men who drowned in the *White Ship* was a relative of the emperor who had been attending the king's court. These links and this level of contact were logical: the two Henrys had made a strategic marriage alliance, which would be of little use to either of them if they did not communicate with and support each other.

One of the subjects of their correspondence during the early 1120s was Louis VI, king of France, who was becoming a dangerous opponent. The kingdom we now know as France had until the early twelfth century been a fairly loose collection of lands held by counts who owed nominal allegiance to the king, but the king did not rule in person over much of his realm: his direct authority was confined to the royal holdings around Paris and the Île-de-France. Indeed, his official title at this time was 'king of the Franks' rather than 'king of France'. However, Louis VI was a driving force for change. Since his accession in 1108 he had gained the support of many French vassals and was now uniting them into something which resembled a national consciousness. The name 'Francia', which had previously only denoted the land between the rivers Meuse and Loire, came to represent the French kingdom as a whole, a kingdom with Paris as its capital. Louis's dynasty, the Capetians, was secure on the throne, having occupied it in direct hereditary succession since 987, and he was busy strengthening that position by producing sons: no fewer than six of them in the decade between 1116 and 1126, which was no doubt a source of personal irritation for the two heirless Henrys, quite apart from the political implications.

Following the *White Ship* disaster of 1120 and the loss of Henry I's only legitimate son William Adelin, Louis had formulated a plan to drive Henry from Normandy and replace him with William Clito, Henry's nephew, the son of his elder brother Robert Curthose. King Henry had defeated the coalition of the French king and his vassals, but to be on the safe side he encouraged his son-in-law Emperor Henry to invade France from the other side; this was, after all, what marriage alliances were for. As it transpired, this planned invasion suited Henry V anyway; as mentioned earlier, he had designs on the Low Countries in order to keep open the Empire's links to the sea. Emperor Henry started his preparations for invasion in late 1123, and in the spring of 1124 he assembled an army to march on Reims. However, in an ominous sign of unity from the French, the noblemen there rallied behind Louis VI ('from all sides we met together in strength at Reims', writes Abbot Suger, describing 'the service of so great an army of strong men' that 'join[ed] all the forces of its members together') and the threat of their combined forces was enough to cause Henry to cancel his invasion.

Matilda had remained in Germany during this episode (the continuation to Frutolf's chronicle notes that Henry left her 'near the borders of Lotharingia'); empresses might have played a greater role in running their husband's affairs than many other consorts, but their duties did not include riding into battle. Instead she concentrated on less martial matters. Matilda had always been conventionally pious, adhering to the tenets of the church and employing household chaplains, and her name appears on a number of documents relating to churches and abbeys. In May 1125 we can place the imperial couple together at Duisburg, where, at his wife's request, Henry made grants to the abbey of St Maximin at Trier, a place Matilda may have remembered fondly from her visits with Archbishop Bruno while she was under his tutelage as a girl. The elderly Bruno had died the previous year, so perhaps this request had a special significance for her.

Henry and Matilda spent Whitsun at Utrecht, but Henry was already ill. He had been suffering for some months with what the continuation to Frutolf's chronicle called 'a disease he had long concealed', which historians now think was cancer. There was no effective treatment for this in the twelfth century, and Henry's condition deteriorated swiftly. He died on 23 May 1125, with Matilda at his bedside. Benoît de Sainte-Maure is the only chronicler to make personal mention of her at this time, and he tells us that she felt 'a great sadness' at Henry's passing. This is not surprising; they had, after all, been an effective team and he had been the most important person in her life since she was a little girl. Henry placed the imperial insignia in Matilda's hands, entrusting them to her until a new king could be elected – and an election there would undoubtedly be, for their eleven-year marriage had produced no children. Henry's body was then conveyed to the cathedral at Speyer, where he was laid to rest alongside his father, grandfather and great-grandfather, the other emperors of the Salian line.

Henry's personal heir, to whom he left his family lands and holdings, was his sister's son Frederick, duke of Swabia, who was one of the contenders in the election that was held in the early autumn of 1125. He may well have been Matilda's favoured candidate, but she had no say in the matter and the election was won by Lothar, duke of Saxony, who had been one of Henry's political opponents and who now became Lothar II. As a childless widow (and one now under the rule of a king less favourably disposed towards her, at that) Matilda's options were limited. She could have retired to a convent, but she does not appear to have considered that seriously at this point – understandably, as she was still only twenty-three and could marry again. Robert de Torigni notes that 'the people of that country wished to keep her among them', but marriage to anyone, after having been the wife of the emperor, was bound to be a step down, and she declined several offers from various members of the German nobility. She could withdraw to her dower lands and live in seclusion as a widow, but that would have held no appeal to a young woman of energy and ambition. It therefore appeared that the only way to go forward was to go back: late in 1125 Matilda resigned her dower lands in Germany, handed over the imperial insignia to the archbishop of Mainz and made her way to Normandy. She had severed her ties with the Empire, but she did bring with her a few precious reminders of her life there: two jewel-encrusted golden crowns and the mummified hand of the apostle Saint James, on whose feast day she had been crowned at Mainz Cathedral fifteen years before. She also brought with her the title of empress, which she would never relinquish and which would help and support her in the years to come.

A new phase of Matilda's life was about to begin.

≫ CHAPTER TWO ≪

CRISIS IN ENGLAND

I N ORDER TO UNDERSTAND MORE clearly the Anglo-Norman world to which Matilda was returning after her fifteen-year absence, and the changed royal and political circumstances that she would encounter, we need to leave her temporarily, step back and take a brief overview of some relevant events.

Since William the Conqueror's death in 1087 the crown of England had passed in turn to two of his sons, neither of whom was the oldest. At the time of his death William was estranged from his eldest son, Robert Curthose, who had revolted against him, but this does not account entirely for his being overlooked for the crown. The practice of the dukes of Normandy for several generations had been that all sons should have some kind of share in the inheritance, with the tendency being to leave the patrimony, the inherited family lands, to the eldest son, and any additional gains made through conquest or marriage to the second. Third or subsequent sons could be given money or smaller parcels of land, or be placed in the church. Under this system the idea of leaving Normandy to Robert and England to his younger brother William Rufus was logical; however, it was unusual – to say the least – for the supplementary gain to be a kingdom, and thus for the second son to inherit more lands and a greater title than the first. Robert may therefore have justifiably felt himself short-changed. However, he was not in a position to challenge William Rufus, who was rapidly crowned William II of England. This was partly due to his comparative lack of funds – England provided a great deal more resource than

Normandy, which meant it would be difficult to finance an expedition against it – and partly as Robert turned out to be somewhat ineffectual as duke. Orderic Vitalis's damning comment that 'all men knew that Duke Robert was weak and indolent; therefore troublemakers despised him and stirred up loathsome factions when and where they chose' is perhaps a little on the harsh side (he was, after all, writing during the reign of Henry I), but certainly Robert experienced many more problems than did his father in keeping peace in the duchy.

Following a couple of ineffective efforts at revolt in his name by magnates who would prefer to see England and Normandy united under one ruler, and a more successful but not complete attempt by William Rufus to conquer Normandy, the brothers made peace and each agreed that the other would be his heir if he died without issue. As they were both unmarried and with no legitimate children at the time, this seemed a fair situation for both of them.

Following the call to crusade preached by Pope Urban II in late 1095, Robert was one of the first and highest-ranking among those who responded. He pawned the whole of Normandy to William Rufus for the sum of 10,000 marks in cash in order to equip a force, and set off in the autumn of 1096. Freed from the administrative aspects of running a duchy and there-fore able to concentrate more fully on his military exploits, Robert was a successful crusader, demonstrating personal courage and dedication to the ideal: Henry of Huntingdon says he was 'invincible' in the field, while Wace says that he 'performed many fine deeds there . . . he won great renown as a result of his exploits'. William of Malmesbury claims that Robert was offered the crown of Jerusalem after the capture of the holy city in 1099 but declined it ('not through awe of its dignity, but through the fear of endless labour'), to which Henry of Huntingdon, with admirable hindsight, adds that because of this, 'God was offended against him, and nothing favourable happened to him thereafter'. With Jerusalem now in Christian hands Robert's mission was accomplished, and he began his journey home via Constantinople and southern Italy, where he married Sybil, daughter of the count of Conversano. With William Rufus still unmarried and childless, Robert could now hope to return to Normandy with an enhanced reputa-tion and the possibility of fathering a son who would inherit both kingdom and duchy in due course.

However, by the time Robert reached Normandy in September 1100, circumstances had conspired against him. William Rufus had died unexpectedly in a hunting accident the previous month, and with Robert not in a position to stake his claim, he found that his youngest brother Henry, who had been on the spot in the New Forest, had hurriedly secured the royal treasury at Winchester, rushed to London and had himself crowned as king of England.

What is important to note here is that at this time it was the act of coronation which effected the transformation from man (or, much more rarely, woman) to monarch. The death of a king did not mean that the throne passed automatically to his nearest heir or designated successor; rather it signalled an interregnum until a new king was crowned – and once he had that crown on his head, he was the king, regardless of who he had been before. This means that, following his coronation and anointing, Henry's kingship was considered divinely approved, and it could not be unmade. Whether Robert liked it or not, his youngest brother was now Henry I, king of England.

Robert landed in England in July 1101, leaving his wife in charge of Normandy (where her administrative abilities as she acted as her husband's representative were much praised by Robert de Torigni). However, armed conflict did not ensue: in negotiations, Robert was persuaded to accept Henry's claim to England, and each recognised the other as his heir if they should remain childless. This was similar to Robert's agreement with William Rufus ten years previously, but this time it was much less favourable to Robert: he was some fifteen years older than Henry and thus unlikely to outlive him, and, unbeknown to him, Henry's young queen Edith-Matilda was already pregnant.

Robert returned to Normandy, where he celebrated the birth of a son, William, in October 1102, and mourned the death of his wife to childbirth complications several months later. Henry's first child Matilda had been born in February 1102, but as she was a girl there was still some slim hope for Robert and his English claims; they were dashed in the summer of 1103 when Queen Edith-Matilda gave birth to a son, also called William. He was to be, says Wace, 'highly esteemed and much loved'. As noted in the introduction, both the young Williams were given soubriquets slightly later in life, but we will refer to them as William Clito and William Adelin throughout, in order to differentiate them. As it happens both names had approximately the same meaning, 'man of royal blood': 'Adelin' was a Norman-French corruption of the Anglo-Saxon *Ætheling*, often used to designate the accepted heir to the throne, and 'Clito' derived from the similar Latin term *inclitus*.

Robert's attention was by now caught up in trying to make peace among the warring factions in his duchy. He was unable to do so effectively, and some of the Norman magnates began to make overtures to Henry. By 1106 there were two distinct factions in Normandy and open warfare had broken out. The climax of the conflict came in September of that year when Henry was besieging the castle of Tinchebrai in lower Normandy; Robert brought his army up behind the besieging forces in an attempt to relieve the castle, but in the ensuing battle he was captured. Henry had him sent to England and confined; he would spend the remaining twenty-eight years of his life as his brother's prisoner.

After the battle of Tinchebrai Henry moved to the ducal castle at Falaise, where he encountered William Clito, who was just coming up to his fourth birthday. In a rare – and perhaps later regretted – act of generosity, Henry released the boy, confiding him to the care of Helias de Saint-Saëns, who was married to a much older half-sister of William, an illegitimate daughter of Robert Curthose's youth whose own name has not come down to us. At the time William Clito seemed no threat to the king: Henry was in full control of both England and Normandy, his brother was in custody, and he had a son of his own who would succeed him. At least, that was the plan.

Over the next few years Henry set about cementing his position. He made a marriage alliance for Matilda with Emperor Henry, as we have seen, and strategically married off his illegitimate daughters in England and Normandy. He made peace in both kingdom and duchy, and it is crucial to note that he did this by acting firmly and authoritatively, even ruthlessly when the need arose. Being an effective twelfth-century monarch was in no way synonymous with being universally popular and well liked, and Henry succeeded where his more affable brother Robert had signally failed. Some of the acts that Henry perpetrated, or allowed to be carried out in his name, make difficult and distressing reading now. For example, on hearing complaints that coins were circulating which were of inferior value – either because they had been clipped or because, instead of solid silver, they were made of silver-plated base metal – he had every coin minter in England who might be accused or even suspected of such adulteration rounded up, whereupon their right hands were cut off, and they were castrated. During a dispute between two lords in Normandy, Eustace de Breteuil and Ralph Harnec, Henry arranged an exchange of hostages: Ralph's son for Eustace's two daughters. Orderic Vitalis tells of the sickening events that subsequently took place: Eustace had Ralph's son blinded and sent him back to his father; Ralph appealed to Henry; in the interests of 'justice', Henry allowed Ralph to take vengeance by putting out the eyes and cutting off the tips of the noses of Eustace's young daughters. What makes this – if possible – even more horrific is that the two girls were actually Henry's own granddaughters: Eustace's wife was Henry's illegitimate daughter Juliana. History does not record the subsequent fate of any of the three mutilated children.

However incomprehensibly harsh Henry's actions may seem today, they achieved the desired result at the time, which was peace throughout the lands under his control. William of Malmesbury's comment that Henry brought peace and stability and was beloved by the common people because he 'restrained the rebellious by the terror of his name' and 'suffered nothing to go unpunished which delinquents had committed repugnant to his dignity' is in marked contrast to his damning verdict on Robert Curthose: 'None could be more pleasant . . . yet, through the easiness of his disposition, was he ever esteemed unfit to have the management of the state.' Henry's ruthlessness was more effective, so while Matilda was growing up in the Empire, completing her education in Germany and acting as regent in Italy, her father was laying the groundwork both for his own personal reputation as king, and also for the success of his dynasty.

Dynastic concerns were at the forefront of Henry's mind. He might have gained the kingdom of England and the duchy of Normandy by unorthodox means – he was not his father's eldest son and could not claim to have been designated as heir by either William I or William II – but he had no intention of allowing any question over the succession after his own death: both territories would pass undisputed to his son and heir by hereditary right. When justifying his own claim to kingship Henry made much of the concept of *porphyrogeniture*: meaning 'born in the purple', this system gave precedence to any sons who were born to a reigning king, as opposed to *primogeniture*, which gave precedence to the eldest son. Henry was the only one of the Conqueror's sons to have been born after his accession to the English throne; at the time of the births of Robert Curthose and William Rufus their father had been merely duke of Normandy. Primogeniture, although becoming more prevalent in Normandy, had not been a deciding factor in the accession of English kings up until this point.

All of this was going to be simpler from now on, in Henry's plan, as William Adelin had the best claim all round. He was Henry's eldest legitimate son, and he had certainly been born in the purple: son of a reigning king and representative of the Anglo-Norman dynasty, and descended not only from the Celtic kings of Scotland but also the ancient Anglo-Saxon line, via his maternal grandmother. He was Henry's great hope – and also his only hope, given the possibly ill-advised decision for the king and queen to have no further children after his arrival.

William Adelin was educated and trained for the throne from his earliest years ('with the fondest hope and surpassing care', according to William of Malmesbury). His initial education, like Matilda's, came from his mother Queen Edith-Matilda, but he was removed from this female province at an early age in order to be schooled in the male-dominated worlds of governance, politics and the martial arts. In 1113, when he was ten years old, William began to attest royal documents, and now he was in the public sphere arrangements were made for his marriage. Henry, as both king of England and duke of Normandy, needed to be almost constantly on the move, and the tenor of his activities in the duchy would depend to a relatively large extent on his relationship with the count of Anjou, whose lands bordered Normandy to the south. Since 1109 this had been Fulk V, who by 1113 was in his early twenties with two young daughters, and count not only of Anjou in his own right but also of neighbouring Maine in right of his wife. He was thus a pivotal figure in the lands between Normandy and France, so the betrothal of his elder daughter, another Matilda (confusingly also sometimes referred to as Alice or Isabelle), to William Adelin was an astute move all round. The agreement was finalised, but as the parties in question were then aged ten and two, the actual marriage would have to wait.

In the meantime, William Adelin was slowly being introduced to the processes of government and succession. He received the homage of the barons of Normandy in 1115 and those of England in March 1116. Following the death of his mother on 1 May 1118 he was officially Henry's regent in

England during the king's sojourns in Normandy, though it is difficult to judge from the surviving evidence exactly how much personal control he exercised. In 1119 Henry and Fulk agreed to the formal marriage of their children, and this took place in June of that year, with Fulk bestowing the county of Maine on the young couple as his daughter's dowry. William Adelin would not be in line to inherit Anjou itself as Fulk and his wife had by this time two sons, Geoffrey and Helias; however, he is listed in a charter of 1119 as *rex designatus*, 'king-designate', so there seems no doubt that he was generally accepted as heir to the English throne. Henry's plans were all coming together. His own kingship was undisputed; his daughter was crowned and earning plaudits overseas; his alliances with the Empire and with Anjou were secure; Maine was in his son's hands; his son was recognised as heir to all his holdings; his illegitimate children were acting usefully on his behalf in a variety of ways; his own ruthlessness had ensured peace. But the one uncharacteristic act of mercy and generosity of his reign was about to come back to haunt him, in the shape of William Clito.

In the summer of 1119 William Clito was a young man of sixteen. After the capture and subsequent imprisonment of his father he had spent a few peaceful years in the household of his half-sister and her husband Helias de Saint-Saëns, but when Henry I came into conflict with the French king Louis VI in 1109 over Henry's obligation to pay homage to him as duke of Normandy, Henry realised that Louis had in William Clito a ready-made candidate to put up in opposition to him, so he attempted to have his nephew arrested. Helias managed to spirit him out of Normandy, and after a stay in France he travelled to Flanders in 1113, where he was sheltered by the count, who was at that time Baldwin VII. William and Baldwin were second cousins: Baldwin's grandfather Count Robert I had been the brother of Matilda of Flanders, wife of William the Conqueror and William Clito's grandmother. William stayed in Flanders for some years, being knighted by Baldwin in 1116, and Baldwin began to launch raids into Normandy on William's behalf. By 1117 there was full-scale warfare between King Henry I and a coalition which included William Clito, Baldwin, King Louis VI, some of the Norman barons, and also Fulk of Anjou, his daughter's betrothal to Henry's son William Adelin notwithstanding. William Clito's supporters were not trying to place him on the throne of England, but they did see him as the natural heir to Normandy following his father's imprisonment. Henry, of course, wanted to keep both his kingdom and his duchy, and pass them on to his son.

The pivotal moment in the war came in the summer of 1119. Flanders had withdrawn from the conflict following the death of Baldwin VII and the accession of his cousin Charles the Good (the same Charles who would later deny Matilda safe passage across his territories when she wanted to visit England). Henry I lured Fulk back to his side by celebrating the wedding of their children – despite the fact that the bride was still only eight years old, well below the accepted canonical age for marriage – and then he soundly defeated a force that included both Louis VI and William Clito at Brémule (in the Norman Vexin, a border region between Normandy and France) on 20 August. The encounter seems to have come about almost by accident, with each party unaware that the other was in the vicinity, but once Henry realised that a small army including both Louis and William Clito was nearby, he split his own host – which included three of his sons, a young William Adelin and the more experienced Robert and Richard fitzRoy – into two: four hundred of his knights dismounted and formed up into two divisions, while the remaining hundred remained mounted. An impetuous, ill-disciplined charge by Louis's knights, who all remained mounted, was easily beaten back by the well-organised formation of infantry, and a large number of them were unhorsed, causing confusion. Although the encounter is generally called the 'battle' of Brémule, it was in reality not much more than a skirmish: it was all over within an hour and only three men were killed. However, 140 or so French knights were captured, and both Louis and William Clito were forced to flee the field without their horses; the result was decisive enough for the French king to agree to negotiate on the question of Normandy.

A peace treaty was brokered in October 1119 by Pope Callixtus II (no doubt glad of a short break from the travails of the Investiture Controversy and the current promotion by Emperor Henry V of the antipope Gregory VIII) but it was not entirely successful. William Clito appealed for the release of his father, who had now been Henry's prisoner for thirteen years, and promised that they would both go to Jerusalem and never return; Henry refused. Henry in turn offered William Clito a place at his court and a position as earl of three counties in England if he would give up his other claims;

William declined. He then had no choice but to resume his exile from Normandy, leaving Henry very much in the ascendant. But the situation was about to change in a drastic manner.

On the afternoon of 25 November 1120 Henry was in Barfleur, a Norman port, along with much of his household and many English and Norman nobles. He was preparing to sail to England on the evening tide when one Thomas fitzStephen, captain of a newly refurbished vessel named the *White Ship*, offered him passage. Thomas claimed that his father had piloted William the Conqueror's ship across the Channel in 1066, and that he would be honoured to convey William's son. Henry declined, having already made other arrangements, but, seeing that many of the young people of the court were keen to travel on such a fine ship, he agreed that Thomas could convey, among others, his sons William Adelin and Richard fitzRoy; his illegitimate daughter Matilda, countess of Perche; his nephew Stephen of Blois, count of Mortain; his niece Matilda of Blois, Stephen's sister; and Matilda's husband Richard, earl of Chester. Altogether there were some three hundred passengers and crew aboard. The royal party was adolescent and riotous, and included neither the very young – Matilda of Anjou, the nine-year-old wife of William Adelin, was not with him – nor those who now felt themselves to be better placed among the wiser heads at court. In this latter group were the king's eldest illegitimate son Robert fitzRoy (now a sober man of about thirty and a substantial magnate thanks to his recent marriage to the heiress Mabel fitzHamon), and Theobald, count of Blois, King Henry's nephew; both of them travelled on other vessels. Shortly before the *White Ship* was due to sail Stephen of Blois, Theobald's younger brother, disembarked, deciding to wait for passage on another vessel, either because he was suffering from a stomach upset or because he thought that 'there was too great a crowd of wild and headstrong young men aboard', as Orderic Vitalis puts it.

The rowdiness of the party was increased by the supplies of wine on board, which William Adelin ordered liberally dispensed to both passengers and crew. By the time the *White Ship* set off it was a dark, moonless night with little wind, they were well behind the rest of King Henry's fleet and most of those on board were drunk. Knowing that the ship was sleek and fast, William and his companions urged Thomas fitzStephen to race out of the harbour to try and catch the rest in order to overtake them and arrive in England first.

Thomas obliged, setting his oarsmen to work to compensate for the lack of wind, but neither they nor the helmsman were paying sufficient attention to their tasks, and on its way out of the harbour the port side of the *White Ship* smashed into a rock which lay just under the surface of the water.

Everything now happened very quickly. The planking of the ship's hull was stove in; water came gushing through; the ship capsized. Those on deck were thrown into the cold sea, while those lodging below were trapped by the rapidly rising water. The women stood virtually no chance of survival, dragged down by the weight of their long dresses and unable to swim, and they screamed as they were pulled under; those in the harbour heard them but could see nothing in the darkness. Some of the men fared better for a short while, but there was no possibility of a rescue effort from the shore and they were too far out to swim back. Soon their desperate cries for help were also silenced as their thrashing ceased and they slipped beneath the freezing waves. 'Thus the conquering sea ... destroys the king's sons and ends wordly honour,' writes Robert de Torigni.

Just one man survived: he was a butcher from Rouen named Berold, who spent the night clinging to floating spars and wreckage. There were later some stories in circulation, possibly put about by this same Berold, that William Adelin had survived by being put in a small boat, but that he turned it back upon hearing the shrieks of his half-sister and was drowned when the boat was overwhelmed by others trying to save themselves; also that Thomas fitzStephen initially survived but then chose to drown on learning of William Adelin's death, to avoid the wrath of the king. But these are probably apocryphal tales, and in the case of the former, meant to eulogise a lost youth. The heir to the throne perishing in an attempt to rescue a lady in distress, heedless of the risk to himself, made a better story to be told and retold in the castles and on the street corners than the tale of the irresponsible and drunken youth whose actions contributed to three hundred needless deaths, including his own.

There seems to be little doubt that the wreck of the *White Ship* was caused by human error. It was somewhat late in the year for a Channel crossing – King Henry had previously never made the journey later than September – but both his brother William Rufus and his father had crossed in December without mishap, so the late November journey was not unreasonable. And the weather was favourable, as evidenced by the safe arrival on English shores of the other ships in the fleet. After disembarking at Southampton Henry headed to Clarendon, there to await the later arrival of his son and heir. But time passed, and William did not appear. As the awful tidings finally trickled into the court, those who heard them were too terrified to tell Henry. 'The magnates wept bitterly in private and mourned inconsolably for their beloved kinfolk and friends, but in the king's presence they struggled to restrain their tears,' says Orderic Vitalis. But the king could not remain in ignorance forever. Eventually Theobald of Blois found a young boy, an innocent who could not be blamed by Henry, and had him cower in tears before the king to give him the dreadful news. Henry immediately fell to the ground, overcome by his anguish. 'He was conducted to his chamber,' says Orderic Vitalis, 'and gave free course to the bitterness of his grief.'

Henry was not alone in his misery, for many of the lords had lost relatives and friends. 'O God, what a catastrophe and what sorrow there was!' laments Wace. 'No ship,' says William of Malmesbury, 'was ever productive of so much misery to England.' The king's personal losses were extreme. Two sons, a daughter and a niece had all perished, as well as many other young people of his court and household of whom he was no doubt fond. His grief was profound and would be lifelong. On that subject, incidentally, we often read of Henry I that after the *White Ship* disaster 'it was said that he never smiled again', but these words are not taken from any contemporary chronicle; rather they originate from the nineteenth-century poem 'He Never Smiled Again', by Felicia Hemans. William Adelin was eulogised, as this representative epitaph from Wace shows: '[William] gave and spent generously and dwelt with his father, who loved him very much. He did what his father asked and avoided what his father forbade. The flower of chivalry from England and Normandy set about serving him and had great hopes of him ... but He who is in control of the destiny of all things had arranged matters differently.'

In addition to his personal qualities, William Adelin was also symbolic of the resolution he was supposed to have brought to the inheritance issues in England and Normandy. On this subject William of Malmesbury says that 'it might be expected that the hopes of England, like the tree cut down, would through this youth again blossom and bring forth fruit, and thus put an end to her sufferings: but God saw otherwise, for this illusion vanished into air'. Henry of Huntingdon, on the other hand, is markedly less sympathetic about

William's loss. He puts the deaths of those on the *White Ship* down to 'the glittering vengeance of God' for their sins and extravagant lifestyles, adding that 'they perished and almost all of them had no burial. And so death suddenly devoured those who had deserved it, although the sea was very calm and there was no wind.'

King Henry was not just personally bereaved; he was also politically disadvantaged, and twice over. Firstly, he had lost his crucial alliance with Anjou. Little Matilda, widowed at the age of nine, was returned the following year to her father Fulk; she did not marry again but later – apparently of her own volition – became a nun at Fontevrault, rising to the rank of abbess before her death in 1154. Henry did not help his relations with Fulk by failing to return Matilda's dowry along with her (as the marriage had not been consummated, the bride's father was entitled to the return of his property to bestow elsewhere), but he had other things on his mind. He would now need to concentrate on his second and potentially catastrophic problem: after all his plans, all his work, there was now no obvious heir to the throne of England.

Hindsight was no more useful in the twelfth century than it is now, and there is no telling how many times Henry berated himself for having only one son with Queen Edith-Matilda. All his hopes had been invested in just one boy, a risky strategy. And due to the extreme youth of Matilda of Anjou, William Adelin's widow, there was no possibility of a grandson on to whom Henry could transfer his affections and his plans. As noted in Chapter 1, Henry's daughter Matilda and the emperor also remained childless at this time, so no definite grandson could be relied upon there either. Henry would have to consider other options.

The one positive point in the king's favour was that the situation did not prove the catalyst for any kind of Anglo-Saxon revival. The Normans had held the throne of England for fifty-four years, and had so effectively replaced any Saxon in a position of rank with one of their own lords that there was nobody left to foment a rebellion. There was a single surviving male member of the old Anglo-Saxon royal line: Edgar the Ætheling, son of Edward the Exile, great-nephew of Edward the Confessor, and uncle of the late queen Edith-Matilda. As a boy he had been elected king of England by the Witenagemot (an assembly of noblemen) after the death of Harold

Godwinson at Hastings, but he had later submitted to William the Conqueror and relinquished his claims to the throne. He was by now something of a nonentity – an elderly man, probably in his late sixties, living quietly in Scotland – so no thought needed to be given to him. In fact he would die, childless, sometime before the end of 1126, thus wiping out the direct male Saxon line forever.

Henry's new heir would be an Anglo-Norman, but who? His one surviving brother Robert Curthose was still alive, but naming him was inconceivable. Not only might it give rise to ideas that his claim to the throne, as the elder, was greater than Henry's in any case, but his personal circumstances made it impossible. He was nearing seventy and had been in prison for fourteen years, away from any kind of court position or responsibility. His selection would be hopeless and was unthinkable on every level, so Henry would have to turn to the next generation. The obvious candidate, and the one whom many people assumed would be named heir to both England and Normandy, was William Clito. As the only son of the Conqueror's eldest son, his claims would surely override those of anyone else; he was eighteen, healthy, popular and a veteran of a number of military campaigns. But Henry was adamantly opposed to this move; he had not spent much of his life fighting against his brother only to cede all his gains to his brother's son, particularly when that son was a long-time protégé of Louis VI of France. And again, there was the possibility that if William Clito were named heir, the question would be raised as to why he was not king and duke already.

Henry, of course, had other sons of his own. The eldest was Robert fitzRoy, now the holder of extensive lands in the English West Country and in Normandy, and shortly to be named earl of Gloucester. He had been unwaveringly loyal to his father and was an able soldier; both William of Malmesbury and Simeon of Durham mention Henry's reliance on Robert's advice in military matters. As a grown man of proven capability – albeit a very self-effacing one – there was a thought that he might make a good king, but ideas on illegitimacy had moved on in the years since 1066; reforms in the church meant that it now had much tighter control over the institution of marriage and that it frowned ever more heavily on those who were born outside of it. The state of bastardy that Robert shared with his grandfather William the Conqueror now barred him very effectively from consideration. Robert himself accepted this fact with equanimity: he would never put himself forward as a candidate for the throne, and would later resist attempts from others who wished to do so on his behalf.

The other possibilities for Henry to consider were his remaining nephews. William the Conqueror and his queen had produced nine or ten children. As already noted, William Rufus was childless; the only other son, Richard, had died in his teens, predeceasing his father, with no offspring. Of William's five or possibly six daughters only one had produced children of her own: the youngest, Adela. She was the nearest in age in the family to King Henry, probably only a year or so between them, and they had known each other well when they were growing up (which was not always the case with royal siblings). She had married Stephen, count of Blois, been widowed, and had in 1120 four surviving sons – William, Theobald, Stephen and Henry – as well as a number of daughters. The youngest son, Henry, had been placed in the church at the age of two, and as a clergyman was discounted from consideration. We know little of the eldest son, William: he might have expected to inherit his father's lands, but he had been passed over in favour of the second brother, Theobald. The chronicler William of Newburgh gives us a clue to the reason, saying that Adela 'wisely set aside her first-born because he was deficient in intelligence and seemed second rate'. When read alongside William's soubriquet of 'the Simple', it may be inferred that he was disabled in some way, but this has never been substantiated. He was married in adolescence to the heiress of Sully, and became count there in right of his wife, living quietly and playing no further public or international role.

Theobald was named count of Blois at the age of twelve, on the death of his father, and was later sent by the ambitious Adela to Henry I's court. He was joined by the remaining brother, Stephen, who was first knighted by the king and then invested by him as count of Mortain, probably in 1111 and 1113 respectively. Theobald and Stephen proved both loyal and useful to their uncle, fighting on his behalf in his campaigns in Normandy, and they were highly regarded by their contemporaries. In 1120 they were around thirty and twenty-eight years of age respectively, and of increasing influence.

The only other possible candidate among the Conqueror's grandchildren was Matilda, far away in the Empire. She suffered from the misfortune of being female, of course, but Henry I had a natural inclination to be succeeded by a child of his own, so she was given greater consideration than might otherwise have been the case. However, she was married, and as far as anyone knew in late 1120 the emperor, still only in his early thirties, might live for many years and therefore require his wife at his side. Naming Matilda as heir now would effectively mean leaving the kingdom of England and the duchy of Normandy to the emperor, and, while this might discomfit Louis VI of France, it was not what Henry I had intended when he had married his daughter overseas.

As we saw earlier, Henry's immediate reaction to the disaster was not to name another heir straight away; instead he married again with the intention of fathering another legitimate son, and chose as his bride Adeliza of Leuven. She did not come with a large dowry of either land or money, but neither of those was Henry's primary concern at the time. Of greater importance was that she was a young woman in her early child-bearing years who was both beautiful and intelligent, who would make Henry an agreeable companion and hopefully bear him a son as soon as possible. Henry of Huntingdon waxes lyrical on Adeliza's appearance: 'O queen of the English, Adel[iz]a, the very muse who prepares to call to mind your graces is frozen in wonder. What to you, most beautiful one, is a crown? What to you are jewels? A jewel grows pale on you, and a crown does not shine. Put adornment aside, for nature provides your adornment, and a fortunate beauty cannot be improved.'

Looks were important: Henry was not about to choose himself an ugly bride. But nor did he base his choice solely on appearance – an added attraction to this particular match was the fact that the lands of Adeliza's father, Duke Godfrey, were strategically placed between Flanders and Germany, thus providing Henry with an alliance that gave him more direct contact with the Empire. Adeliza's ship navigated the winter crossing of the Channel without incident; she arrived safely at Dover, was escorted to Windsor, and married Henry there on 29 January 1121.

The next four years were a time of trouble for King Henry. As already noted, his planned meeting with Matilda in 1122 had to be aborted because of the interference of Charles, count of Flanders, and this happened almost at the last minute: Henry had already travelled to Kent to meet her when the news arrived that she was not coming. His subsequent schemes with Emperor Henry for an invasion of France also came to nothing, thanks to the growing unity of the French king and his vassals.

Henry's alliance with Fulk of Anjou, as we have seen, had been broken by William Adelin's death; in 1123 the situation was made more serious by the marriage of Fulk's second daughter, Sybil, to William Clito. Clito was given the county of Maine – part of the previous settlement with William Adelin that had lapsed upon the latter's death – as part of the marriage deal, which strengthened his position on the borders of Normandy. A rebellion in Normandy itself led by the count of Évreux, Fulk's uncle Amaury de Montfort, was potentially serious. Henry's initial reaction was to send across the Channel, in April 1123, two of his most capable barons: his son Robert fitzRoy, now earl of Gloucester, and Ranulf le Meschin ('the Young'), who had succeeded – at some cost, as we will see later – to the earldom of Chester following the death of his cousin Richard in the *White Ship* disaster. Henry himself followed in the summer of the same year, in order to put down the rebellion and push back the simultaneous incursions of William Clito from the south. Henry was engaged in siege warfare in Normandy for the rest of the year and into the following spring.

In March 1124 some of Henry's forces were sent by Ranulf of Chester to ambush the rebels near a place called Bourgthéroulde, about 10 miles south-west of Rouen. Although Ranulf did not accompany them, and neither Robert of Gloucester nor Henry was present, the host scored a significant victory. The infantry and archers were well placed, and a charge of knights by the rebels was mown down before the lines could meet. Battle was then joined as Henry's men took advantage of the disarray, and some eighty rebels were captured. On hearing news of his victory, Henry rejoiced, and he was determined to be ruthless in order to crush the rebellion once and for all. Amaury de Montfort had escaped (he later fled to France), but rather than ransoming all the nobles who had fought against him, as was common practice for those captured in battle, Henry sentenced three of the ringleaders to be blinded. The sentence was carried out on two of them; the third chose to commit suicide by dashing his brains out against a wall in his prison cell rather than suffer the punishment. Orderic Vitalis has the count of Flanders questioning Henry's sentencing of one of the captives, to which the king replies that 'God has delivered him into my hands for chastisement, in order that he may be forced to renounce his evil ways, and that others who hear of the punishment of his audacious conduct may be profitably corrected'. Chilling words, but once again Henry's mercilessness was effective; as Robert de Torigni notes, 'the duchy of Normandy and the kingdom of England were completely at peace' for the rest of Henry's reign.

The king also scored a coup later in 1124 when he persuaded Pope Callixtus to annul the marriage of William Clito and Sybil of Anjou on the grounds of consanguinity. Given that precisely the same complaint could have been made about William Adelin's earlier marriage to Sybil's sister Matilda, Henry's concern was unquestionably political: he needed to sever William Clito's link with Anjou. His request to the pope was accompanied by a substantial donation to the papal treasury, and the papal bull declaring the marriage invalid was issued on 26 August. His alliance dissolved, William Clito was forced to resume his wandering life of exile.

Henry was still in Normandy in the late spring of 1125 when news reached him of the emperor's death. This immediately added a new dimension to the question of his heir, his marriage to Adeliza having so far failed to produce a child, despite her travelling everywhere with him in order to increase the chances of conception. Once again Henry could now consider the possibility of being succeeded by his own, legitimate child.

Father and daughter had, of course, not met in person since Matilda left England shortly after her eighth birthday, so – although there had been correspondence and Henry would have been aware of her conduct and achievements in the Empire – it is difficult to see that Henry could have taken into consideration Matilda's personal qualities. It was her bloodline, rather than her competence, that initially moved her to the head of the queue. Father and daughter were reunited in Normandy in the autumn of 1125, and Matilda could begin to see what the future held for her.

CHAPTER THREE

HEIR TO THE THRONE

For Matilda, the return to Normandy must have been something of a shock. Her first problem was the very basic one of language: she was a German-speaking woman in a court in which the Anglo-Norman dialect of French was the *lingua franca*, and she would need to adapt. She had, of course, spent her very early youth in the self-same court and would therefore have a residual memory of the language, but fifteen years of studying German and using it day in, day out as her first language meant that she would have forgotten or lost much of her knowledge of her mother tongue; she must have had numerous frustrating communication problems until she reacquired some fluency.

A second issue, and one that was to influence the chroniclers' depictions of Matilda both now and later, was court etiquette. The bluff informality of King Henry's household was in marked contrast to the stiff decorum and ritual Matilda was used to at the imperial court, to say nothing of the fact that she had for many years been accustomed to the deference accorded to her as empress. Managing her expectations as to the reception she could expect in her new home, with a new status – and all the while coping with a profound bereavement and trying to communicate in a forgotten language – must have represented something of a challenge. The mentions in various chronicles of Matilda's so-called haughtiness and arrogance begin from around this date, but given the combination of culture shock and linguistic issues, it is probably not surprising that Matilda did not immediately slot back into her allotted place as the king's submissive daughter. Her formative years in the Empire were not so easily forgotten.

Matilda did find one close ally in her father's household: her stepmother Queen Adeliza. The two women were much of an age, and although they may not actually have met when they were children, their shared experience of Matilda's intercession on behalf of Adeliza's father in 1110 connected them, and Adeliza was probably more familiar with the Empire than anyone else at the Anglo-Norman court. They formed a friendship that was valuable to Matilda as she came to terms with being uprooted for the second time in her life, and which would prove to be beneficial in future years.

There were others at the court with whom Matilda needed to acquaint or reacquaint herself. Chief among these was her half-brother Robert, earl of Gloucester; last seen by Matilda when he was a youth in his late teens, he was now in his mid-thirties, a great landholder in his prime and the king's right-hand man in both war and peace. Her cousins Theobald and Stephen of Blois were also in Henry's household, the latter now count of Boulogne via a very advantageous marriage to Matilda, the heiress thereof, arranged by his uncle. Matilda of Boulogne was, as it happened, a cousin of Matilda, their Scottish mothers having been sisters (she was not, however, related by blood to her new husband Stephen; he was also Empress Matilda's cousin, but on her father's side). Boulogne was a county of both economic and political importance, situated on the Channel coast and controlling much of the wool and wine trade between England and the Continent from its port at Wissant (the other ports of Dunkirk, Calais and Ostend having not yet assumed their later significance): this marriage was a mark of King Henry's particular favour to Stephen, increasing his wealth and his standing.

Another man at court who would play an important role in Matilda's life in the years to come was Brian fitzCount, illegitimate half-brother of Conan, duke of Brittany. Brian had been brought up in the king's household and was now the holder of large estates in Berkshire and Wiltshire via his marriage to the heiress of Wallingford (who, almost inevitably, was another Matilda). Brian had served the king since his youth, in both Normandy and England, and was a close friend and associate of Robert of Gloucester, who was of a similar age and whose English lands neighboured his own. What all four of these men had in common was that they owed a great debt of gratitude to King Henry: Theobald would have inherited his county of Blois in any case, but his enhanced national and international role was down to the patronage of the king; Robert, Stephen and Brian owed their wealth and positions entirely to him, and their loyalty was therefore guaranteed.

The court remained in Normandy for most of the following year, during which time Matilda settled more firmly into her new position, getting to know the various individuals who surrounded her and acclimatising herself to the political situation. She was also able to witness her father's kingship at close quarters and to start to learn about the tantalising possibility of a new role: that she might be not just a queen consort but a ruler in her own right. This would be a great step up and a formidable challenge. Matilda had exercised authority before, but only on behalf of her husband; wielding power herself would be a very different matter. And she must, even at this stage, have anticipated resistance to the idea of a woman taking the throne; she would need to be ready for it. But she was in an excellent position to see at first hand how effective was Henry's autocratic, firm and occasionally cruel style of leadership, and she could learn.

Henry and his household returned to England in September 1126, about a year after Matilda had left Germany. She was then able to meet another figure from her past: her maternal uncle David, always kind to her and now in a much more influential position as king of Scots. He travelled south to offer his support to her ahead of the deliberations that Henry was about to undertake.

King Henry had been ruminating on the subject of the succession for some time, as well he might. In his chronicle Benoît de Sainte-Maure appears to imply that Henry had made up his mind to name Matilda as his heir before he returned to England, but it seems more likely that the matter was still under his consideration. During the autumn of 1126 he took advice from a number of important counsellors: among those who travelled with him from Normandy were Geoffrey, archbishop of Rouen, Conan, duke of Brittany (who was married to Henry's illegitimate daughter Matilda), and Rotrou, count of Perche, formerly another son-in-law but widowed when his wife, yet another Matilda, drowned in the *White Ship* disaster. Once in England Henry was joined not only by King David but also by other magnates and churchmen who had remained to govern England in his absence; he had many opportunities to take advice and engage in discussion.

The witness lists of various charters of Henry's that were drawn up during the autumn show that Matilda was with him constantly; this meant that they had now been in each other's close company for over a year, more than enough time for the king to get to know his adult daughter personally, and to form a new understanding of her capabilities. Her positive showing in this regard, when added to her blood right as his only legitimate child, and also when set against Henry's absolute opposition to recognising any claim of William Clito (who, as we have seen, had refused his overture and offer of three counties seven years previously), tipped the balance in her favour. A further consideration was that Matilda was the only candidate who could possibly claim porphyrogeniture, so in using this argument Henry would be re-substantiating his own claim to the throne ahead of his elder brother, while dismissing the claims of William Clito on the same grounds. Henry made up his mind: he would take the momentous step of naming Matilda as his heir to England and Normandy.

Matilda, of course, had not been unaware of her father's deliberations, and she had begun to manoeuvre herself into a more favourable position almost as soon as she set foot back in England. She had by now become close to Robert, earl of Gloucester, and she lobbied the king to remove the long-imprisoned Robert Curthose from the custody of Roger, bishop of Salisbury, and place him instead in the keeping of her half-brother. From Matilda's point of view Robert Curthose was the most important and potentially threatening prisoner in England, so to have him in the hands of the man she now trusted above all others would be advantageous. King David added his support to Matilda's plan and Henry agreed; Robert Curthose was moved to his nephew's castle of Bristol and then on to Cardiff, where he would remain confined for the remainder of his life. Matilda could not do much about the looming threat over the Channel of William Clito, but having William's father more or less in her power was a great step forward for her cause.

The barons of England assembled for the king's Christmas court at Windsor, and once the initial festivities were over they moved to London, where they convened for a ceremony on 1 January 1127.

As monarch, King Henry's designation of an heir could be considered his own business, but he knew that the path ahead would be smoother if he could persuade, rather than force, his barons to accept his daughter. He made an opening speech, the composition of which might appear confusing without some background that can be gleaned from the work of William of Malmesbury. At an earlier point in his *Chronicle of the Kings of England*, William includes a scene from the deathbed of Edward the Confessor in which Edward makes a prophecy that a green tree, when cut, could be grafted to another and could, 'without any assistance, become again united to its stem, bud out with flowers, and stretch forth its fruit as before'. This was, according to William, a metaphor for the joining of the two branches of Anglo-Saxon and Anglo-Norman royalty brought about when Henry I married Edith-Matilda; he uses the analogy of the green tree when he discusses the birth of William Adelin, who was the fruit of the grafted stock.

Matilda, of course, shared the same descent, and King Henry made much of this in his speech, for he had to tread carefully: any case that relied too heavily on Matilda's patrilineal descent from William the Conqueror would inadvertently make a stronger argument for Robert Curthose and William Clito. So, as William of Malmesbury goes on to tell us, Henry passed fairly briefly over the fact that Matilda's grandfather, uncle and father had been kings, and then went on to wax lyrical on 'her maternal descent for many ages back', from the ancient Saxon and Celtic kings, before he 'compelled' those present to take an oath. Neither William of Malmesbury nor John of Worcester, who give the fullest accounts of the event, specifies the precise wording of the oath, but they both agree that the lords swore that they would accept Matilda as their sovereign if Henry should die without a legitimate male heir. The *Peterborough Chronicle* also notes that 'there he [Henry] had archbishops, and bishops, and abbots, and earls, and all those thegns [lords] who were there, swear England and Normandy after his day into the hand of his daughter'.

This was not a mass oath-taking in which all the participants spoke together. The king, his wife and his daughter sat in front of the assembled throng, who were called out one by one (by Roger, bishop of Salisbury, who was officiating) to stand forward and swear in person, before all the witnesses. In this way nobody could later claim that he had been present but had kept quiet and not taken the oath. The fact that everyone was to be called individually caused some debate about the order in which this should be done, as this reflected the participants' precedence. As the senior churchman present, William of Corbeil, the archbishop of Canterbury, went first, followed by the other bishops including Roger himself; but although the abbots thought they should come next, the most senior of the laymen in attendance, David, king of Scots, was called. Always a supporter of his niece, he no doubt swore his oath loudly and willingly. When the abbots complained about being positioned behind a layman, the king told them that what was done could not be undone – in other words, that they should shut up and get on with it, which they did.

But the disputes were not over. Next to swear would be the noblemen of the rank of earl or count, and here again there was some jostling for position. The two greatest landholders under the king were Robert of Gloucester and Stephen of Blois, the one his eldest son but illegitimate, the other legitimate but only his nephew. Interestingly, William of Malmesbury and John of Worcester give different reasons for the dispute, with William claiming that they were arguing over who should go first, while John says that each was being overly courteous and trying to give precedence to the other. In any event it was Stephen who swore first, his legitimacy giving him priority. There is no doubt at all that he took the oath, and the fact that he had publicly sworn to uphold Matilda's right to the succession would be noted in subsequent years.

The apparent unanimity of the ceremony papered over the fact that opinion at court was divided. There were some barons who would have favoured William Clito as heir, although it is debatable how many of them would have known him personally; their preference rested primarily on his martial reputation and on him being the eldest son of the Conqueror's eldest son – and, of course, a man. The inclination for a male candidate extended also to the churchmen, and there was some suspicion that Roger, bishop of Salisbury, might be one of them, which casts further interesting light on Matilda's petition to have Robert Curthose moved from his custody to Robert of Gloucester's. Did she suspect that Roger might be a Clito sympathiser, or did his sympathies for Clito become greater after this event, which he presumably considered an insult?

As Matilda watched each man stepping forward – and we may imagine her straight-backed, dignified and suitably imperious as they did so – she would have taken careful note of their attitudes, of those who swore enthusiastically and those who looked less willing. She would remember them all. Nobody would dare refuse to take the oath while King Henry's ferocious gaze was upon them, but what would happen when he was gone and his forbidding presence no longer loomed in support of her? Who would still be on her side? A publicly sworn oath was a thing of great significance and it strengthened her position considerably, but Matilda can have been under no illusion that the path ahead would be easy, or that it might not change rapidly after the king's death. Indeed, it might change much earlier than that if Queen Adeliza were to bear a son, for the barons were swearing to uphold Matilda's rights only if Henry left no legitimate male issue. Adeliza was present at the ceremony, which must have been something of a humiliation for her as it had, in effect, been necessary to convene it due to her 'infertility'. But she was treated with great respect, an announcement was made that her income was to be increased, and both her position and her relationship with Matilda survived intact.

Once the ceremony and the Christmas court were over, the barons dispersed back to their own estates, there to reflect on the unique situation in which they now found themselves: if Henry's plans came to fruition, the next monarch to whom they would be subject would be not a king, but a queen.

There was no official or legal bar to female rule in England or Normandy. However, custom and precedent weighed heavily in both places, and the fact that there had been no previous queen or duchess regnant was a point very much against Matilda.

There was one recent example of female rule in lands that may have been familiar to the English and Norman barons: Urraca, queen of León and Castile. Urraca (born in 1079) was the only surviving child of King Alfonso VI and his queen, and had been declared heir to the throne as a child. She had been married at the age of eight, had later borne two children and then been widowed. During the early 1100s her father wavered and designated his illegitimate son Sancho as his successor, but Sancho's death in 1108 reinstated Urraca as heir, and Alfonso assembled his nobles to swear that they would accept her. Urraca had succeeded to the throne in 1109, married again and reigned – initially in her own right and latterly as regent for her son when he reached a suitable age – until her death in the spring of 1126. As trade and news passed between the Anglo-Norman realms and the Iberian Peninsula, the precedent of Urraca's seventeen-year reign cannot surely have been unknown.

Also at this time, the heir to the throne of Jerusalem was Melisende, eldest of the four daughters of King Baldwin II. That her status was recognised is evidenced by Melisende's style on her father's charters as *filia regis et regni Jerosolimitani haeres*, 'daughter of the king and heir to the kingdom of the Jerusalemites'. She would later accede to the throne of Jerusalem alongside her husband, and we will hear more about her in due course.

At the level of the nobility, it was relatively common for women to inherit lands and estates: the vagaries of fertility, childhood mortality, wars and accidents meant that many noble families were left without a legitimate male heir. However, although there were very isolated cases of women ruling in their own right (such as Matilda of Canossa, whom we met in Chapter 1), the normal procedure was for the heiress's overlord to give her in marriage to a favoured man who would rule *jure uxoris*, 'in right of his wife'. As we have seen, Robert of Gloucester, Stephen of Blois and Brian fitzCount had all benefited from such an arrangement.

The question of Matilda's next marriage therefore hung over the succession issue. There was no doubt in the minds of the king and the barons that she would need to marry again, in order to produce an heir. Henry was desperate for his legitimate bloodline to continue or he would not have taken the radical step of naming a female heir in the first place; and the barons were unlikely to continue to support a candidate whose own death, if childless, would land them in exactly the same position again a few years down the line.

The choice of a new husband for Matilda would, of course, be in her father's hands rather than her own; there is no way of knowing whether he even discussed the possible candidates with her, although there is some evidence that he confided in Robert of Gloucester. The king would need to consider carefully, as there were potential pitfalls in every direction. A husband sourced from abroad – perhaps the son of one of Europe's other kings – would mean that the barons might find themselves subject to a foreigner in the years to come; however, the alternative of a home-grown husband would mean raising one of them far above all the others. Either option might prove to be unpopular if the wrong man were chosen. There was also the question of his potential status: Henry had made the barons swear to support Matilda, but there had been no mention of her future husband being king. But how could a married woman, who was by the laws of both church and land subject to her husband, take precedence over him? The best-case scenario, as far as Henry was concerned, would be if Matilda could produce a legitimate son or sons who were grown (or at least half-grown) before he himself died; the succession issues would then be simplified in his mind: the kingdom and the duchy could be passed on directly to the next generation. If he were to die a little sooner than expected, the barons might be more willing to accept the nominal and temporary rule of a woman if she were regent rather than regnant. Of course, Matilda probably had other ideas on the subject, and indeed the fact that a hypothetical young and untried boy was to be preferred to a grown and experienced woman says something about the contemporary notions of gender and capability that she would seek to overthrow in subsequent years.

In any case, Henry was now in his late fifties, so action needed to be taken quickly; the choice of a suitable husband for his daughter became his paramount concern. As he turned over the options in his mind he could not help but return to the question of the all-important alliance with Anjou. So far he had both lost and gained in that respect: his son's marriage to Count Fulk's elder daughter had ended before it could usefully begin, but he had succeeded in blocking his nephew's marriage to Fulk's younger daughter by having it annulled. Henry had no more sons and Fulk no more daughters, but the alliance could still be re-forged in a slightly different way. An agreement was reached that Matilda would marry Geoffrey, Fulk's elder son and heir. There was never going to be a candidate who was perfect in the eyes of all Henry's barons, but there could surely be little objection – not in the king's hearing, anyway – to an alliance that would secure the southern borders of Normandy.

The only man who would be seriously inconvenienced by the match was King Henry's nephew Theobald of Blois. His discontent was on two fronts: firstly, the house of Blois was a long-standing and natural rival of the house of Anjou, with which it had disputed control of Touraine for many years; and, secondly, Theobald was now also count of Champagne, having inherited that title from an uncle, which meant that he was the lord of a great expanse of territory in France which bordered those lands which would now be allied to England. The earlier marriage between King Henry's son and a daughter of Anjou had not been a threat, for the wife carried no claims to inheritance. But the marriage of Henry's daughter to the son and heir of

Anjou brought with it the spectre of Geoffrey one day ruling over England and Normandy. This would put Theobald in a very difficult position in northern France: he would either have to submit to a scion of the house that had long been his enemy (and who might, therefore, not be disposed to treat him favourably), or have to rely more heavily on Louis VI and his heirs, thus compromising his own independence. But for now there was nothing he could do, except possibly complain in confidence to his brothers Stephen and Henry, the latter also now in England as abbot of Glastonbury and shortly to be appointed bishop of Winchester.

None of Theobald's potential anxieties were of any concern to King Henry, who had other things to worry about: before his plan could be carried out, there were some not inconsiderable issues to overcome. Firstly, given that Henry had arranged the annulment of William Clito's marriage to Sybil of Anjou on the grounds of consanguinity, and that Matilda and Geoffrey were related to precisely the same degree, objections could have been raised. But nobody said anything; throughout England, Normandy and even France everyone was either too polite or too intimidated to gainsay the king. The other issue, of course, was Matilda's own reaction to the proposed marriage, for she now found herself in a very trying situation indeed.

There is no doubt that the match was unattractive to her on a personal level. Firstly, there was the matter of the age difference: at this point, the spring of 1127, she had just turned twenty-five and Geoffrey was thirteen. She had lived in and travelled throughout western Europe; he was an untried youth. Secondly, the difference in rank was substantial: she was the daughter of a king and the widow of an emperor (to whom this boy would no doubt be very unfavourably compared in her mind); he was merely the son of a provincial count. And, thirdly, Matilda may have been in two minds about the whole question of a second marriage anyway. She had been subject to men all her life, but her designation as heir to England and Normandy had raised the enticing possibility that – for the very first time – she would have her own agency, the control of her own fate; a marriage would negate that. She had enjoyed the status of noble widow, with the slightly greater personal freedoms which that entailed, for a year and half and was just becoming accustomed to it. Why would she want to marry again? Might her status as daughter of the king, widow and empress be enough on its own to force through her claim to England's crown?

There is some contemporary evidence that Matilda actually voiced her objections. Robert de Torigni tells us directly that she was unwilling to acquiesce to the marriage; and a letter from Hildebert, archbishop of Tours, to Matilda expresses the wish that she would stop causing distress to her father through her 'disobedience'. It is clear that her personal wishes were against it. But Matilda was a sensible woman, an intelligent woman, and she realised that her position would be hugely weakened if she did not go along with her father's plans. On the one hand there was always the possibility that failing to follow his wishes would result in him removing her from the succession; and on the other, the barons would be much less likely to accept her if she did not produce heirs. On top of this was the contemporary notion that a monarch was above all a military leader; and something Matilda would never be able to do was to ride into battle at the head of her troops. She would need a man to take on that role on her behalf, and realistically and practically that man needed to be a husband. Matilda faced a straightforward and somewhat stark choice: however much she disliked the prospect, if she did not marry, and marry according to the king's will, any chance of acceding to the throne would disappear. And so, as she would on multiple occasions during the rest of her life, Matilda put her ambitions ahead of her personal desires, and agreed to the match.

It was precisely at this time, the spring of 1127, that Matilda's situation was made more critical: her major rival for England and Normandy was in the ascendant.

William Clito and his increasingly influential backer, Louis VI of France, had held out hopes that Clito would be named as Henry's heir in England and Normandy. Both, therefore, had been keeping a low profile and not making any moves against Henry while he was seemingly still undecided. Their hopes were dashed by the oath-taking ceremony of January 1127, and Louis sprang into immediate action as soon as the news reached him. Before the month was out he had arranged for his protégé to be married to Jeanne de Montferrat, the half-sister of Louis's own queen, and had agreed to give the couple the French Vexin as a dowry. This was an area north of the Seine which lay on the border between France and Normandy, so it would give Clito a foothold of his own as he sought to re-establish himself once more.

William Clito was by now exactly the sort of man to make a suitable and successful twelfth-century lord. He was descended from kings and dukes; he was a fit and healthy twenty-four years of age; he had a reputation for gallantry and daring; and he was a hugely experienced military leader, having spent most of his youth engaged in campaigns to regain his patrimony. The fact that he had not met with unequivocal success was due more to a lack of resource than to any personal failings – indeed, when his actions are examined in relation to the means at his disposal we can see that his accomplishments were actually disproportionate. Henry of Huntingdon, describing one engagement in which Clito took part, gives a flavour of the way he was perceived by his contemporaries: 'William made up for the small size of his forces by his inextinguishable prowess. All his armour stained with enemy blood, he hacked into the enemy's squadrons with his lightning sword. The enemy could not withstand the awesome weight of his youthful arm, and took flight in terror.' Clito was popular with his followers, who were in the main equally young and spirited; his position also elicited sympathy from many who were not his direct supporters. Now with the firm backing of Louis VI, he rode with confidence from his new lands in the Vexin to Henry's border castle of Gisors to make another formal claim to Normandy.

William Clito was finally on his way up, and just a few weeks later in March 1127 he had an unusual stroke of luck when Charles the Good, count of Flanders, died childless and without naming an heir. Charles was murdered at the altar of a Bruges church as he knelt during Mass, an event that caused uproar on both a local and national level; King Louis VI, in his position as overlord of Flanders, moved quickly to punish the guilty, quell the violence and influence the choice of successor. He arrived in Flanders within a fortnight to organise a hearing. There were two principal candidates for the title: William Clito, whose grandmother Matilda (wife of William the Conqueror) had been the daughter of Count Baldwin V; and Thierry of Alsace, whose grandfather had been Baldwin V's son and Matilda's brother. Thierry's claim of descent through the male line carried more weight in hereditary principle, and his candidature was (unsurprisingly) backed by King Henry, but it was Louis – in a better position than Henry to exert influence over those who were his vassals – who won out, and William Clito was named count of Flanders. Finally, he was no longer a landless and disinherited wanderer, but a powerful magnate in his own right with resources of his own and an alliance through marriage with the French king. He was a threat to Henry's dominance in Normandy; he was a threat to Matilda's succession both there and in England. That he was thinking seriously about conquest can be seen from the evidence of a charter he granted on 14 April 1127 to the town of Saint-Omer, in which he promised to confer privileges on the townsmen if he should ever rule over England.

William Clito began preparing himself for war.

Once more Matilda stood on England's shore awaiting a journey across the sea for a marriage not of her own choosing. But although events seemed to be repeating themselves, this situation was in some ways the reverse of the previous one: then she had been a lonely little girl, but the future ahead was glittering; now she was a grown and experienced woman, but she was about to lower her status substantially. There was nothing to be done: she was once more the powerless female at the mercy of male relatives, so she would have to steel herself and make the best of it. Matilda was accompanied on the crossing in May 1127 by Robert, earl of Gloucester and Brian fitzCount, who then rode with her to Rouen, Normandy's capital, for the formal betrothal ceremony. If she spent the days and nights of the journey railing against her position or wishing that she had put up more of a fight against her father, none of the chroniclers mentions it.

It was at the betrothal ceremony that Matilda and Geoffrey met each other for the first time. She may have been agreeably surprised by his appearance, for even at this young age he was known as Geoffrey le Bel, 'the Handsome'; but, good-looking or not, he was a child more than a decade her junior who was of inferior status, and she presumably had to work hard to conceal her distaste. She did, and the ceremony passed without incident. The wedding itself would not take place yet as the groom was considered too young – fourteen was the accepted canonical age for marriage for boys – and there were other details to hammer out. Foremost among these was that Geoffrey's father Fulk was arranging to step down as count of Anjou and hand the title over to his son, as he was about to embark on a great and ambitious adventure of his own.

As we noted earlier, the heir to the kingdom of Jerusalem was Melisende, daughter of King Baldwin II. Baldwin had been seeking a husband for her from among the nobility of Europe, someone who was an able warrior and who could play the significant military role that the situation in the Holy Land required. After taking advice from the crowned heads of Europe he chose Fulk, by now a widower of around forty, who had a solid political and military reputation, and who had visited Jerusalem before. Fulk agreed to the match – which would, after all, make him in time the king of Jerusalem, the highest honour that could possibly be bestowed upon a western European Christian – and began to arrange his affairs. As his absence would be permanent, he needed to make sure he left his children in safe hands and his estates in good order. The effect on Matilda was slight in personal terms but at least she would begin her second marriage as a countess rather than a countess-in-waiting, and she would be the premier woman in Anjou with no mother-in-law to overshadow her.

The next step in elevating Geoffrey to a more appropriate rank came on 10 June 1128 when he was knighted by King Henry in Rouen. A detailed description of the event appears in the work of a chronicler called John de Marmoutier, but he was writing some sixty years later at a time when knighting ceremonies had become much more elaborate affairs, so it is possible that his descriptions of a ritual bath, a tunic of cloth-of-gold, golden spurs and so on are anachronistic embellishments. However, even in 1128 a knighting at the hands of a king was an event of significance, enhancing Geoffrey's standing, and it was no doubt a sumptous occasion.

Geoffrey had turned fourteen the previous summer and so was now of an age to be married; a week of feasts and tournaments followed the knighting, and then the wedding was celebrated in Le Mans on 17 June. Matilda was handed over by her father, with Robert of Gloucester and Brian fitzCount in attendance. She was now, in law, the property of her teenage husband, but she would have to grit her teeth and bear it in the name of future ambition. The newlyweds enjoyed (or endured) three weeks of great celebrations before moving to the Angevin capital of Angers, where they were welcomed with more jubilation. Fulk left almost straight away to travel to Jerusalem, where his own marriage was celebrated at Whitsun in 1129; Fulk and Melisende would later become king and queen of Jerusalem on the death of Baldwin II in 1131. Robert of Gloucester and Brian fitzCount returned to England, where they were kept busy by the king for the next year or so in the less glamorous task of undertaking a financial audit of the royal treasury at Winchester. Matilda and Geoffrey were left to try to make their marriage work somehow, against the backdrop of the threat from her cousin in the north.

* * *

Meanwhile, the perennially luckless William Clito's fortunes had taken a downward turn once more. Since William's accession to the county of Flanders King Henry had been devoting considerable resources of time, money and influence to causing trouble for his nephew. He used his alliances in the surrounding lands of Lotharingia (held by his father-in-law Godfrey) and Boulogne (in the hands of his nephew Stephen) to put pressure on Clito's borders, and he sent Stephen over in person to foment further discord against the new count. In the meantime he used a combination of bribes and economic sanctions against the towns of Flanders to turn them against Clito. Most of their wealth was founded on trade with England: such measures could have a severe impact on the prosperity of the whole region.

William Clito, as might be expected, did not take this lying down. He did not have anything like as much resource as his uncle, but he had his own reputation for prowess and a loyal band of knights. He waged a campaign throughout the summer of 1127, and Orderic Vitalis tells us that 'in August he [Clito] led an army against Stephen, count of Boulogne, and in an attempt to force him into subjection began to lay waste his lands relentlessly with fire and sword'. Stephen apparently lost his stomach for the fight as he arranged a three-year truce, leaving William to concentrate his attention elsewhere over the winter.

But he needed help. In March 1128 Clito wrote a letter to Louis VI: 'Behold my powerful and inveterate enemy, namely the king of the English, who has long grieved at my success. Now he has brought together innumerable knights and vast amounts of money; and out of pure spite he labours to take away from you and from ourselves a section of the most faithful and powerful men of your realm, confident in the number of his men and still more in the quantity of his cash.' Louis initially responded to this missive by heading back to Flanders in order to assist Clito, arriving in April 1128, but after a shrewd military manoeuvre by Henry I, now in Normandy in person, he was forced to retreat. King Henry, according to both the contemporary Henry of Huntingdon and the later chronicler Roger of Howden (writing at the end of the twelfth century), went with his army to Épernon, between Paris and Chartres, and stayed there for eight days, 'as safely as if he were in his own kingdom'. This was far too close to Paris for Louis's comfort; he needed to look after his own interests first and so he withdrew abruptly to his capital, at which point Henry left Épernon and returned to Normandy. But his point had been made, and William Clito was once more on his own.

By now Henry's economic sanctions against the towns of Flanders had begun to cut more deeply, and the result was a general rebellion against Clito. But he did not give up: with the depleted means at his disposal he marshalled his forces and began a series of sieges of opposing strongholds. His tireless efforts ('by his invincible prowess, Earl William made up for the deficiency in his forces, which were few in number,' says Roger of Howden) were just starting to gain him the upper hand when Fortune, so long his enemy, struck him a final blow. Clito was assailing Thierry of Alsace's castle of Aalst in east Flanders in July 1128 when he was wounded in the hand, necessitating what he thought was a temporary withdrawal from the fray. But, as Orderic Vitalis tells us, due to inflammation of the wound 'he was compelled to retire to his bed ... his whole arm up to the shoulder turned as black as coal'. He died five days later.

William Clito had lost his mother before his first birthday and his father before his fourth. He had spent most of his childhood in nomadic exile and in danger. The whole of his twenty-five-year life had been spent in trying to regain the lands and titles that had been taken away and that he saw as rightfully his. He may have yearned for a simpler and more stable existence – his somewhat plaintive plea to King Henry in 1119 that if his father were released, they would both go to the Holy Land and never return, hints at this – but he never gave up on his quest. Clito was generally looked on by contemporaries with favour and sympathy, and the epitaphs left to us by chroniclers reflect this. John of Worcester says his death provoked universal grief; Wace calls him 'noble' and says that he was 'greatly loved by his knights' and that his death caused 'great sorrow'. Roger of Howden says that 'this most noble youth, during his short life, earned endless glory'; Roger may have been drawing on the earlier work of Henry of Huntingdon, who tells us in similar wording that 'in his short life this most noble of youths earned eternal fame ... Mars has died on earth, the gods lament an equal god'. And Orderic Vitalis strikes a sombre note when he writes that 'This young prince was born to misfortune, from which he was never altogether free as long as he lived. He was brave, handsome and high-spirited; desperately fond of warlike adventures ... he was the cause of more misery than profit to the multitude who adhered to him.'

Following William Clito's death the county of Flanders passed to Thierry of Alsace, by now an acceptable compromise candidate whose accession was recognised by Henry I, Louis VI and Emperor Lothar. Thierry ruled as count of Flanders for the next forty years, finally bringing peace to the region following the successive violent, childless deaths of the last four counts in a row. In a perhaps unexpected twist, he later married Sybil of Anjou, the younger daughter of Count Fulk, who had previously been the wife of William Clito in their short-lived and annulled union. Sybil, of course, was at this point also Matilda's sister-in-law.

The news of William Clito's death sped south to Anjou, where Matilda was able to digest its profound implications. Her major rival for the kingdom of England and the duchy of Normandy was gone: suddenly, unexpectedly, miraculously. There were no further complications in the shape of a son or younger brother, for Clito had no siblings and neither of his marriages had produced children. His followers, bereft of their leader, divided into two camps: some sought reconciliation with King Henry, which was granted as Henry's best interests were served by the peace this offered; the rest took the standard twelfth-century exit clause for landless or broken-hearted young nobles and headed for the Holy Land. A monk named Simeon of Durham wrote of King Henry that 'his enemies on every side were either conquered or reconciled; prosperity everywhere smiled on him'.

The threat to Matilda had vanished. Surely, her unhindered succession to the English crown beckoned. William Clito had been Matilda's cousin but it is unlikely that they ever met, and any very small amount of personal regret that she might have felt, or considered that she ought to feel, at his untimely death must have been tempered by an overwhelming relief. But there was surely also some frustration that the event had not happened sooner. For by the time she heard the news, it was too late to protest against her marriage to the boy Geoffrey, which had taken place just six weeks earlier.

The union was a disaster from the very start, due to the overwhelming personal and political complexities of the relationship. Matilda and Geoffrey were not helped by having been left to their own devices: Fulk, who would have been able to influence his son, had gone, and so too had Earl Robert and Brian fitzCount, who might have acted as a steadying influence on

Matilda. Instead, the couple, unable to empathise with each other, became locked in a vicious circle of mutual dislike.

The many commentators, both medieval and modern, who have examined the early stages of the marriage tend to veer towards explanations that support their own preconceived opinions, placing the blame on one party or the other according to their preferred narrative. But it seems likely that the fault for the initial breakdown of the marriage lay on both sides. Geoffrey probably did not appreciate how hard it was for a queen and empress to find herself in her current marital situation, and appears to have made little attempt to understand. Matilda would not have been happy at being subject to the control and the whims of a no doubt hormonal and unpredictable teenager; but, on the other hand, she might have paused to think that a young boy suddenly thrust into the responsibility of leadership and command, without the guiding hand of his father, might appreciate some help from an older and wiser political head. Of course, this is necessarily all speculation: maybe Matilda did offer such help but he refused it on the grounds that he did not want to be (or be seen to be) under the thumb of his wife. Whatever the precise causes, the couple's personal problems continued to escalate.

There were other, more political issues to deal with as well. Geoffrey had no idea of the nature of the role that King Henry intended for him. His most ambitious expectation must have been that he would be king and duke *jure uxoris*, in much the same way that his own father would be king of Jerusalem in right of his wife. But was this Henry's intention? Only one chronicler seems to support this view, Simeon of Durham writing that it was agreed that Geoffrey should succeed to the kingdom of England if Henry died without a legitimate male heir. However, if we judge Henry by his actions, this appears to be far from the truth. Following the marriage he continued to associate Matilda with him in charters but made no attempt to link Geoffrey with power, which would have been an odd course of action if he had considered Geoffrey to be a king-in-waiting. Orderic Vitalis may be nearer the truth when he opined that Geoffrey was to be merely a 'stipendiary commander on his wife's behalf' – providing her with sons and with military support while restricting his own ambitions to Anjou. Geoffrey himself seems to have concentrated his attentions on Normandy rather than England; as a representative of the house of Anjou this is perhaps not surprising. Certainly he never travelled to England and it does not seem as though King Henry and Geoffrey ever met in person after the wedding festivities were over. The most likely answer is that Henry was seeking to keep his options open. After all, he could not predict how long he might live, and the situation might change as the years went by.

The difficulties of the marriage became such that the pair separated within a year. Matilda moved away from Anjou (opinions are divided on whether she did this of her own volition, choosing to leave her husband, or whether he in effect threw her out – again, commentators tend to present the episode according to their own prevailing view) and was back in Normandy by the autumn of 1129. The couple had not conceived a child within the first year of their marriage, but whether this was the cause of the tension or whether it merely added to it is a moot point. The king was not there as he had by this time travelled back to England.

There was stalemate for a year. Matilda stayed in Normandy, continuing to call herself the empress rather than the countess of Anjou, and sending letters of complaint to her father. With no lands to rule, no formal govern-mental role to play and no close family about her, she had ample time to reconsider her position, but she made no move to return to her husband, a course of action that might appear either principled or stubborn, depending on the point of view of the onlooker. Geoffrey, meanwhile, made no attempt to follow her but stayed in Anjou, developing his military skills with a campaign against various rebel factions in the county, and consoling himself with a mistress: his illegitimate son Hamelin was born in 1130. King Henry also made no particular move; now that the threat posed by William Clito had been eliminated, he had more leisure to consider his options.

Henry finally stirred in the summer of 1131. He had crossed to Normandy for reasons unrelated to Matilda's marital woes: the recently elected Pope Innocent II was making a tour of western Europe and in late spring Henry had received him and the papal entourage in Rouen, a glittering occasion. He evidently then made some effort to communicate more closely with his daughter, as both their names appear together on a grant he made to the abbey of Cluny, indicating that they were not estranged. When he travelled back to England in the late summer he took Matilda with him, though we have no way of knowing what the precise negotiations were that enabled them to reach this point. As it was, the decision almost resulted in utter disaster: the Channel was very rough for the time of year, and shipwreck threatened during the journey. With the king, the queen, Matilda and Robert of Gloucester all on board, the entire royal family could have been wiped out at a stroke. Amid the shrieking storm they all prayed for deliverance and Henry vowed that if they lived he would collect no danegeld (an English tax) for seven years, and would make a pilgrimage to the shrine of Saint Edmund in East Anglia. They did survive and, according to John of Worcester, the king later fulfilled his promise.

Once the party was safely back on firm English soil Henry reiterated Matilda's position as heir to the throne at a council on 8 September 1131 at which, as William of Malmesbury succinctly puts it, 'the oath of fidelity to her was renewed by such as had already sworn, and also taken by such as hitherto had not'. It is important to note that this ceremony took place well after Matilda's marriage to Geoffrey, so the barons could not later complain that they were kept in the dark – but also that the oaths made no mention of Geoffrey being king.

At the same council it was decided – by the king and the barons, not by Matilda herself – that she should be returned to her husband. Geoffrey had (according to Henry of Huntingdon) been 'asking for her', and was prepared to receive her 'with the pomp which befitted such a great heroine'. However much this might or might not sweeten the pill, Matilda would have to return to the scene of her humiliation, and live and sleep with her husband long enough to beget heirs. This situation was now becoming critical: she was not to be permitted to forget that she was a woman approaching thirty who had been married twice and never given birth to a child. But if she and Geoffrey could just produce a son or two then conceivably the marriage could revert to some kind of practical alliance that concentrated on the political rather than the personal.

The couple were reunited, both now perhaps more prepared to compromise after their time apart and the opportunity for reflection which this had provided, and things remained calm for a year – or at least calm enough that no chronicler felt compelled to comment on the situation. Geoffrey had put down the rebellion in Anjou so the county was a relatively peaceful place. And then, in the autumn of 1132, came the news that all England and Normandy had been waiting for: Matilda was pregnant.

Pregnancy was dangerous. Matilda, of course, was in a much more favourable position than expectant mothers of lower rank, in that she benefited from adequate nutrition and did not have to undertake physical labour in the fields or workshop, but still, antenatal care at this time was almost non-existent so she would have to make her own way through the new experience. Male physicians were not generally involved in pregnancy and birth, but Matilda would have surrounded herself with her ladies and with matrons who were experienced in these matters and who could offer advice and practical help. Doubtless she also spent much time praying that the child would be a boy, for if she were to give birth to a girl then her own situation would merely be perpetuated or replicated. In the spring of 1133 the time came and Matilda was confined (quite literally shut in her apartments with her attendants) in the castle of Le Mans. The risks to her life and health should not be underestimated: labour was extremely hazardous and a woman giving birth had a greater chance of dying than a knight fighting in a battle. Nobody could predict what might happen in each individual case. The ordeal might go on for days, leading to death from exhaustion; a breech or other difficult presentation was almost certainly fatal, and even if the mother survived the labour she might die of blood loss, complications or infection afterwards. And on top of this were the inconvenient facts that at thirty-one years of age Matilda was considered an elderly first-time mother, without the resilience of youth, and that pain relief options were negligible.

The dangers of death for the newborn were, if anything, even greater: stillbirths were common, premature births carried an extremely high risk, and even with the best care available to those of exalted status which might shield them from cold or malnutrition, rank was no protection against the myriad diseases, infections or accidents that could befall any baby. A reasonable estimate would be that one in eight mothers and one in six babies died during or as a result of the confinement. Matilda was about to risk everything.

Prayers were said throughout Anjou, Normandy and England for the survival of mother and child, and they were answered on 5 March 1133 when Matilda gave birth – to her immense relief – to a healthy son. In one of the least surprising moves of the Middle Ages, the boy was named Henry; he showed traces of his ancestry on both sides, inheriting King Henry's stocky physique (and, as he would later demonstrate, his almost inexhaustible energy) but his father's golden-red hair. A great future awaited the tiny figure if he could survive long enough to claim it: he would in due course inherit England, Normandy and Anjou. Amid the public celebrations,

Matilda's own feelings must have been overwhelming. Any mother might be proud of her newborn, but for her there was the added weight of all that he represented. His birth wiped out the humiliation of her having been considered barren, of not having borne the emperor a son; and it strengthened her position as her father's heir. She wept for joy at his baptism (the only time she is ever reported as shedding tears in public), and Henry would be her favourite child all her life. And he would take his soubriquet from neither father nor grandfather but from his mother: by his own choice he was known later throughout all his lands as Henry fitzEmpress.

King Henry travelled to Normandy in the summer of 1133 to meet his grandson and to share in the celebrations. He was still there in the spring of 1134 when news reached him that Robert Curthose had finally died, still a prisoner in Cardiff Castle, at the age of around eighty. He had not been a threat for many years, sliding into a decline that was accelerated by the catastrophic news of his son's death and the consequent loss of any remaining hope. He was a broken old man who never made an attempt to escape and who spent his time learning Welsh and writing poetry (a poem attributed to him contains the evocative line 'woe to him that is not old enough to die'), but his death at least drew a final line under any claims to the throne other than Matilda's.

After all the years of being considered barren, and no doubt enduring the veiled and not-so-veiled insults that came with it, Matilda was soon pregnant again, and her second son Geoffrey (an Angevin name this time) was born in Rouen in May 1134. But all did not go according to plan: the birth was a very difficult one, and one of the many dangers of the confinement chamber struck. We do not know the exact details, but it is clear that Matilda was considered to be dying: Robert de Torigni tells us that she 'was in such imminent danger by the birth that her life was despaired of'. There was even a well-documented argument between Matilda and her father over where she was to be buried: he wanted her to be interred in the ancestral vault of the dukes of Normandy at Rouen Cathedral, but she preferred the abbey of Bec, for which she had a particular affection. As noted in Chapter 1, Matilda was devout in a way that was normal and conventional for her time, and she had made a number of grants to religious foundations. Bec was a favourite of hers; it had already been the recipient of numerous gifts and would continue to benefit from her generosity, either from the bequest that would accompany her body or from the donations that would continue if she lived. But live she must, for – health aside – Matilda was in the most favourable position she had ever enjoyed: she was the undisputed heir to the kingdom of England and the duchy of Normandy, and was the mother of two healthy sons. Dying now would be the greatest of ironies.

Somehow Matilda pulled through; this was probably in spite of, rather than because of, any medical attention she received. As she convalesced she discovered that at long last she and Geoffrey had a shared interest: their sons' futures. A slight thawing of their relationship ensued. And of course they were not the only ones with a vested interest in the boys; King Henry left Roger, bishop of Salisbury, as his justiciar (the officer in charge of his administration) and regent in England and prolonged his stay in Normandy in order to spend time with his grandsons, who had given him a new lease of life. Henry of Huntingdon tells us that 'King Henry stayed in Normandy to rejoice in his grandsons', a verb not usually used in relation to the king in the latter part of his life. It was fourteen years since William Adelin had drowned, and Henry had now given up hope of Queen Adeliza bearing a son, so his grandsons would be his compensation. His great hope would have been that he could live another fifteen years or so – although, as he was already in his mid-sixties, the odds were against it.

Once Matilda's recovery from birth and illness was complete, she could finally leave her chambers and re-enter the world of politics. It is extremely unlikely that she spent her time being what we would now call a hands-on mother; the custom among the nobility in the twelfth century was to employ a wet-nurse and other female attendants to care for babies and infants. Once the boys were older Matilda might supervise their education in the same way that her own mother had directed hers, but for now she would be satisfied as long as they continued in good health.

Matilda had in any case other things to worry about, as there was conflict brewing between her husband and her father. Henry of Huntingdon makes some attempt to blame Matilda for this, saying that the king was detained in Normandy 'on account of various disputes, which arose on a number of issues, between the king and the count of Anjou, due to the machinations of none other than the king's daughter', but in this particular case it seems more likely that the discord between the two men needed no encouragement from her.

Geoffrey of Anjou, also known as Geoffrey Plantagenet from his habit of wearing a sprig of broom (*planta genista* in Latin), was no longer the boy Matilda had married. He was now in his early twenties, a father, the holder of extensive lands, and a man with years of experience as count and military leader under his belt. King Henry's refusal to associate him with any real royal or ducal power continued, and by this point Geoffrey may well have been coming to the realisation that he was never going to be king of England. However, he still had designs on Normandy, and there were ways in which he could begin to assert himself. The castles of Argentan, Exmes and Domfront, all of which lay in Normandy near the border with his own lands, had been promised to him as part of Matilda's dowry, but the king had as yet not handed them over – some six years after the wedding. Keen as Henry was not to cede any power or territory before his death, if these castles were part of a dowry rather than part of an eventual inheritance then control of them should have been transferred once the wedding was complete (and certainly once the initial rift had been healed and Matilda returned to her husband in 1131), regardless of whether Henry was still living. Orderic Vitalis notes that Geoffrey was of this view, telling us that he 'demanded castles in Normandy, alleging that they were promised to him by the king when he gave him his daughter in marriage'. But Henry, says Orderic, 'had no inclination to allow anyone, while he lived, to have pre-eminence over himself, or even to be his equal', so he refused to budge. Although the question only centred on three castles, they were important in a number of ways: firstly as a symbol of Geoffrey's own increasing influence and rising status, and his independence from his father-in-law; and secondly – and more practically – for the foothold they would provide in any subsequent claim to or campaign in Normandy. Holding the castles would act as security towards Matilda's succession and Geoffrey's ambitions after Henry's death, and Geoffrey became more insistent in his demands. The situation deteriorated: Geoffrey 'gave offence to the king, both by threats and acts of insolence', says Orderic, which made Henry 'much irritated'.

Matilda's position in this, of course, was awkward. Would she side with her father – who might still change his mind about keeping her as his heir – or her husband, with whom she needed to plan the future of her sons? She chose the latter, a sign of how much her situation had changed during the previous five years. Until this point, she had since her marriage spent more time in Normandy than she had in her husband's county, but in the summer of 1135 she removed to Anjou to remain with Geoffrey, while Henry and his troops placed themselves (or 'prowled', as Orderic memorably puts it) along the border. Henry made no overt or aggressive move, but he did enlarge and refortify the disputed castle at Argentan.

In the autumn of the same year, Matilda discovered that she was pregnant once more. This might have provoked mixed feelings: on the one hand it was positive news, as a noble couple seeking power and influence could never have too many children to serve their purposes; but on the other, it brought with it the attendant dangers. It was only a year and a half since Matilda's near-death experience, and she was aware – even more than she had been previously – that child-bearing could be fatal. Being too active, which encompassed any kind of travel, might endanger her, to say nothing of the fact that at this early stage of the pregnancy she might well have been very sick. She would have had to retire to one or other of her residences to rest, thus putting her out of action. The disadvantages of being female in the political world of the twelfth century were many.

In November 1135 Henry pulled back from the Anjou border a little, but only to go to his hunting lodge at Lyons-la-Forêt, further north towards Rouen, for a respite and some sport. Orderic Vitalis gives us quite a precise summary of the subsequent events. The king (who, let us not forget, was now in his late sixties, and with a summer and autumn of exhausting military manoeuvres behind him) arrived on a Monday, planned to hunt the next day but fell ill during the night. Orderic does not specify the illness, but Henry of Huntingdon notes that Henry, against the advice of his doctors, ate a dish of eels (the famous 'surfeit of lampreys' of many later tales) which disagreed with him, and that this was the cause. Orderic continues his narrative: from Tuesday until the following Sunday the king's condition worsened. He knew he was dying. He confessed to his chaplain and sent for the archbishop of Rouen; he was given the last rites. He commanded Robert of Gloucester, who had hurried to his father's bedside as soon as he heard the news, to take £60,000 from the treasury at Falaise to pay outstanding wages and debts, with any left over to be distributed to the poor. This figure was in Angevin pounds and therefore equal to about £15,000 in contemporary sterling, but it still represented a huge sum – enough to pay more than a thousand knights their daily wage for a year. Henry ordered that his body be conveyed after his death to his new and splendid abbey at Reading, now the home of the relic of the hand of Saint James, and a burgeoning pilgrim destination. It is apparent that although he was suffering physically, Henry's mind was clear.

Henry had consistently refused to relinquish any authority during his lifetime, and nobody had been able to wrest it from him. There had been no gradual transfer of power to an heir, as perhaps might have happened had William Adelin lived. Henry's now-imminent death was therefore going to represent a complete break, and so the question of who was to succeed him became even more crucial. And yet he made no further definitive announcement. There was no written testament to put the question beyond doubt; there was only conflicting testimony about what he said before witnesses while he lay on his deathbed. William of Malmesbury says quite unambiguously that Henry named Matilda to those barons and clergymen gathered around him: 'being interrogated by these persons, as to his successor, he awarded all his territories, on either side of the sea, to his daughter, in legitimate and perpetual succession'. But the *Deeds of Stephen*, which begins at this point with Henry's death, makes a very convoluted case that Henry had effectively released the barons from their oaths to Matilda, because although it was 'presumptuous to wish to desire anything contrary to this arrangement' (i.e., the oath of allegiance to Matilda), Henry had 'rather compelled than directed the leading men of the whole kingdom to swear to accept her as his heir', and that as he was dying 'he very plainly showed repentance for the forcible imposition of the oath on his barons'.

As William of Malmesbury and the author of the *Deeds of Stephen* subsequently took opposing sides in the succession conflict, we can safely assume that each interpreted events according to his own agenda. However, it is noticeable that even the *Deeds of Stephen*, rabidly anti-Matilda as it later turns out to be, does not make any specific claim for Henry having named anyone else as his heir. Orderic Vitalis portrays the Norman barons as being essentially rudderless over the ensuing few weeks as they rushed around trying to protect their own lands and pillaging those of others in various private wars; as he is otherwise so well informed about the details of Henry's death, we can assume that if the king had made a specific pronouncement about his heir then Orderic would have said so.

Henry's illness, as we have seen, was sudden; there was no time for Earl Robert to summon his sister. Benoît de Sainte-Maure confirms that Matilda was still in Anjou at this time, but does not say exactly where; if she was in the capital of Angers, then she was some 200 miles away from Lyons-la-Forêt, a week's journey at that time of year even for a single messenger on horseback to reach her, to say nothing of the time it would take for her subsequently to travel north in her current condition and with a suitable retinue. There was therefore no opportunity for a personal reconciliation before Henry died on the night of 1 December 1135, less than a week after falling ill. Instead Matilda continued in ignorance – ignorance that would prove to be catastrophic.

⮞ CHAPTER FOUR ⮜

USURPED

'GRIEVOUS CALAMITY ... UTTERLY DISORDERED ... ABUNDANCE of iniquity ... all manner of wickedness ... violence ... utterly disregarding the enactments of law ... hateful enmity.' The lengthy opening section of the *Deeds of Stephen* may briefly be summarised thus: after King Henry died, all hell broke loose. Henry's consistent refusal to transfer any significant power to an heir during his lifetime had meant that both kingdom and duchy remained peaceful under his iron fist as long as he lived, but the inevitable result was a conflict that would break out as soon as he died. Had he entertained any idea of the scale of the chaos that his demise would unleash on his hard-won lands, he might have considered making different preparations for the event, but it was now too late.

Henry's personal post-mortem fate was at least dignified, and certainly more respectable than that of his father. William the Conqueror had been abandoned by his followers before his body was even cold and then stuffed into a grave too small for the corpse, but no such end awaited Henry. A king's deathbed was a relatively public place; as well as the various bishops and other clergy whose presence was necessary for a Christian monarch's passing, Henry had been attended by five high-ranking noblemen: his illegitimate son Robert, earl of Gloucester; his erstwhile son-in-law Rotrou, count of Perche; William de Warenne, heir to and later earl of Surrey; Waleran de Beaumont, count of Meulan; and Robert de Beaumont, earl of Leicester. These last three were all interesting characters who had rebelled against Henry at various times and eventually been forgiven; we will hear more of them later. All five promised Henry that once he had breathed his last they would accompany his body to the coast with all honour, a promise they kept. A formal procession first made its way to Rouen, where the entrails were extracted from the corpse – not an uncommon practice at the time – to be buried at the church of Notre-Dame du Pré, and the body was embalmed before its voyage back to England. The next stage of the journey took the company 80 miles to Caen, where the winter weather made it too dangerous to risk the long Channel crossing from the Normandy coast; while they were waiting, the body rested at the monastery of Saint-Étienne, burial place of William the Conqueror. The delay was a long one, and it was not until after Christmas that Henry's body was accompanied to England by a contingent of monks; the crossing was accomplished without incident and the king was buried, as he had wished, at Reading Abbey on 4 January 1136.

But by then both England and Normandy were in uproar. As noted in Chapter 2, the death of a king did not result in the immediate accession of an heir, but rather caused an interregnum until a new monarch was crowned; in the meantime there was no firm leadership. This was of particular concern in Normandy, where the quarrelsome nobles took advantage of the situation. Of the weeks following Henry's death, Orderic Vitalis notes that

> Already, everyone covets his neighbour's property and abandons himself to unbridled injustice ... the Normans abandon themselves to robbery and pillage; they butcher one another, take prisoners, and bind them in fetters; burn houses and all that is in them, not even sparing monks or respecting women ... peace is insupportable to these people, and they broke it as soon as they heard of the king's death ... they suppose that there is now no master to restrain them.

Normandy, perhaps even more so than England, needed a firm hand on the tiller; and the longer there was no king or duke, the more the situation would deteriorate. The failure of King Henry on his deathbed either to reiterate his existing wishes or to clarify new ones meant that the matter was more ambiguous than it should have been. But where there was any question over the succession, a major advantage could be gained by someone who had a blood claim and who could think and act quickly, as evidenced by the accessions both of Henry I himself and of his older brother William Rufus. And now someone saw his chance and took it.

Stephen of Blois, King Henry's nephew, was in his county of Boulogne when the news of Henry's death reached him. This was fortuitous for him in two ways: he was informed of the event sooner than Matilda, and he was in the place from which the shortest possible crossing of the Channel could be made. He sailed from Wissant, probably on 5 December, and landed at Dover. He was, according to the monk and chronicler Gervase of Canterbury, turned away from the royal castle at Dover and the walled city of Canterbury, both controlled by Robert, earl of Gloucester – this implies that news of King Henry's death had sped to England ahead of him, and that a rivalry between Stephen and Robert was already recognised or at least suspected. However, this was no more than a minor inconvenience; Stephen headed straight for London, accompanied only by a small retinue, arriving there possibly as early as 8 December, just a week after the old king's death.

Fortune continued to favour Stephen. He was popular in the capital, the citizens wanting to keep on the right side of him: in his position as count of Boulogne, he controlled their all-important trade route to the Continent. In a somewhat irregular procedure, and possibly via a promise to recognise London as a commune (which would give the city more autonomy and freedom from various restrictions and tolls), he secured their 'election' as king. Despite the *Deeds of Stephen*'s claim that the Londoners said 'it was their own right and peculiar privilege that if their king died from any cause a successor should immediately be appointed by their own choice', they had no particular legal rights in this regard. However, this was a promising sign for Stephen that momentum was with him – and, of course, it would have been much more difficult to press a claim to the throne if the Londoners had come out against him. The wind was still at his back.

Stephen did not tarry long in London but next rode straight for the ancient city and important administrative centre of Winchester. This was the site of the royal treasury and also – once again, providentially – the episcopal seat of his brother Henry. Henry's influence would be crucial in the days and weeks ahead; indeed, the *Deeds of Stephen* is clear that it was Bishop Henry 'on whom his [Stephen's] enterprise entirely depended'. It was with Henry's help that Stephen was able to gain the support of another powerful churchman, Roger, bishop of Salisbury – who, as we have seen, had been left as justiciar and regent of England in King Henry's absence. Bishop Henry was naturally going to favour the candidature of his brother (with all the potential for his own advancement which that entailed) and Roger was no friend to Matilda and thus inclined to support a male rival. Between them the two bishops persuaded the treasury chamberlain William de Pont-de-l'Arche to hand over the keys to the royal treasury, which was very full after Henry I's years of efficient revenue-gathering and careful management; Stephen now enjoyed great material resource as well as the support of the Londoners and the bishops. Henry and Roger then sought to win over the highest-ranking churchman in the realm, the all-important archbishop of Canterbury, who was the only man who had the right to perform a coronation ceremony that would be valid beyond doubt.

Here the first potential stumbling block appeared in Stephen's hitherto smooth plan: Archbishop William of Corbeil inconveniently brought up the subject of Stephen's previous oath to support Matilda's claim to the throne. Would reneging on it not be perjury? Stephen and his backers embarked on some fast talking. The oath was invalid because it had been imposed by the king and not given freely; the king knew in any case that his wishes would not be followed after his death and had only insisted on the oath in order to keep peace during his lifetime; and finally, he had repented of the oath on his deathbed. A convenient 'surprise' witness was produced: Hugh Bigod, a member of one of the old Anglo-Norman noble families and a royal steward since the death of his elder brother in the *White Ship* disaster in 1120. According to both Gervase of Canterbury and John of Salisbury, Hugh swore that King Henry had released the barons from their vows on his deathbed, and had instead urged them to support Stephen's claim; Bishop Roger backed up Hugh's statement. However, Roger had certainly not been present at Henry's deathbed, being verifiably in England at the time, and a later papal court in 1139 heard testimony that Hugh had not been there either. Neither Hugh Bigod nor the supposed release from the oath is mentioned in a detailed letter from another Hugh, the archbishop of Rouen (who was unquestionably at Henry's side during his last days) to the pope shortly after the king's death, and he would surely have noted something so momentous. It was true, of course, that Henry and Matilda had been in conflict with each other at the time of the king's death, so Stephen and his companions were no doubt playing on the uncertainties caused by that situation, but even had the king been so irritated with his daughter that he considered disinheriting her, it seems unlikely that he would thereby want to dispossess permanently the grandson in whom he had so 'rejoiced'. Putting all these things together, we may choose to take Hugh Bigod's statement with a very large pinch of salt.

However, King Henry had unwittingly thrown another hurdle in his daughter's path to the throne at an earlier date. His original intention in marrying Stephen to the heiress Matilda of Boulogne was to ensure that a trusted relative was in charge of the area that was most convenient for Channel crossings and that was pivotal for trade. But in arranging the match between a grandson of the Conqueror and a daughter of the united Anglo-Saxon–Scottish royal house, he effectively created the same 'grafting of the green tree' that had been a cornerstone of his speech in January 1127 on the subject of why Matilda should be preferred to William Clito in the succession; Stephen's claim was thereby made stronger.

Stephen was charming. Bishop Henry was persuasive and influential. And Bishop Roger held out the possibility of peace and continuity, having ruled England in King Henry's absence for the best part of the last two years and being willing to continue to serve under Stephen. It was all enough for Archbishop William.

A hastily arranged, simple and sparsely attended (William of Malmesbury notes that those present were 'three bishops, no abbots and scarcely any of the nobility') coronation ceremony took place at Westminster Abbey on 22 December 1135 at which Stephen was crowned and anointed king of England. This consecration was irrevocable; by the time Stephen acted as one of the pall-bearers at Henry's delayed funeral a week later, when the body had finally arrived at Reading, he was indisputably a king.

Stephen's coup had been so swift that many in both England and Normandy were caught out, including some who might have been considered contenders for the throne.

Robert, earl of Gloucester and the eldest illegitimate son of King Henry, was generally considered by contemporaries to be an honourable and just man. It is not surprising that William of Malmesbury should be full of praise for his patron, but even the noticeably pro-Stephen *Deeds of Stephen* admits that Robert was 'a man of proven talent and admirable wisdom'.

After his father's death Robert had accompanied the cortege as far as Caen, and he now remained in Normandy with a considerable amount of the late king's cash in his possession. Many noblemen, finding themselves in this position, might have made a grab for power, but Robert did not, as the *Deeds of Stephen* continues: 'When he was advised, as the story went, to claim the throne on his father's death . . . he by no means assented, saying it was fairer to yield it to his sister's son, to whom it more justly belonged, than presumptuously to arrogate it to himself.' Robert's was the lone voice speaking for young Henry; if the boy had only been older then this might have been a workable plan, and one to which the barons could have been reconciled, but he was at this stage just two years old, so it was too much of a risk and the idea, if it was ever formally raised at all, was dismissed.

Robert remained in Normandy, and in the middle of December he was one of the magnates who met in council to discuss the question of the succession. The outcome of the deliberations was that the group offered the duchy of Normandy to Theobald of Blois, Stephen's brother, on the basis that he was the eldest of the late king's nephews. As we saw earlier, Theobald had been incommoded by Matilda's marriage into the house of Anjou, so the idea of adding Normandy to his territories in Blois and Champagne was appealing. He was on the verge of accepting the offer when a messenger from England reached them, probably sometime between 18 and 20 December. Orderic Vitalis has the details: 'Meanwhile, the Normans, holding council at Neubourg, inclined to place themselves under the government of Theobald . . . but hearing, while they were assembled, from a monk who was Stephen's envoy, that all the English had submitted to him and intended to make him their king, the meeting unanimously resolved, with Theobald's consent, to serve under one lord, on account of the fiefs which the barons held in both provinces.'

The news was evidently a great surprise. Although we may detect a small amount of exaggeration for effect on Stephen's part in saying that 'all' the English had submitted to him, the group of nobles seemed in no doubt that his accession was a fait accompli and one that would be sealed by the coronation a few days later. Orderic notes that Theobald, as the elder of the two brothers, was 'indignant' at Stephen's actions, but it seems he was not angry enough to dispute it. After all, he had been offered only Normandy; England would need to be fought for, possibly at the expense of the ancestral lands and holdings he would leave behind him. He no doubt saw Stephen as the next best candidate after himself: the crown would be in the family, having Stephen as king and duke would ease some of Theobald's own worries in Champagne and Blois, and he could in due course look forward to further preferment. The Norman barons, meanwhile, were happy with the arrangement as most of them held lands in both Normandy and England, and it would make their lives easier to have a single overlord ruling over both. Theobald withdrew to France. Stephen was occupied in England for the time being, so Normandy was left to its own devices.

And what of Matilda? Many miles to the south as she was, Stephen was probably already in England and heading for London before she even heard of her father's death. Her feelings on receiving the shocking news must have been mixed: Henry had not always been kind to her on a personal level, being a king first and a father second, but they had shared a close relationship and he had been a major figure in her life, so her grief was surely profound. However, she too had been trained to put the political before the personal, so she must push her private feelings to one side and decide how best to act. And the crucial, the unavoidable, question we must therefore ask at this point is this: why did she make no move towards England?

One answer may be that she believed that the barons and clergy of England and Normandy would honour her father's wishes, honour their vows, come to her and acclaim her as queen and duchess without the need for further effort on her part. If this is so, then it is an indication of a staggering naïvety, which – given her political acumen and previous experience – is unlikely to be the case. Therefore we must look beyond this possibility. There may have been a physical cause: she was, of course, expecting a child, and William of Malmesbury does note rather coyly that she did not travel to England due to 'certain causes'. We do not know the exact stage of her pregnancy in mid-December 1135, but if we start from the known date of the birth, assume it was not overly premature (the survival of the child indicating that it was not) and work backwards, then we can extrapolate that at the time she heard of Henry's death Matilda was somewhere between eight and twelve weeks pregnant, a peak time for sickness. If she was vomiting constantly and unable to stomach food or drink then even the prospect of a crown might not have been enough to entice her into a winter sea voyage, and it would certainly have affected her judgement.

Matilda's pregnancy was just one of the multiple disadvantages from which she suffered at this point. Had she been present at her father's deathbed, she would have been in a better position to assert her rights. Had she even been elsewhere in Normandy or in England then she would have been nearer to the centre of events. But she was not. Matilda might herself be blamed, at least in part, for these things, as she had chosen to support her husband in his conflict against her father; but then, that same husband had been chosen by her father, against her wishes, and the king had subsequently sent her back to him after she had made one attempt to leave, in order to force her to have his children. She could hardly then be blamed for siding with the man who was the father of her sons and her life partner in the eyes of God and the law. Indeed, one suspects that if she had chosen to support Henry against Geoffrey in the disputes of 1134–35 then she would have been portrayed as a disobedient wife, which would not have done her any favours in contemporary opinion either. The frustrating irony now was that Matilda had done everything that her father wished, only to find that it all worked against her when it mattered, by locating her both physically and politically at the outer edge of the Anglo-Norman world.

But, pregnancy or no, something had to be done. A sea voyage to England might not have been feasible, but the journey to the southern border of Normandy was much shorter. Matilda travelled to the area of the disputed castles; this was in mid-December, so it must have been in response to the king's death rather than to news of Stephen's usurpation of the crown, which cannot possibly have reached her by then. There she had some luck. King Henry's death meant that the castellan in charge of all three castles accepted her, as Orderic Vitalis says, 'as his lawful sovereign, and yielded to her Argentan, Exmes and Domfront, and some other places, which he governed under the king'.

Matilda made her base at the recently refortified Argentan. This was the best site, strategically, of the three: it lay between the other two, had been a favoured residence of Henry I, and was an important administrative and military hub, being both a repository for revenues collected and a centre for the manufacture of mail armour. She did not move physically from Argentan for several months but was in a favourable position to receive news via the various trade, administrative and information networks that converged there. And, immobile as she was, she could still control the surrounding lands: the area dominated by a fortification was not, as is sometimes supposed, a bowshot's length from the walls, but rather a day's ride in any direction. Thus by stationing an active garrison in each of the three castles now in her possession, and overlapping their areas of influence, she had control of an area some 90 miles wide that had the added advantage of encompassing the main route that led south from Caen to Alençon and Le Mans. While Matilda was directing matters from Argentan, Geoffrey, more mobile, made his way to Maine and took control of three fortifications there, extending the couple's influence further.

This incursion into Normandy had both advantages and disadvantages. On the one hand, it gave Matilda a foothold there that she would never lose, thus providing her with a base from which to launch later attempts on the duchy. However, on the other, politically speaking it might also have been considered ill-advised, as it effectively prolonged the war with her father and thus put her in an opposing position to Henry's most loyal adherents, including Robert of Gloucester and Brian fitzCount, who might feel obliged to carry on the conflict on the late king's behalf. Matilda's motives are open to question. Did she feel that the benefits of having at least a portion of the duchy under her control outweighed the potential disadvantages? Or was she in fact a little more hesitant, but unable to prevent the frustrated and bellicose Geoffrey from embarking on his long-held aim of invading Normandy? As it happened, they moved no further at this point; Geoffrey's absence from Anjou prompted a minor rebellion there, and he was forced to return to quell it.

It was while she was at Argentan that the devastating news reached Matilda. Stephen, who had twice publicly sworn an oath to support her, had reneged on his word – had perjured himself before God and man – and seized her crown. Her fury may easily be imagined, particularly when coupled with the extreme vexation of knowing that she could do absolutely nothing about it. Had she been a man, would her claims have been pushed aside without thought, ignored in this way? The answer could only have been a resounding 'no'. She was the only legitimate child of the previous king, 'born in the purple', designated and accepted as heir; she saw herself as the intellectual and political equal of the barons. But recent events showed that they simply could not overcome the barrier of her sex. To them a woman – any woman – was unfit to rule, simply because she was a woman, regardless of how clever or experienced or otherwise suited to the position she might be. Indeed, Matilda's femaleness was currently a curse on her ambitions twice over: the noblemen and clergymen felt that they could use it as an excuse to overlook her with impunity, and she was unable to take direct action against them because of that most female of reasons, pregnancy. Matilda was increasingly immobile and had no choice but to remain where she was; additionally, she realised that the road in front of her was becoming longer and more arduous. Any resource she might have been able to muster would now pale into insignificance compared to the great wealth Stephen would have at his disposal from the English royal treasury. There would be no swift and easy campaign to seize her crown. And, finally, the sting was made more painful by the fact that so far not one baron or bishop had raised his voice on her behalf, despite their own public oaths, sworn to her face.

There were very few ways in which Matilda could make her presence felt more widely while she was immobilised at Argentan. Even making the token gesture of calling herself monarch would be futile: there was no point trying to style herself 'queen of England' when that title had already been bestowed on Stephen's wife by right of his coronation. But Matilda did not refer to herself as 'countess of Anjou' either – instead she took a middle way. Charters of hers are few and far between for this period (which is not surprising: she was not taking an active role in public life and had little patronage to dispense) but two that are traceable are a grant of land near to Argentan and a charter in which she confirms the rights of a church in Angers. In both she styles herself 'Matilda, empress, daughter of the king of the English'; the 'daughter of the king' part implies some entitlement to England but does not go as far as claiming to be queen-designate or even 'lawful heir', as had been the case with William Adelin or with Melisende in Jerusalem. Geoffrey also referred to her using similar titles, perhaps to enhance his own prestige: in a charter of his own that dates from the period between King Henry's death and Matilda's return to England he refers to her as 'Matilda, my wife, daughter of Henry king of the English, lawfully married to me after the death of Henry emperor of the Romans'.

And so Matilda sat in Argentan while the Anglo-Norman political world went on without her. Was it tempting to give up and accept her role as countess of Anjou? With a task of such magnitude ahead, a fight against such overwhelming odds, some might have succumbed; but Empress Matilda, daughter of the English king, descendant of ancient royalty, former queen of the Germans, queen of the Romans and regent of Italy, was no readier to retire to a life of provincial obscurity than she had been a decade earlier when she was first widowed. And besides, even if she yielded to the temptation to feel sorry for herself, she would have to pull herself together to fight on behalf of her sons and their inheritance. Was little Henry, following the long and anguished wait for his arrival during all her childless years, and born as a result of Matilda putting her ambitions ahead of her personal life, to be relegated to a status of mere local importance, to raise his ambitions no higher than succeeding to a French county? This was impossible to contemplate. But Stephen had five children of his own, three sons and two daughters, so both England and Normandy would slip away from the late King Henry's line permanently if Matilda did not take action. It was up to her. Fortunately, this was one area – possibly the only one – where she and Geoffrey could find common ground, so she could at least expect to rely on his help. But there was nothing practical to be done until she had survived the forthcoming birth, so she kicked her heels at Argentan through the spring and early summer of 1136 while Stephen went about consolidating his position.

There was a single ray of light for Matilda, for one man on the other side of the Channel had stood by his oath to her and now acted. As soon as David, king of Scots heard that Henry I was dead, he mustered an army and invaded England. We should not, of course, lose sight of the fact that this action was in his own interest as well as Matilda's – few Scottish kings would turn down the opportunity to make inroads into the north of England – but still, he was the only one of all the oath-takers of 1127 and 1131 even to seem to act on her behalf. Describing the invasion, Richard, the prior of Hexham, wrote that David 'took security and hostages from the great men and the nobility of the region that they *maintain their faith to the empress*' (my emphasis). Unfortunately for both uncle and niece David's invasion turned out to be a damp squib. He had some initial success, despite the winter weather: throughout the second half of December his forces attacked on a wide front, and by late January 1136 he had captured castles along an axis that ran from Norham through Alnwick and Wark to Carlisle, and had reached as far south as Newcastle, which he took before the end of the month. He then headed for Durham. But Stephen was able to react quickly and, with the significant cash now at his disposal, he gathered and equipped a sizeable force including many mercenaries, marched north and met David at Durham in February.

Outnumbered and far from his own border, David chose not to fight but instead agreed a treaty. He would keep the castle of Carlisle and his twenty-one-year-old son Henry would be installed as earl of Huntingdon (a title which had previously been David's, but in right of his late wife), along with half the lands thereof. There was a vague promise that if Stephen should ever consider reinstating the earldom of Northumbria – which had been in abeyance since 1095 – then Henry would be given first consideration; his mother had been the daughter of the Anglo-Saxon earl Waltheof, who had been executed in 1067. David would return the other castles he had captured to Stephen. Once the treaty was sealed David returned to Scotland, but he had not yet finished fighting for Matilda's cause.

By Easter 1136 most of the other barons had reconciled themselves to Stephen's rule, for what other realistic option was there? Matilda's absence made her an increasing irrelevance, Theobald of Blois had accepted the situation and returned to France, and Robert of Gloucester had made no move on his own behalf. Rather than stirring up trouble, it was better for the magnates to accept the status quo, however irregular its beginning, and to see what they could make of it.

If Matilda had suffered from impotent fury at hearing the news of Stephen's usurpation, others were bemused. We should clarify at this point that the use of the word 'usurp' refers more to Stephen's reneging on his oath than to his overturning of hereditary precedence, as, despite King Henry's efforts, this was not yet the defining principle in the English succession. But it is difficult to see on precisely what grounds Stephen was claiming the throne, other than that he was in the right place at the right time. He could hardly claim hereditary right, over the legitimate child of the previous king; nor male primogeniture, as he had a living older brother, Theobald. Henry's much-trumpeted principle of porphyrogeniture did not apply: Stephen was the son of a count. He was a male candidate descended from the Conqueror, yes, but one who traced his descent in the female line, which made it difficult to see why Matilda's son Henry should not be preferred, even if she herself was not.

The simple and defining reason for Stephen's success was that, since the death of Edward the Confessor seventy years before, the crown of England had been there for the taking each time the incumbent died. Anyone with a reasonable blood claim and the resources to back it up could have a go; being in the right place at the right time had worked before and it worked now. Stephen had all the advantages that came with being a legitimate adult male; and a legitimate adult male, moreover, who could talk smoothly, who could win people over with his genial and open-hearted nature, and who had influential supporters in the church. Still, the speed of his actions meant that there was plenty of contemporary confusion about how events had transpired, and exactly what Stephen's justification had been, which is illustrated in the chronicles.

The most specifically pro-Matilda writer is Benoît de Sainte-Maure. His chronicle ends with the death of Henry I, but he does just have time to squeeze in a comment that Stephen 'became king through deception, and by most grievous wrongdoing, for the empress was the heir'. Others do not go quite as far as this, but they do mention the oath of allegiance that Stephen had sworn to his cousin. John of Worcester says that all those who took the oath would become perjurers when they supported Stephen, but frustratingly he drops the subject after that. He does also note that Stephen became king by 'election', thus indicating that he was not attempting to claim hereditary right. Henry of Huntingdon tells us that Stephen was 'a man of great valour and boldness, and trusting to his vigour and effrontery; although he had sworn the English realm's oath of fealty to the daughter of King Henry, he tried God's patience by seizing the crown of the kingdom'. William of Malmesbury makes much of supposed bad omens when he notes that Stephen, 'after the king of Scotland, was the first layman to swear fidelity to the empress' and then says that on the day Stephen disembarked in England there was 'a terrible peal of thunder, with most dreadful lightning, so that the world seemed well-nigh about to be dissolved'.

The *Deeds of Stephen* justifies Stephen's acts, as we have seen, by asserting that the Londoners claimed an ancient right to choose the king, citing the need to choose quickly because of the danger to the kingdom if it were to be left leaderless for too long: 'For, they said, every kingdom was exposed to calamities from ill fortune when a representative of the whole government and a fount of justice was lacking. It was therefore worth their while to appoint as soon as possible a king who, with a view to re-establishing peace for the common benefit, would meet the insurgents of the kingdom in arms and would justly administer the enactment of the laws.' Even in this work, though, there is a hint that some preferred Stephen simply because he was not Matilda – not because they thought he was a perfect candidate. The *Deeds of Stephen* notes in passing that Stephen was someone who, 'exalted . . . by the fame of his wise brothers, will, supported by their assistance, bring to greater perfection whatever is thought to be lacking in him'. Hardly a ringing endorsement.

It is left to the hindsight of Roger of Wendover – who was writing a hundred years after the event and thus basing his account on a précis of earlier works rather than eyewitness testimony – to spell out the simple reason why Stephen was preferred: 'All the bishops, earls and barons, who had sworn fealty to the king's daughter and her heirs, gave their adherence to King Stephen, saying that it would be a shame for so many nobles to submit themselves to a woman.'

By the time Stephen summoned his barons to Westminster for the Easter court of 1136, he probably felt that his position was secure. In order to provide a spectacle demonstrating his kingship and confirming the support of the church (given that so few of the nobles had been at his actual coronation), he processed into the abbey wearing his crown, with the archbishops of Canterbury and York on either side of him; his wife was then crowned as Queen Matilda. On a more practical level, he had dealt with the Scottish situation to the satisfaction of his followers; and as a final triumph he now also had in his possession a letter of support from Pope Innocent II recognising his accession to the throne.

This last is not quite as impressive as it sounds. Although the question of the English succession would be debated at length in 1139 (and this is a point to which we will return in Chapter 5), at this stage it is possible that Innocent had not given the matter his full attention but rather accepted the fait accompli. Stephen's coronation had, after all, been approved and carried out by the archbishop of Canterbury, who was also a papal legate and thus a personal representative of the Holy See; to gainsay the archbishop's authority would create a rift in the church, which Innocent presumably wished to avoid. He would also have hoped for some advantage for the church from the situation. The archbishop of Canterbury had ensured that Stephen took an oath at his coronation to restore and maintain the liberties of the church; Henry, bishop of Winchester had spent the days between the securing of the archbishop's consent and the ceremony itself drawing up a text which would solve or regulate some of the common points of dispute between church and state. It should not surprise us that the agreed text on the points at issue came down firmly in favour of the church. Chief among them was the 'canonical' election of clergymen – that is, the freedom of churchmen to select a candidate for a bishopric or abbacy without interference from the state or its laymen. This echoed the Investiture Controversy, mentioned in Chapter 1, that had caused so much friction and conflict throughout western Europe for decades. Stephen, of course, had been in no position to argue if he wanted his coronation to go ahead, so he had accepted the wording of the document; this had no doubt been conveyed to the pope at the same time as the news of the accession, thus sweetening the pill.

However, although Stephen may at this point have felt a little more secure – given that three months had elapsed and he was still in possession of the crown – there were still those who did not approve of his seizure of it. David, king of Scots, seemed quiet but was busy making further plans for action, and both Earl Robert of Gloucester (who was not present at Stephen's Easter court and whose actions we will explore in more depth later in this chapter) and Brian fitzCount were lukewarm to say the least. Others rebelled more openly, among them Baldwin de Redvers, a West Country lord who held the honours of Plympton in Devon, Christchurch in Hampshire and the Isle of Wight.

Baldwin was also the castellan of Exeter Castle; that is, he did not own it but held it for the king. Dissatisfied with Stephen, Baldwin now claimed lordship over the city of Exeter and the surrounding countryside in his own name. This was bad enough, but when he followed up in practice by garrisoning the royal castle at Exeter with his own men and stockpiling provisions there, the issue grew too serious to be ignored. Stephen could not overlook such a challenge to his kingship, so he responded by sending an advance party of two hundred cavalry (who could move much faster than a larger army made up of a mixture of horsemen, infantry and others), and followed with the rest of his force shortly afterwards, reaching Exeter in June. Even with the king in front of them in person, the garrison refused to surrender. There was no longer any possibility of dismissing the situation lightly or spinning it as any kind of misunderstanding: it was a rebellion against the crown, and Stephen had to respond appropriately if he were to nip it in the bud. His forces encircled the castle and began a siege. According to the *Deeds of Stephen*, he tried everything, showing no lack of personal courage:

> Day and night he vigorously and energetically pressed on with the siege of the garrison; sometimes he joined battle with them by means of armed men crawling up the rampart; sometimes, by the aid of countless slingers, who had been hired from a distant region, he assailed them with an unendurable hail of stones; at other times he summoned those who had skill in mining underground and ordered them to search into the bowels of the earth with a view to demolishing the wall; frequently too he devised engines of different sorts . . . to shake or undermine the wall.

The siege engines of this period, however, were not the huge and effective machines of later centuries, so they had little effect; the castle was both well fortified and well provisioned and it held out for three months through the summer. But then the inevitable happened, and the garrison's supplies of water began to run out. They were forced to use wine, not only for drinking but also for cooking, baking bread and even firefighting; and when the supplies of wine began to run out too, they were compelled to consider surrender.

In his camp Stephen was enjoying the taste of forthcoming victory. But it was at this point that he made a crucial mistake, the first of many related to his easy-going nature. After the trouble the garrison had caused, and the huge expense of the siege (the cost ran into thousands of pounds, and Henry of Huntingdon noted that Stephen 'used up much of his treasure'), not to mention the inconvenient monopolising of the king's attention when he had matters to deal with elsewhere, a harsh response was both expected and required. Many of Stephen's men, including his brother Bishop Henry, who was present, argued for severe measures in order to punish the rebellious and to serve as a warning to others. This was sensible in the context: the late King Henry had ensured peace in his lands by acting swiftly, decisively and even cruelly in such situations, such that none dared to rebel after. But Stephen was a different man. He accepted the surrender of the garrison and then rather tamely allowed them to leave with honour. The same courtesy was extended to those garrisoning Baldwin's other castle at Plympton, and – almost inexplicably given the circumstances – Baldwin himself was allowed to go free.

This demonstration of either clemency or weakness (depending on your point of view of Stephen) was widely discussed by contemporaries. The *Deeds of Stephen* naturally puts the most positive spin on it: 'That he might win their closer attachment and have them more devoted to his service he allowed the besieged not only to go forth in freedom but also to take away their possessions.' The king preferred 'to settle all things in the love of peace and concord rather than encourage the schism of discord in any wise'. But immediate peace and mercy were not always in the long-term interests of the kingdom, as Henry of Huntingdon points out: 'Taking the very worst advice, he did not execute punishment on those who had betrayed him. For if he had done so at that time, there would not have been so many castles held against him later.' Here we see some early echoes of the damning verdicts on Robert Curthose, and what his affability had cost him. Baldwin de Redvers was indeed to return to haunt Stephen: on leaving Devon he repaired to his base on the Isle of Wight, where he immediately stirred up another rebellion, and later 'left England as an exile and went to the count of Anjou', according to the *Deeds of Stephen*. Geoffrey and Matilda 'received him and his followers with honour', and Baldwin would become one of Matilda's firmest supporters in the years to come.

However, that was in the future. For now Stephen had put down the rebellion, and he was able to spend the winter in the south-east of England where his family lands lay. By March 1137 he felt confident enough to make the crossing to Normandy for the first time since his coronation, and there he held his Easter court, probably in Rouen. In May he held a meeting with the now-ailing Louis VI of France; Louis was only fifty-five but he was deservedly earning the soubriquet by which he would later be known, 'the Fat', and he was not in good health. He was 'failing not in mind but in body . . . worn out by his corpulence and by the continual strain of his tasks', says Abbot Suger. Some five years previously he had lost his eldest son and heir, Philip (already crowned as 'junior king' according to the custom of the Capetians), in a riding accident, so his second son Louis had been promoted to the position. Louis senior was still well enough and resourceful enough to have secured a recent diplomatic and political triumph that would later have repercussions for England and Normandy: the powerful duke of

Aquitaine, William X, had died just a month previously, and on his deathbed he had named Louis as the guardian of his fifteen-year-old daughter and heiress, Eleanor. The king wasted no time arranging a profitable alliance, and the younger Louis was even now on his way south to marry the girl. One of the richest and most extensive duchies on French soil would now be united with the Capetians and the crown, and Louis VI was no doubt confident of his house's future as he met the English king. Stephen, too, was now involving his children in the political game; at the meeting his seven-year-old eldest son Eustace gave homage for Normandy to the French king. This embedded Stephen and his family more firmly in their royal position, thus making Matilda's mountain ever harder to climb.

However, although Stephen by now felt more confident in his kingship, and on the surface all seemed peaceful, he had erred in sending out the message – in England at least – that a rebel could defy the king and escape with his life and liberty. This was not the right lesson to teach those magnates who might either be regretting their hasty decision to recognise him as king or who might see opportunities for gain in a continuation of conflict against him.

One such was David, king of Scots. His initial invasion of England in December 1135 had been too hasty; the swiftness with which he had acted indicated that it was in response to King Henry's death and before he had been more fully informed of the situation in Normandy. David had perhaps expected that the Norman barons might declare for Matilda or that she herself would sweep north from her position in Anjou, so that he would be one half of a pincer movement which would capture Normandy and England between them. But Normandy, after the barons' initial flirtation with Theobald, had accepted Stephen, so David's had been a lone gesture. However, he had not given up. The *Deeds of Stephen* says that, 'inflamed by zeal for justice, both on account of the ties of kinship and because he owed the woman the fealty he had promised, he determined to set the kingdom of England in confusion'. The truce sealed at Durham in the spring of 1136 expired in December 1137, just as Stephen was returning from Normandy, and David now acted. Initially he sent envoys to Stephen on a possibly bogus pretext, asking to reopen the question of the earldom of Northumbria (which, as we have seen, was referred to in the negotiations of 1136), but when his request was rejected out of hand he reacted by marching south with his son Henry, despite the winter weather.

Scottish forces besieged the castle of Wark for several weeks, and David sent his troops on a murderous rampage through Northumberland and the county of Durham. This was roundly condemned by contemporaries: the *Deeds of Stephen* says that the Scots were 'barbarous and filthy, neither overcome by excess of cold nor enfeebled by severe hunger, putting their trust in swiftness of foot and light equipment ... among foreigners they surpass all in cruelty'; Prior Richard of Hexham, who was an eyewitness to the campaign, added that they were 'more atrocious than any pagans, respecting neither God nor man'. We should note that criticism of the Scots as 'barbarous' was something of a cliché among English writers at this time, so the campaign and its supposed atrocities may not have been quite as vicious as they claim, but there was, nevertheless, much loss of life and property.

Stephen needed to react quickly, and he did; he was on his way north with an army early in the new year of 1138, and had reached the area devastated by David's men by the beginning of February. This time he made no attempt at negotiation, but rather bypassed David, entered Scotland and began to lay waste to Lothian. David was forced to withdraw back to his own border, but Stephen had no intention of being drawn into a pitched battle at this stage. He was low on supplies (February was not a good time for foraging and living off the land) and in unfamiliar terrain, so the odds would not be in his favour; he turned south again. David responded by launching more raids against the coastal areas of Northumberland and Durham throughout April. In Stephen's absence the hostilities continued throughout the spring and summer, including an engagement at Clitheroe in Lancashire in June in which the Scots were victorious, and another siege of Wark throughout the summer at which they had less success.

King David then profited from two strokes of good fortune. Firstly, a further revolt against Stephen had broken out in Herefordshire and Shropshire, and Stephen's attention was focused there, giving David more or less a free rein. And, secondly, a prominent northern baron, Eustace fitz-John, came over to him; this gifted the Scottish king not only more troops but also control of the castles of Alnwick and Malton. Thus David had quite a large army when he moved again in late July and early August, with the intention of penetrating further south than before, deep into England.

The barons of northern England were not a united group. They lacked the presence of the king who might bring them together, and they were suspicious of each other and unwilling to submit to each other's leadership. But the threat from the Scots was too dangerous to ignore, so Thurstan, the aged archbishop of York, took charge and mustered a force. He was too old and infirm to travel himself, but he sent an army up the Great North Road accompanied by symbols of the support of the church: a wagon mounted with a ship's mast on which flew the banners of three saints of local importance, Saint Peter (to whom York Minster was dedicated), Saint John of Beverley and Saint Wilfrid of Ripon. This host met David's force near Northallerton on 22 August 1138 in an engagement which is sometimes called the battle of Northallerton but more often the battle of the Standard, in recognition of the holy banners of the English. The result was a resounding defeat for the Scottish king and, although he was not captured, he was forced to retreat behind his own border and come to terms. Richard of Hexham notes that Stephen's wife, Queen Matilda, was instrumental in the peace negotiations – she was, after all, David's niece.

But David had once more failed his other niece, with the result that Stephen seemed ever safer on his throne.

Let us return now to Matilda, whom we last saw immobile and frustrated in the castle of Argentan in spring 1136 while she awaited the end of her pregnancy. She was confined there in the height of summer, and gave birth without too many complications on 22 July to a boy who was named William. With three healthy sons, she and Geoffrey could now count themselves reasonably secure in terms of the survival to adulthood of a male heir; this gave them the option of ceasing their marital relations if they chose to, and it is probable that they did so as they had no more children after producing three in three and a half years. Safe from the possibility and dangers of pregnancy, Matilda could start to make further plans.

Although the birth had been successful, both parties surviving unscathed, Matilda would still have needed some time for recovery. This 'lying-in' period was standard practice for mothers of all social classes, and in Matilda's present case her recuperation would have given her some time to consider her options. She was well aware by now that there would be no swift and decisive campaign for the crown. She controlled no port in Normandy, had no safe route to the coast; to attempt an invasion of England at this point, without proper back-up and against Stephen's wealth of resource, would be absolute folly. The most likely outcome of that potential course of action would be her capture – and possible lifelong incarceration, as had been the case for her uncle Robert Curthose – and the consequent loss of opportunity for her sons, who would be forced into a Clito-esque life of exile. Matilda had not spent years manoeuvring herself into her current position only to throw it all away. The immediate situation was not favourable, but she would need to take a long-term view.

Matilda's recovery from the birth was quicker and more straightforward than her previous experience, and by the autumn of 1136 she was fit enough to take action in support of Geoffrey's current campaign. As we noted, he had not remained at Argentan with her, but had instead made gains in Maine and had then returned to Anjou to quell a rebellion. He was now back in Normandy and engaged in a siege at Le Sap, a small fortification in central Normandy roughly equidistant from Caen, Alençon and Évreux; Matilda rode in person to bring him an additional troop of two hundred men, arriving in early October. However, the reunion with her husband was as unsuccessful and anti-climactic as might be expected from such a turbulent relationship. The siege was ineffective; Geoffrey was wounded in the foot, possibly on the very day she arrived, and was unable to continue to fight in person; dysentery threatened the camp; he announced that he was giving up and going home. During the short campaign he had allowed his men to act with savagery (Orderic Vitalis says that they 'made themselves hated for ever by their brutality') and they were repaid by attacks from the locals on their column as they retreated south. This did Matilda no favours: she was coming to be seen as the wife of the invading Angevin count rather than as the daughter of the old duke and the rightful inheritor of Normandy.

Matilda made little progress during the next twelve months, although some trouble was stirred up on her behalf by Baldwin de Redvers, whom we met earlier in this chapter and who had by now made his way across the Channel from England. France suddenly became less of a threat to all parties when Louis VI died on 1 August 1137; he was succeeded by the seventeen-year-old and somewhat monkish Louis VII – as noted earlier, he was Louis's second son and therefore not originally intended for the crown. Young Louis was already struggling to control his new acquisition, Aquitaine, and had little time to spare for what was essentially an internal conflict in Normandy.

By the spring of 1138 Matilda's cause was flagging. Although Stephen could not claim to be fully in control of Normandy, he had been king of England for over two years and had put down – albeit with mixed eventual results – several rebellions against him. He was embedding himself further into his position and had three surviving children (his second son Baldwin and his younger daughter Matilda had both recently died, aged around six and five; they were buried together at Holy Trinity Priory in Aldgate), including two sons. The elder of these, Eustace, was already being associated with Stephen's rule, as we saw earlier when he gave homage for Normandy. Matilda, still stuck on the southern fringes of the duchy, needed a boost. And then, in the early summer of 1138, she received one.

Robert, earl of Gloucester, had never been easy in his support for Stephen. He had been almost the last of the barons to recognise him as king, and then only reluctantly. He was not present at Stephen's Easter court in England in 1136, being in Normandy at that time. As William of Malmesbury tells us, he found himself in a very difficult position: 'If he became subject to Stephen, it seemed contrary to the oath he had sworn to his sister; if he opposed him, he saw that he could nothing benefit her or his nephews, though he must grievously injure himself.' There was no option to abstain: Robert would have to jump one way or the other. His sister was his nearer relative, and he had sworn to uphold her rights; however, she had been in conflict with their father at the time of his death, and Robert was nothing if not loyal to his father. Stephen was his cousin and also therefore a close relative, but the two men had been rivals for a long time so agreeing to serve him now would be humiliating. Plus there were practical considerations – Robert had his own lands and family (a wife and seven children) to think of. What was the potential damage to them? But he had to decide, and he went – for now at least – with the status quo. William of Malmesbury continues: 'He did homage to the king, therefore, under a certain condition; namely, so long as he should preserve his rank entire, and maintain his engagements to him; for having long since scrutinised Stephen's disposition, he foresaw the instability of his faith.'

The fact that Stephen was prepared to accept such an equivocal oath demonstrates both that Robert was in a strong position and that Stephen was tending towards ineffectualness – one cannot, for example, imagine

Henry I accepting homage on such terms from anyone. Interestingly, William of Malmesbury also contends that Robert was secretly for his sister all the time; the barons had, in the main, gone over to Stephen, but Robert 'therefore was extremely desirous to convince them of their misconduct, and recall them to wiser sentiments by his presence; for he was unable to oppose Stephen's power ... he had not the liberty of coming to England unless, appearing as a partaker of their revolt, he dissembled for a time his secret intentions'. This is William's justification for Robert's later actions: that he paid homage under duress and only to dissemble, so that (in a similar way to those who justified their support for Stephen by saying that their oath to Matilda had been extracted through coercion by King Henry) he could later claim that his oath to Stephen was not binding. We should not forget, however, that William was something of an apologist for Robert. The *Deeds of Stephen* details the same events, but the author interprets them differently: 'When, after being many times summoned to the king's presence by messages and letters, he at length appeared, he was received with favour and distinction and obtained all he demanded in accordance with his wish, on paying homage to the king; and when peace finally had been made with him, almost the whole kingdom of England had gone over to the king's side.' Stephen and Robert were never going to be easy allies, but it is open to question how much of their subsequent rift was based on genuine dislike and how much on misinterpretation of their original agreement.

After Robert paid homage to Stephen, Stephen was initially unwilling to let him out of his sight. Robert therefore remained with the king for several months and was a member of his party at the siege of Exeter in the summer of 1136. However, once he was able to leave court to travel back to his own lands, he became a little more elusive. He did not accompany Stephen when he sailed to Normandy in March 1137; Robert apparently had unspecified matters to attend to on his own estates in the West Country and so did not cross the Channel until a month later, handily missing the Easter court at which Stephen assembled his Norman barons. Robert had great holdings in Normandy as well as in England; he was particularly strong in the regions of Caen – through which Stephen passed after his Channel crossing – and in Bayeux, where his illegitimate son Richard was bishop. The governance of these extensive estates gave him all the excuse he needed to settle himself back into Normandy, remaining there after Stephen had returned to England.

Also present in Normandy at this time was the exiled Baldwin de Redvers. Together with his friends Stephen de Mandeville and Reginald de Dunstanville (who was another, and probably the last, of Henry I's illegitimate sons and therefore a much younger half-brother of Robert and Matilda) he continued to agitate on Matilda's behalf. His efforts were not successful in any meaningful sense, as he did not have enough men to stage a full rebellion, but he was causing sufficient trouble to attract Stephen's attention once more. It was the spring of 1138 and Stephen was both embroiled in his campaign against David, king of Scots and distracted by the uprising in Shropshire, so he was not in a position to cross the Channel himself to deal with the man he might now be wishing he had executed; instead he sent Waleran de Beaumont, count of Meulan, and William of Ypres (the commander of his mercenaries) over to Normandy.

At this point some kind of definitive rift occurred between Stephen and Robert, which led to Robert taking the all-important step of renouncing his homage in May 1138. It is possible that he claimed that Stephen had plotted to kill him in an ambush, although this may be a fabrication or at least an exaggeration, as the account of it appears only in the work of William of Malmesbury. Whatever the precise reason, and regardless of whether there was one specific trigger event, Stephen seems to have been incrementally depriving Robert of influence; this is perhaps unsurprising given their previous relationship, but it was contrary to their homage agreement and serious enough to goad Robert into action. He publicly and widely accused Stephen of breaking his oath to Henry I and of usurping the throne; and he declared unequivocally that Matilda was the rightful heir to the crown of England. He went so far as to issue a *diffidatio*, or formal defiance, as William of Malmesbury describes: 'He sent representatives and abandoned friendship and faith with the king in the traditional way, also renouncing homage, giving as the reason that his action was just, because the king had both unlawfully claimed the throne and disregarded, not to say betrayed, all the faith he had sworn to him.' Others might have made a more surprise move when changing sides, in order to maximise gain, but not Robert. We may attribute this partly to his reputation as an honest and upright man who wanted to do the right thing, but the *diffidatio* also served a political purpose: as Robert was accusing Stephen of falsehood and shady dealing, he (and by extension Matilda) needed to claim the moral high ground.

The wonderful news galloped southwards to Matilda. Robert's defection and his support of her cause changed her fortunes at a stroke, holding out the promise of numerous castles and men on the ground in England. And in the immediate short term, it gave her access through Caen and a safe passage to the sea. Matilda and Geoffrey wasted no time: by June 1138 they were moving through Normandy with an army at their back, picking off a number of Stephen's smaller castles in the duchy as they went. The main obstacle in their path was Falaise, the great ducal stronghold and birthplace of William the Conqueror, which stood directly in the way between Matilda's base at Argentan and Robert's at Caen; Geoffrey laid siege to it, but was beaten back after eighteen days.

The setback was temporary. Matilda's forces were growing; she bypassed Falaise while keeping up to date with her uncle David's actions on her behalf in the north of England and the rebellion against Stephen in Herefordshire and Shropshire, which was keeping him occupied there. Meanwhile, Stephen had broken off his firefighting efforts long enough to react to Robert's renunciation of homage by confiscating all the latter's English estates. But confiscating lands in theory was a very different matter from seizing them in practice: to compound his other woes Stephen was engaged in a fruitless siege of Robert's castle of Bristol all through the summer.

By the autumn of 1138 Matilda had made it through to Robert's lands, had been (no doubt joyfully) reunited with him, and had also, according to the evidence of charter witness lists, made contact with her other half-brother Reginald. They all spent the winter of 1138–39 and the spring of 1139 making preparations. Matilda needed to cover all bases, so as well as military preparations she also sent envoys to the pope, who (as we will see in Chapter 5) would take them seriously enough to instigate a papal hearing on the question of the English crown. Orderic Vitalis details some of Matilda's activities during the spring, and it is important to note that he portrays the campaign as hers, not her husband's, with the troops owing their allegiance directly to her: '*the countess's retainers* captured Ralph of Esson, a powerful lord, in Lent and handed him over to *their lady*' (my emphasis).

By the summer of 1139 everything was in place, but careful arrangements needed to be made ahead of the sea crossing; Matilda did not want to be met by a large army and a potentially decisive battle as soon as she set foot on English soil. Stephen's forces had dealt once more with King David, as we have seen, and he had finally extricated himself from the situation in Shropshire (he had evidently learned a lesson from the Exeter debacle two years previously, this time hanging the entire ninety-three-man garrison of Shrewsbury Castle after he captured it), so he was at liberty to move to wherever the need seemed greatest. Thus Matilda and her supporters made plans to split up to fight her campaign on different fronts. Geoffrey would remain in Normandy – presumably by choice as, in guarding their rear as the others invaded England, he would also be able to make some headway with his own ambitions – while the others would cross the Channel. Baldwin de Redvers, probably accompanied by Reginald de Dunstanville, took ship first: he sailed in August, landed at Wareham in Dorset and marched immediately to garrison the almost impregnable stronghold of Corfe Castle. This had the effect of drawing Stephen to Corfe, away from the south-east of England.

Matilda and Robert now set off. Until recently the obvious destination for them would have been Dover, but after Stephen's announcement that Robert had forfeited his lands in England, Dover was one of the few places that had fallen, taken by Stephen's queen Matilda and her ships from Boulogne. The loss of Robert's fortress precluded the possibility of landing there; it would also be too risky to sail the long way round, all along the south coast, around Cornwall and then up to Bristol. However, they had another plan and another ally, so it was with confidence that Matilda finally sailed for England, after almost a decade away, at the end of September 1139.

CHAPTER FIVE

RETURN TO ENGLAND

A<small>T THE TIME OF HENRY</small> I's death at the end of 1135 his queen, Adeliza, was around thirty years of age, possibly slightly younger. As a still-nubile, childless and enormously rich royal widow with extensive lands and estates, she would need to consider with some care her options for the future. Initially she retired to the Benedictine convent of Wilton Abbey; not to take holy orders, but rather to find a place of refuge where she could mourn in peace and dignity, as befitted a new dowager queen. It was not unusual for noblewomen to spend some part of their lives as convent guests without ever becoming professed nuns, particularly girls who were sent to gain an education or women who did not want to be forced into hasty marriage or remarriage, and who therefore appreciated the all-female environment.

Adeliza next appears in official records in December 1136, when she was present at a ceremony of dedication at King Henry's tomb in Reading to mark the first anniversary of his death. After a further period of mourning she emerged from the cloister and was married again, probably in 1138, to William d'Aubigny, previously one of Henry's advisors, who became lord (and later earl) of Arundel in right of her holdings. She would, incidentally, go on to bear her new husband seven children, thus putting the lie to the somewhat baffling 'infertility' that had characterised her marriage to the equally fecund Henry. By the summer of 1139 Adeliza and William – who, like his peers, had accepted Stephen as king – were living peacefully at the castle of Arundel on the Sussex coast. Adeliza had evidently been keeping up a correspondence with her stepdaughter Matilda during her years of widowhood, and, au fait with Matilda's plan to sail across the Channel, she now offered Arundel as a safe place to land in England. For all that Adeliza may have been drawn to support Matilda for personal reasons – they had a long and friendly history, begun in childhood, and Matilda had been the chosen heir of Adeliza's late and respected husband – she cannot have been unaware of the wider implications of her action.

Matilda and Earl Robert arrived on 30 September 1139, bringing with them 140 knights and some 3,000 infantry. This was a relatively small force, but speed and secrecy were all-important at first; they needed to gain a foothold and to make contact with Robert's significant following in England, and this was best done without a large and unwieldy army that would take days to disembark. Although it was 5 miles from the sea, Arundel could be reached by ship via the navigable River Arun and was therefore a port. Matilda and her half-brother were thus on friendly territory as soon as they set foot on land, and they were able to act immediately. Robert and a small group of a dozen armed knights set off without delay to ride to his stronghold of Bristol; this was a journey of some 120 miles, but they hoped to be behind the sheltering walls there before Stephen could catch up with them, possibly even before he heard of their arrival. Meanwhile, Matilda made her way up the hill to the imposing and well-defended castle, where she was welcomed by her stepmother.

After the rigours of the journey, Matilda was now able to sit, eat and talk in comfort while she took stock of her situation. The initial phase of her quest, the very first step in the recovery of her crown, had finally been achieved after a four-year wait. Once more her personal life had been put to one side – she had left behind her husband, whom she probably did not miss much, but also her sons, now aged six, five and three, whom she perhaps did – but it was all in the service of a greater cause. To her mind her sons would benefit more from her gaining England and Normandy than they would from her physical presence in Anjou and acceptance of a lesser status. She was not to see them again for a number of years, but she could rest in the knowledge that they were safer where they were.

Indeed, now she had a brief period of leisure to contemplate the subject, it might have occurred to Matilda that, for the first time in her life, she was in a relatively favourable position with regard to the men around her. As we have noted previously, she could not stand alone in her quest – the social, political and legal milieu put this out of the question – but she currently had the male members of her family more or less where she needed them. She was married, and had the necessary attendant status without the actual irritating presence of her husband at her side, and without being subject to his rule. She had three sons, so she had fulfilled both her feminine, wifely duty and her royal hereditary obligation. The men with whom she chose to associate herself most closely in her titles and styles – her father King Henry and her first husband Emperor Henry – both added to her social standing while being conveniently dead and thus unable to influence or direct her. The living and present men whom she needed to ride into battle for her were headed by her illegitimate brothers, one a decade younger than her, with plenty of energy, and one a decade older, bringing with him a wealth of military and political experience; neither of them could pose a threat to her claim to the throne. Matilda was, finally, almost free of male control.

However, there was another group of men who had recently thrown further obstacles in Matilda's path: the pope and the other prelates at his court. Stephen, as we have seen, had previously received a letter of support from Pope Innocent II, but there was a suspicion that the matter had not been properly considered, so Matilda had sent envoys to Rome early in 1139, before she prepared to sail for England. Her intention was to challenge Stephen's usurpation of the English crown on the grounds that she was Henry I's heir both by hereditary right and by the oaths sworn to her. Stephen sent a delegation of his own to defend his cause; the arguments for both sides were heard in April 1139 at the Second Lateran Council, a gathering of nearly a thousand churchmen from across Europe. Interestingly, neither party was headed by an English prelate: Matilda's case was presented by Ulger, bishop of Angers, and although Stephen's delegation included Roger, bishop of Coventry, his main representative was Arnulf, archdeacon of Sées in Normandy.

Ulger dutifully put forward Matilda's case. He expected Arnulf to counter his arguments of heredity and oaths, and had prepared his responses accordingly, but he was to be wrong-footed. Arnulf's reply was totally unanticipated: rather than attempting to argue that Stephen's hereditary right took precedence over Matilda's, or that the oaths from the barons and churchmen were not valid, he took a step further back into the past and made the startling accusation that Matilda herself was illegitimate and therefore had no right to claim to be Henry's heir at all. His argument rested on the fact that Matilda's mother, Edith-Matilda, had been a professed nun; therefore, her marriage to King Henry was invalid; therefore, any children born to the couple were illegitimate.

This wholly unexpected line of attack threw Ulger into disarray, and he was unable immediately to make the obvious reply: that Edith-Matilda had been resident in the convent of Romsey Abbey, where her aunt Cristina was the abbess, and had been educated there, but had not taken any vows (not an uncommon scenario at the time, as we have noted); and that the question of her vocational status had been thoroughly investigated at the time of her betrothal and had been proved to the satisfaction of Anselm, the then arch-bishop of Canterbury, who had been happy to celebrate the marriage and to crown Edith-Matilda as queen. Arnulf's argument was specious at best, but it was so audacious that it took the wind out of Ulger's sails and made his case for Matilda seem weaker.

There are two principal surviving accounts of the proceedings. One is by John of Salisbury, in his *Memoirs of the Papal Court*; he was writing a couple of decades afterwards and had the benefit of hindsight. He brings up the question of the oaths that had been sworn to Matilda by the barons and prelates, saying that Arnulf claimed they had been made under duress and that Henry had changed his mind on his deathbed; he also depicts Ulger replying to this accusation in a robust fashion, saying that it was proved false and that it was evident that the key 'witness', Hugh Bigod, had not been at Henry's deathbed. However, none of this appears in the only contemporary eyewitness account of the occasion, which was written by Gilbert Foliot, a monk of the Cluniac order who would shortly be elected abbot of Gloucester. In his version Ulger is not nearly so quick-witted and does not put Matilda's case forward with such vigour. What seems evident either way is that Ulger lost the argument; both Gilbert and John agree on the final outcome of the case, which was that the pope saw no reason to overturn his original deci-sion, that he recognised Stephen's coronation as a fait accompli and that he now confirmed Stephen as king of England and duke of Normandy.

The disappointing news reached Matilda in Normandy by the summer of 1139, so she was fully cognisant of her lack of papal support before she sailed for England in September. As she enjoyed the opulent surroundings of Arundel Castle, anticipating further news from Earl Robert, she could put legal arguments to one side and rest her hopes on a military solution; she may well have preferred this, the prospect of action, to the endless talking and waiting of the past few years. And action there would be: Matilda knew that Stephen would not leave her in peace for long.

Since we last saw him in the summer of 1138, Stephen had been spending most of his time firefighting, trying to stamp out the minor local rebellions that had broken out up and down his realm. The *Deeds of Stephen* tells us that 'the king hastened, always armed, always accompanied by a host, to deal with various anxieties and tasks of many kinds which continually dragged him hither and thither all over England. It was like what we read of the fabled hydra of Hercules; when one head was cut off two or more grew in its place.' This was both tiring and expensive, but at least he could feel that he was in control of his response: he was, as we have noted, a competent soldier and director of sieges. However, his travails during the last year or so had been not only military but also political and ecclesiastical: the favourable relationship he had previously enjoyed with the church began to disintegrate, and he encountered a number of what we might categorise as 'bishop problems'.

Stephen's brother Henry, bishop of Winchester, had been a pivotal figure in Stephen's successful campaign to secure the crown, and he might well have expected further reward and preferment both on this basis and due to their fraternal ties. On 21 November 1136, after Stephen had been on the throne for almost a year, the ideal opportunity for the king to demonstrate his gratitude presented itself: William of Corbeil, the archbishop of Canterbury, died, leaving the position – head of the church in England, as well as the traditional most valued advisor to the king – vacant. On hearing the news, Bishop Henry prepared himself for advancement (he was in France at the time and remained there throughout the winter of 1136–37, anticipating a summons to Rome), but the call never came for him. In fact it did not come for anyone else, either: the see was still vacant two years later. An election was finally called at Christmas 1138, at which point Theobald, abbot of Bec, was appointed archbishop. He was consecrated and enthroned on 8 January 1139.

Theobald has been depicted by some commentators (both contemporary and modern) as a 'surprise' candidate, perhaps put up for election simply because he was not Henry, but his position as abbot of the influential foundation at Bec gave him a considerable standing in the church. Still, his selection over the head of the man who was both bishop of Winchester and the king's brother requires some explanation. Theobald was very different in character to Henry, being a quiet, scholarly type rather than a politician; this may have been a more appealing prospect both to the monks and to the king. Significantly, Theobald also enjoyed the support of Waleran de Beaumont, count of Meulan, whom we met earlier at the deathbed of Henry I and who was, by now, a very powerful figure in the Anglo-Norman world.

Waleran and his brother Robert were the sons of the late Robert de Beaumont, earl of Leicester, one of William the Conqueror's companions in 1066 and subsequently an advisor to Henry I; he had died in 1118. Exceptionally for the time, Waleran and Robert were twins; very few twins survived birth and infancy, so the existence of an adult pair was unusual enough for contemporaries to comment on it. They were fourteen when their father died, at which point Waleran, the elder, inherited the family lands and seat of Meulan in the Norman Vexin, while Robert became earl of Leicester in England. They also had a younger brother, known as Hugh the Poor (the soubriquet relating to his lack of paternal inheritance, rather than because he was an actual pauper). Their half-brother from their mother's second marriage, William de Warenne, was earl of Surrey; their first cousin Roger de Beaumont was earl of Warwick.

Waleran and Robert had been wards of Henry I during their minority, living at his court; after reaching his majority and succeeding fully to his lands and title Waleran had rebelled against Henry in 1123–24, in support of William Clito and Amaury de Montfort, and was on the losing side at the battle of Bourgthéroulde. After his capture he accompanied Henry and Matilda to England in 1126, when Matilda made her first return across the Channel after being widowed, but in Waleran's case it was as a captive to be imprisoned away from Normandy, so it is doubtful whether the two of them met or spoke at that juncture. He was later pardoned, and by the end of Henry's reign a decade later he was back in full royal favour. He rose swiftly during the early years of Stephen's reign, and by 1138 had secured not only the earldom of Worcester for himself but also that of Bedford for his brother Hugh; he was at one point betrothed to Stephen's infant daughter Matilda, but she died at the age of four or five before the wedding could take place.

Despite this minor setback to his ambitions, Waleran continued to rise in favour and influence, and the Beaumont bloc as a whole was not to be trifled with. Waleran was a patron of the abbey of Bec and there is little doubt that he backed Theobald for the archbishopric of Canterbury, to the detriment of Bishop Henry. Henry did not make any hasty public move in early 1139; however, he was seething at the slight and it is safe to say that he was not best pleased with his brother. The election had, of course, been canonical and carried out by the monks of Canterbury (Stephen had promised to refrain from lay investiture as part of his coronation oath), but it would be naïve to think that the king of England could not have exercised an influence one way or the other, had he so wished.

This was not to be the last of Stephen's 'bishop problems'. If the Beaumonts had the lay aspects of power in England sewn up, then another family was in a similar position among the clergy. Roger, bishop of Salisbury, was still the justiciar and therefore the *de facto* second-in-command to the king and regent in his absence; during his long tenure he had amassed a substantial store of personal wealth as well as control of a number of castles. Hardly less influential, and no less rich, were Alexander, bishop of Lincoln, and Nigel, bishop of Ely, both of whom were Roger's nephews – nepotism being a literal concept in the twelfth century. Nigel was also Stephen's treasurer, and another family member, Roger le Poer, was the chancellor. Roger was officially referred to as Roger of Salisbury's nephew, but it is likely that he was actually the bishop's illegitimate son. William of Malmesbury, in his slightly coy way, says that the younger Roger was 'a nephew or perhaps even a closer relative' of the elder; both Orderic Vitalis and John of Worcester come straight out and refer to Roger le Poer as Bishop Roger's son, so the situation was presumably common knowledge. In any case, between them the extended family controlled the entire English chancery and exchequer.

The rivalry for power between Bishop Roger's clan and the Beaumont faction was always going to come to a head. In 1139 Waleran began to hint to Stephen that perhaps Roger's power was becoming a threat to the king's own, and that, as Roger held castles in the West Country, he might be in a position to assist the rumoured forthcoming invasion by Matilda. There was no firm evidence either way, but relations deteriorated rapidly. An incident occurred while the royal court was at Oxford in June 1139 – an incident possibly manufactured by Waleran himself, as the *Deeds of Stephen* says it was 'at the instigation of the crafty count of Meulan' – during which there was a fight and at least one man was killed by Roger's supporters. Stephen could not tolerate such behaviour at his own court without losing face, so he summoned all three bishops to answer charges about disturbing the peace of the kingdom. Nigel of Ely fled to the castle of Devizes and there prepared for a siege, but the others were arrested. Stephen marched against Devizes and, in a rare show of belligerence, threatened to hang the now ex-chancellor Roger le Poer in front of the walls. Amid the tears of Bishop Roger outside the gates, and those of his mistress (who was by implication Roger le Poer's mother) inside, Nigel was persuaded to surrender it, and Bishop Roger's other castles at Sherborne, Malmesbury and Salisbury followed suit. All four men relinquished their royal offices, to be replaced in post by protégés of the Beaumonts. Bishop Alexander's castle of Newark was given up (but only, according to Henry of Huntingdon, after Stephen 'imposed on the bishop an unlawful fast, swearing on oath that he would be deprived of all food until the castle was surrendered to him'), shortly followed by his other stronghold of Sleaford. Both fell into the hands of Robert de Beaumont, earl of Leicester.

Stephen gained a great deal of treasure from the seizure of the castles and their contents, which he used to good effect, replenishing his treasury and sending to France a lavish offer for Louis VII's teenage sister Constance as a bride for Stephen's eldest son Eustace. Of course, Stephen had no ecclesiastical power to deprive the three bishops of their sees, so they were able to return to them, albeit in a state of relative penury and extreme dissatisfaction. Roger, the elderly bishop of Salisbury, would be dead by the end of the year, 'worn out by sorrow as well as old age', says Henry of Huntingdon, his demise perhaps hastened by the stress of the summer's events.

Despite his victory, Stephen now became mired in further conflict with the church over his coronation charter, in which he had promised that 'justice over ecclesiastical persons and all clerics and their belongings ... should be in the hands of bishops'. His brother Bishop Henry, still smarting from his non-appointment to the see of Canterbury, had in the meantime gone one better and secured himself a commission as a papal legate – a direct representative of the pope and therefore outranking the archbishop in the church hierarchy. It was with this status in hand that he actually summoned the king to appear before a church council due to be held at Winchester on 29 August 1139.

The anointed king of England, unsurprisingly, did not find it amusing to be summoned anywhere, least of all by his own younger brother. He sent several earls to Winchester to enquire why he should need to respond, but Bishop Henry was ready for them, according to William of Malmesbury: 'The legate [Bishop Henry] answered in brief that one who remembered that he owed obedience to the faith of Christ should not complain if he had been summoned by Christ's ministers to give satisfaction when he knew himself guilty of an offence such as our times had nowhere seen; for it belonged to pagan times to imprison bishops and deprive them of their property.'

As it transpired, the earls were persuaded that there was a case to be answered, so Stephen (still not attending in person) sent his chamberlain to argue that the bishops had been arrested not as bishops but as servants of the king, as they were the holders of royal offices. This case was eventually upheld by the court on the grounds that the castles were lay property and did not belong to the church, so they should have been relinquished on request to the king. If bishops Roger, Alexander and Nigel wished to 'prove by canon law that they were entitled to have them', as William of Malmesbury puts it, then they could attempt to do so. This represented a victory for Stephen, but we should also note that the wording used by the council, the implied criticism that men of the cloth should not accumulate material wealth or build fortifications, was also a dig at Bishop Henry, who had amassed more castles than the other bishops combined. The council broke up with both sides dissatisfied: Henry because he had lost, and Stephen because he had effectively set a precedent that the church was entitled to sit in judgement upon him.

It was in this state of confusion that news reached Stephen of the invasion of Baldwin de Redvers on the south coast; he immediately set off for Corfe, perhaps glad of the opportunity for action rather than legal argument, but perhaps also wishing that he had been less lenient with the rebel baron three years previously. Corfe was extremely well fortified and Stephen realised he would only be able to take it via a protracted siege, 'thinking to reduce the enemy by siege engines or starve them out', as the *Deeds of Stephen* tells us. He was not at leisure to conduct this personally, as this would trap him in one location for many weeks, so he had an offensive retaining wall built around it, in order to prevent the rebels from issuing forth and causing trouble in the surrounding countryside, and left the siege in the hands of subordinates. He had bigger fish to fry: while he was outside Corfe the news reached him that, despite the 'careful watch, night and day,' on all the approaches to the harbours' which the *Deeds of Stephen* tells us he had set around the south coast, Matilda and Robert had landed in Arundel.

This was the most serious crisis of Stephen's reign to date. He had been putting down rebellions for several years, but they had been sporadic, unco-ordinated; now that Matilda, his rival for the throne, was actually on English soil with an experienced commander at her side, his hold on the crown was markedly less secure. Corfe and Baldwin de Redvers would have to wait: Stephen set off to march the 90 miles to Arundel.

Matilda had not been at Arundel for very long – probably about a week – when Stephen's troops appeared on the horizon. Normal practice at the time was for a garrison to undertake regular patrols in the countryside surrounding the castle, so these men would have brought back word of the approaching army in good time for the gates to be closed against it. Matilda could stand on the high battlements of the Norman gatehouse in relative safety and watch from a distance as the host came closer and its size and strength could be judged accurately. She may or may not have caught sight of Stephen in person for the first time in eight years, but the interaction between them that would shortly be forthcoming would give her an opportunity to size him up as an opponent.

In truth, her options were limited. To head swiftly back to the river, out to sea and back to Normandy would be an admission of defeat and failure, unthinkable after such a short time on English soil. And if she took ship, where else could she go? Stephen had watches set on all the south-coast ports, so attempting to land elsewhere in England would be problematic and dangerous. No, she would have to stay where she was, which meant settling in and preparing to withstand a siege. This was a more favourable alternative than running away; Matilda had some 130 knights (allowing for the dozen or so who had gone with Robert to Bristol) and 3,000 infantry with her, and the castle was in a very defensible position atop a hill. The river protected one side of it, and the ground on the other side was flat and marshy, meaning that conditions underfoot were less than ideal for large numbers of troops or horses, for camping or for heavy siege machinery. Stephen would have to set up camp farther back and assail the stone walls on their high motte from afar; any attempt at a frontal assault would be easily visible. If he wanted to starve them out he would have to blockade not only the landward side but also the river and the route to the sea, to stop supplies coming in from that direction. A siege of any great length would be expensive and would also allow time for Earl Robert to muster his forces, assuming (as Stephen was aware but Matilda could not yet know for certain) that he had reached Bristol in safety.

But of course, Arundel Castle was not Matilda's to command, in a siege or otherwise. She was in the hands of Adeliza and her husband, William d'Aubigny, who now found themselves in an awkward position. William had, until now, been a supporter of Stephen, and being so recently enriched and ennobled he would have been cautious about jeopardising his position and his acquisitions. William is a low-key figure in the chronicles at this point, almost absent from discussion of this episode: the writers tend to focus on Stephen and Matilda, and on Adeliza, in whose right William held the castle in the first place. An important and hitherto overlooked point to note about Adeliza is that if we look carefully at her age, the date of her marriage to William and the number of children she had borne before the end of her child-bearing years, she was quite possibly pregnant with her first child in October 1139. After all her years of infertility with King Henry, this would have been a big event in her life and one which would have made her more cautious in her dealings.

Stephen opened negotiations with Adeliza, who was unwilling actually to take up arms against the king. The question of handing Matilda over was raised and considered. William of Malmesbury criticises Adeliza for not providing a safer and more permanent refuge for her stepdaughter, saying that 'through female inconstancy, she had broken the faith she had repeatedly pledged by messages sent to Normandy', but it is difficult to see what else might be done once the king, the Lord's anointed, had appeared at her gates in person and with an army. To refuse to consider his overtures would be open rebellion, and – maybe with a potential heir to worry about – Adeliza was unwilling to risk her health, wealth or position in a long siege.

But what was the alternative? She needed to think fast. John of Worcester describes the reply she gave: 'The ex-queen was awed by the king's majesty, and was afraid that she might lose what rank she had in England, and solemnly swore that no enemy of the king had come to England through her doing, but that, saving her dignity, she had provided hospitality to those ... who were known to her.' This was a good line, for how could Stephen disprove it without calling the dowager queen a liar? And after all, it was not strictly illegal for Matilda to be in England, not if she were merely there as a social guest of her stepmother, as Adeliza claimed. A potential impasse loomed: Stephen could not find an excuse to attack and Adeliza would not surrender Matilda. Another solution would have to be found. There is no knowing exactly how many envoys went back and forth between castle and camp, but eventually Stephen's man brought an astonishing offer: Matilda could leave in safety, and Stephen would give her safe conduct to travel to join Robert at Bristol. Robert had indeed reached his destination in safety along with his small group of men, having eluded Stephen's troops by taking lesser-known routes in order to avoid detection. This was welcome news to Matilda, and she accepted the offer.

On a superficial level, this appears to have been a huge error of judgement by Stephen, and indeed some chroniclers interpreted it this way. His rival for the throne was trapped at the very edge of England, and could be easily surrounded; she could have no communication with the outside world and was at his mercy. But yet he let her go. Was this another example of his easy-going nature letting him down when it mattered? Henry of Huntingdon thought so, saying that 'either because he trusted treacherous advice, or because he thought the castle impregnable, he allowed her to go to Bristol'. Orderic Vitalis is scathing in his assessment: 'It may be remarked that this permission given by the king was a sign of great simplicity or carelessness, and prudent men regret that he was regardless of his own welfare and the kingdom's security. It was in his power at this time to have easily stifled a flame which threatened great mischief, if, within a policy becoming the wise, he had at once ... crushed the deadly efforts of those whose enterprise threatened the country with pillage, slaughter and depopulation.'

However, when we examine the situation more carefully, we can see that there is a little more to it. Firstly, on a practical level, it could be argued that Stephen was better off having Matilda and Robert in the same place.

Arundel Castle could only be taken by a long siege, and if Stephen were pinned down there for many months this would offer Robert a free rein to organise his own rebellion in the West Country, to raise troops on his sister's behalf, and perhaps to advance behind the king and trap him between two armies, a very dangerous position indeed. Better, then, to herd them both into the west, away from the capital and the strategically and economically important towns and castles of the south-east, and a greater distance from any potential support or reinforcement that might be sent by Matilda's husband Geoffrey from Normandy or Anjou.

Secondly, there were political and social aspects to consider. Matilda might be in England with the intention of unseating Stephen from the throne and making herself queen (or, more accurately, as we shall discuss later, a unique type of 'female king'), but the fact remained that she was a woman – and a woman of high rank at that, the daughter of a king, the widow of an emperor and both Stephen's own and his wife's cousin – and that therefore there were certain standards of behaviour that must govern his conduct towards her. Moreover, she could claim to be the invited guest of the dowager queen, the second highest-ranking woman in the realm after Stephen's wife, and the widow of the king who had done so much to raise Stephen to prominence in the first place. Were he to besiege them both, threaten them, attack them, starve them, his reputation would be irrevocably tarnished. And this would have further implications: a king ruled only with the support of his barons, so if Stephen were to act harshly, he ran the risk of alienating those who had (or who could use the opportunity to claim that they had) a conscience. Matilda's sex had finally done her a favour.

Adeliza suffered no subsequent repercussions. She continued to live peacefully at Arundel for another decade, bearing seven children; sometime around 1150 she retired to a convent in Flanders, where she died in 1151. Her body was brought back to England to be buried alongside Henry I at Reading.

As a mark of respect and to guarantee his word and Matilda's safe conduct, Stephen arranged for an escort to accompany her to Bristol; her two principal companions on the journey would be Waleran de Beaumont and Henry, bishop of Winchester. But if allowing Matilda to travel westwards was not the massive blunder it has sometimes been interpreted as, sending Henry to escort her certainly was, especially given that Waleran left them at Calne in Wiltshire: they rode the rest of the way without him, free to discuss matters of mutual interest.

There is, disappointingly, no record at all of what Matilda and Henry may or may not have said to each other during the journey, but it is inconceivable that they did not converse with each other during what was a journey of five or six days. As we have already intimated, Bishop Henry's allegiance to his brother came a distant third in his priorities behind his loyalty to the church and his own personal ambition – not necessarily in that order – and, although he may not have been absolutely set on betraying his brother at this stage, it was certainly in his interests to inveigle himself into Matilda's good graces in case the balance of power should tip her way. Indeed, the *Deeds of Stephen* suggests that it was on Henry's advice that Stephen allowed Matilda to leave Arundel in the first place. From Matilda's point of view the situation also opened up various intriguing possibilities. Henry – her cousin, let us not forget – had been one of those who had sworn the oath to uphold her claim to the throne back in 1131. Was there perhaps some way of working on his conscience to this effect, and capitalising on his more recent dissatisfaction with Stephen? He was a clever and influential man who would be useful to have as an ally.

Much of the narrative of Matilda's first couple of weeks in England traditionally depicts her as more or less passive: Robert brought her across the Channel, Adeliza took her in, Stephen let her go, Henry escorted her to Bristol. But we should perhaps give her more credit and consider the possibility that she had, in fact, scored a carefully planned tactical triumph. Matilda had spent her entire life in royal courts, and was not stupid. She was well aware of social mores and distinctions, particularly those that related to the treatment of women of rank; and, although she had not seen Stephen in a number of years, she had previously known him well and had presumably made some effort to keep up with intelligence about him since his coronation. She may have used all of this knowledge and experience to gamble, predicting that this would be Stephen's reaction.

Regardless of the extent of Matilda's own agency in this episode, the fact is that her landing in Arundel and travelling to Bristol paid off. Stephen's generosity, ill-advised or not, backfired when it was the catalyst for a number of important defections to his rival's cause. Those who came to Matilda to offer their service and allegiance in person once she was safe within her brother's walls might not have done so had they needed to wade through a besieging army outside Arundel.

Matilda arrived in Bristol in mid-October 1139. The West Country would be her base for some time: it was, admittedly, not particularly close to the centres of power of London and Westminster, but it was a great deal nearer than Argentan, and it was a secure location surrounded by lands held by her supporters. It was here that two men who were to be of pivotal importance in her campaign appeared: Miles of Gloucester and Brian fitzCount.

Miles of Gloucester was not related to Earl Robert: his toponym derived from the fact that he held Gloucester Castle as sheriff of that county. Sheriffs (*vicecomites*) were, as the Latin name implies, subordinate in each shire to the earls (*comites*), and they tended to take on the bulk of the administrative and judicial duties. Miles was the third generation of his family to act as heredi-tary castellan; he was at this point probably in his mid- to late forties, was married with seven or eight children, and was the holder not only of Gloucester Castle by right of his office, but also of lands of his own scattered throughout the West Country, the Marches and south Wales. The marriage of his eldest son to a local heiress had brought lands in Herefordshire into family control, so Miles's area of influence was wide. He was also a kinsman of Gilbert Foliot, the recently appointed abbot of Gloucester, and was on good terms with him.

Along with many other barons Miles had been hesitant about Stephen's seizure of the throne but had come to terms with the situation; he had been at Stephen's Easter court in 1136, and with him at the siege of Shrewsbury in the summer of 1138. He had not immediately declared for Matilda when Robert of Gloucester renounced his homage in 1138, but this may have indicated pragmatism rather than ambivalence – Earl Robert was far away in Normandy at the time, so any declaration of Miles's would have been unilateral in England and would have left him hopelessly exposed. However, once Robert returned and Matilda arrived in person, this provided a real and practical alternative to Stephen's rule and Miles had no hesitation in declaring for her; he met her at Bristol and offered his submission. He was an exceptionally able military commander and tactician, and Matilda imme-diately accepted him into her service. She awarded him the castle of St Briavels (which was approximately equidistant from Bristol and Gloucester,

119

but on the other side of the Severn) together with the Forest of Dean – it is debatable quite how practical a gift this was in the present circumstances, but the fact that Matilda took upon herself the authority to grant lands and castles was a symbolic show of her claim to be the true monarch.

Brian fitzCount was, of course, an old friend of Matilda. They had both been at Henry I's court as children, and he had been one of her companions during the difficult period when she travelled to Normandy for her marriage to Geoffrey of Anjou. As we have seen, he was raised to prominence under Henry I and to wealth by his marriage to Matilda of Wallingford. He had briefly been on the opposing side to the empress during her conflict with her father in the year leading up to his death, but under the circumstances Brian could hardly be blamed for remaining loyal to the king who had always supported his interests. After Henry's death Brian had come to terms with Stephen's accession, but it is likely that his sympathies lay with Matilda. He had not even waited for her arrival in Bristol to declare for her: he rode out and met Robert halfway on his journey from Arundel, arranging that he would return to Wallingford to fortify, garrison and provision the castle there; its position in the Thames valley would make it the eastern-most outpost of the area under her control.

A lot of nonsense has been written over the years – mainly by novelists, but also by one or two historians – about Brian's motives for supporting Matilda, and his personal feelings for her. But he was, as we shall see, a loyal and upright man (loyal to his wife as well as to his liege lady and his compan-ions), a knight and baron of integrity, and also a much underrated intellec-tual who wrote fluently and copiously about his faith and his rationale for supporting the true successor to Henry I.

Brian was not at Bristol when Matilda arrived, having returned directly to Wallingford, and news soon reached her that Stephen's army was besieging it. This was not a breach of the king's word or his safe conduct: his promise had been to escort Matilda (in her pseudo-fictional guise as Adeliza's guest) safely to Robert in Bristol, nothing more. Matilda's subsequent acceptance of service and homage indicated her challenge to Stephen for the crown, so he was naturally then entitled to take action against her and her supporters without incurring any damage to his reputation.

The besieging army at Wallingford – left there by Stephen, who was himself pushing on towards South Cerney, Malmesbury and Trowbridge, which was held by Miles's son-in-law Humphrey de Bohun – had erected two temporary fortifications on the opposite bank of the river to the castle, and was intent on starving the garrison out. Under the circumstances this was the best they could do: the castle would be difficult to take by assault, being a stone motte-and-bailey construction on the banks of the Thames and protected on three sides by a double moat. There was also the additional consideration that Stephen would not have wanted to cause too much damage to the fortification: his intention was not to destroy it, but rather to capture it so he could garrison it himself. Therefore starvation was a better initial tactic than bombardment by siege machinery, as it would damage only the people and not the building.

However, this approach was necessarily a long-term one, so it offered time for a rescue effort to be mounted, and this is exactly what happened. Miles of Gloucester ('a man of the greatest spirit and active and very ready for mighty enterprises', as even the *Deeds of Stephen* admits), keen to demonstrate his loyalty both to his friend and to his new liege lady, sprang into action. Riding at the head of his troops, he eluded the part of Stephen's army that was marching westwards, slipped around behind them, and made a surprise dash for Wallingford. Once there, he and his men made 'a bold and vigorous attack', assailing and destroying the wooden siege fortifications, killing or capturing those within, and relieving the castle to allow Brian and his men out.

Thanks to Wallingford's position as the eastern outpost of Matilda's sphere of influence, around 50 miles from London, Miles and Brian now found them themselves, theoretically at least, within striking distance of the capital. News of the defeat at Wallingford sped to Stephen, and in a panic about the possibility of losing his capital, he turned back – having got nowhere near Matilda, who was still at Bristol – and headed for London himself. This gave Miles free rein back in the west again (ready to 'devote himself wholly to troubling the king and his followers', as the *Deeds of Stephen* puts it), so he made a swift attack on Worcester, seat of the king's favourite Waleran de Beaumont. John of Worcester, an eyewitness to the raid (he notes that it started 'when we were engaged in the church at lauds, and had already chanted prime') tells of the attack coming from the north side of the city, using the present tense in order to emphasise the immediacy of the crisis:

There being no fortifications on that side, the entire host rushes tumul-
tuously in, mad with fury, and sets fire to the houses in many parts. Alas!
A considerable portion of the city is destroyed ... immense plunder is
carried off, consisting of chattels of all kinds, from the city, and of oxen,
sheep, cattle and horses from the country. Many people are taken in the
streets and suburbs, and dragged into miserable captivity ... whatever
their cruel foes fix for their ransom they are forced to promise on oath
to pay.

Miles might not have been winning any friends, but he understood that
in a war those with fewer resources needed to use them cleverly; he had
both tactical intelligence and the practical skills to put his plans into action.
His attack was swift and effective, netting his troops both money and much-
needed supplies. So rapid was his raid on Worcester that he had been and
gone by the time Waleran could arrive to defend his city; all the earl could
do was commiserate with the citizens' losses, and then retaliate in kind by
attacking Sudeley Castle, 20 miles away, and sacking the land around it.
'And if it be enquired what the earl did there,' continues John of Worcester,
'the reply is such as it is scarcely fit to record: returning evil for evil, he
seized the people, their goods, and cattle.' Stephen arrived, also too late; he
was at this juncture on the back foot, rushing reactively from place to place.

Miles's success bought Matilda some time in which to consolidate her
position. She did suffer from the disadvantage that she could not charge
into battle or direct a siege from the front, rallying her men in person as
Stephen did (although she might, as she had done at Le Sap, ride at the
head of troops on the march); but then again, this meant that she was much
less susceptible to death or capture, and in fact it was useful to have the head
of the party static in one place so that news and intelligence could be
brought to her. We should emphasise that although Matilda could neither
don armour nor fight in combat, she was not a passive figure in these events,
sitting quietly and working on embroidery while Robert, Miles and Brian
did everything for her. Matilda's years of experience at various royal courts
across Europe, and in Anjou, meant that she had as good a grasp of strategy
as any non-combatant could hope to have, and she could be an active participant in planning her own affairs. She was the senior figure in the party.
Military generalship involved more than merely riding into battle; the

political and strategic decisions taken around the command table were as important as manoeuvres in the field, and Matilda knew this. It was, after all, her crown.

Interestingly, it would seem that the impression Matilda left in England was a military one. In the 1220s a chronicler known as the Anonymous of Béthune wrote a text entitled the *Histoire des ducs de Normandie et des rois d'Angleterre* (*History of the Dukes of Normandy and the Kings of England*); he includes a section on Matilda arriving in England and then goes on to note that 'she left Bristol and campaigned throughout the land, making war upon King Stephen in the most severe manner ... The empress rode with the army every day, and gave the best and most valuable advice; in all the army there was no baron as astute or as experienced in war as she.'

The joint efforts of Matilda and her three principal lieutenants had initial success: by the time she had been in England a month she had established a secure base for her campaign, welcomed to her side a group of magnates who would form the nucleus of her party, and set the groundwork for a long-term campaign. She provided a personal focus for all those who were disaffected with Stephen for whatever reason, while at the same time offering a position on the moral high ground: if they deserted the man they had accepted as king and came over to her, they were not traitors but were simply making amends for the earlier breaking of their oaths to her (which she could magnanimously forgive as long as they stayed with her now) and they could claim to be acting in good faith by supporting old King Henry's true heir. How many of them started out motivated to act *against Stephen* rather than *for Matilda* is debatable; not all of them knew her personally before they defected to her cause. But just as she needed them for their support, their castles and their troops, so they also needed her: there was no point rebelling against the king unless there was a viable alternative. Matilda's main objective, while her commanders were active in the field, would be to win over the barons and prelates she needed while starting to plan how she would govern them.

An important part of this strategy was that Matilda must position herself as monarch, not as rebel. This being the case, Bristol was not the most suitable long-term base for her. It was a castle held in person by her brother Robert as part of his earldom of Gloucester, which meant that as long as she stayed there she was his guest, which might imply a subordinate position. It was with this in mind that she moved, sometime before the end of 1139, to the castle of Gloucester. This, of course, was held by Miles, but the crucial difference was that it was a royal castle and that he held it by virtue of his position, that is, as a servant of the crown. Miles continued to be one of her most valued advisors (the *Deeds of Stephen* says that he 'always behaved to her like a father in deed and counsel'), but here he was the subordinate accommodating his liege lady, who headed her own household. None of this implies any kind of rift with Robert: it was simply a further example of the political needing to be put before the personal.

Another way in which Matilda emphasised the legality of her position was in having her own coins minted. These silver pennies bore her likeness, not Stephen's, on the obverse; they were struck at Bristol and Cardiff, both mint towns and both under her party's control. The coins probably had a limited range of circulation, not making their way far out of the south-west, but their implication was clear.

The two sides, separated geographically with Matilda in the south and west while Stephen controlled the south-east, the Midlands and the north, were now positioned almost as though they were pieces on a chess board; an apt analogy as kings, queens, knights, bishops and castles were all to play important roles in the war.

Castles were of pivotal importance. As we have noted, their area of influence extended some 20 to 30 miles in all directions, as they provided a secure base from which to range. Defensive architecture was at this time ahead in the race against offensive weaponry, and capturing castles was difficult: it could be done, but it was arduous, expensive and time-consuming. In basic terms this meant that anyone who owned or held a castle, particularly a stone one (there were still some wooden ones around at this time) was in a very favourable position indeed. They had an obvious advantage over anyone lower down in the hierarchy – who could be attacked at any time because they had no solid walls behind which they could retreat – but they were in far less danger either from their peers or from their social superiors. Castle-holders could range around the local countryside by day and then sleep behind closed gates at night; stores could be kept and stockpiled in safety, both for the benefit of the garrison and to stop them falling into the hands of marauding enemies. The holder of a castle, even if besieged and outnumbered, could normally manage to negotiate a settlement as the besieging party would rather come to terms than have to spend months camping outside the walls, with all the attendant dangers such as hunger, disease and loss of campaign momentum.

It would seem that everyone who owned or held a castle was at this time engaged in fortifying or improving their defences. The annals of Winchester record that 'Bishop Henry built in Winchester a town house which was rather a palace, with a strong tower; also the castles of Merdon, and Farnham, and Waltham, and Dowton, and Taunton ... the earl of Gloucester [fortified] those of Gloucester, Bath, Bristol, Dorchester, Exeter, Wimborne, Corfe, and Wareham; Brian [fitzCount], Wallingford and Oxford ... there was no man of any standing or substance in England who did not either build or strengthen a fortification.'

We have already seen that Stephen had been experiencing problems with bishops, and this was to return to haunt him in the early stages of the war. Although Matilda's lack of success in appealing to the pope meant that the church stood officially with Stephen, his harsh treatment of some of the bishops in the previous few years had alienated them.

Nigel, bishop of Ely, was naturally disaffected with Stephen following his arrest and the forced surrender of Devizes Castle; in December 1139 he additionally learned of the death of his uncle, Roger, the bishop of Salisbury, and this seems to have spurred him to defect to Matilda. He did not travel immediately to the West Country but rather remained in Ely (at this time an island surrounded by fenland), hired mercenaries and used them to attack and harry the lands of neighbours who supported Stephen. Stephen was pulled away from his campaigns in the West Country to quell this rebellion. Despite the complex geographical and topographical situation he managed to retaliate with success: he used a number of boats lashed together to form a pontoon bridge across the marsh, reached the castle of Ely and captured it. Bishop Nigel escaped to Gloucester, where he declared for Matilda in person.

Henry, bishop of Winchester and papal legate, suffered another setback to his ambitions in the spring of 1140. Following the death of the bishop of Salisbury, that see had fallen vacant, and Bishop Henry had a favoured candidate to slot into the position: his nephew Henry de Sully, the son of his eldest brother William (who, as noted in Chapter 2, was known as 'the Simple' and had been overlooked in the family inheritance before being married off to the heiress of Sully). But Waleran de Beaumont had more leverage, and his own cousin Philip de Harcourt, who was already chancellor (having replaced Roger le Poer), was appointed instead. Orderic Vitalis tells us that Bishop Henry, seeing that he was not going to get his way, 'left the king's court in high dudgeon', but he was not finished: he managed to get the appointment quashed. Philip was never enthroned as bishop of Salisbury, although he did later become bishop of Bayeux in Normandy. Meanwhile Henry's relationship with Stephen, and more particularly with Waleran, deteriorated.

The knights on the chess board, including those of all ranks from earl and baron to local lord, were the most mobile pieces and the most fluid in their allegiances. There were those few who declared immediately for Matilda and remained loyal to her throughout: these were principally those who had family ties to her or who had risen to prominence under Henry I but seen their fortunes decline under Stephen. Equally, there were those who remained loyal to Stephen throughout the war; most notably those who owed a meteoric rise to him personally. There was a third group – including two notable earls whom we will meet in Chapter 6 – who switched allegiances as it suited them, and a fourth who made no early declaration but waited to see which way the game was heading before jumping one way or the other. Among this last group were Hugh Bigod (perhaps surprisingly, given that his 'evidence' about Henry I's deathbed had been pivotal in putting Stephen on the throne in the first place), and John Marshal, holder of Marlborough Castle, whose motives were at this point so obscure that William of Malmesbury and the *Deeds of Stephen* call him a supporter of Matilda while John of Worcester has him down as an adherent of Stephen.

The problem for all parties was that there was no overwhelming momentum that could force a quick and easy victory for either side. Stephen could claim more followers and much greater resource, but he relied heavily on Waleran de Beaumont and his clique, on his own 'new men' – those he had raised to the rank of earl during a slew of new appointments in 1138 – and on mercenaries led by William of Ypres, who were unpopular with his own supporters as well as his enemies. Matilda, on the other hand, had very little patronage to dispense – only that of royal lands under her control – but she could make promises for future gain, in the form of what we might call 'licences to conquer', where an adherent was told he could keep a particular castle or area of land if he could take it from Stephen. Also of note is the fact that some of Matilda's newest supporters were referred to as the 'disinherited': those whose lands had been confiscated by Stephen so that he could use them to reward his close confidants. They had no cause to love Stephen and, by now, very little to lose, so they came to Matilda and she accepted their homage.

To return to our chess analogy, Matilda also had a king on the board: her uncle, David, king of Scots. His allegiance was definitely for her (rather than merely against Stephen), but since his defeat at the battle of the Standard in 1138 he was in no position to supply anything more than moral support for the time being. And if Matilda had a king, Stephen had a queen: his greatest ally was his wife Queen Matilda, a determined woman of whom we shall hear more later. Her contacts – and her ships – in Boulogne, where she was countess in her own right, were of vital importance, as was her determination to uphold the rights of her children.

The other pieces on a chess board, of course, are the pawns; unfortunately for them, they were to fare less well throughout the war. The evidence from charters of this period shows that the rate of town foundation – a marker of economic development – dropped during Stephen's reign; the disruption to travel and trading networks caused by the war meant that there was a downturn. This, of course, affected the finances of individuals and families, which at best meant some belt-tightening and at worst caused penury and starvation. And that was before the actual violence was factored in: men with no particular interest in the conflict could be called up to fight and die for their lord, and the situation was equally dangerous for those who stayed at home. They had no castles, no walls to retreat behind; they were left out in the open at the mercy of whichever side happened to be devastating their area at the time. Most of the common people would have had little interest in who sat on the throne as long as they might grow their crops, work at their trades and raise their families in tranquillity. But the peace of Henry I's reign was dead and gone, and it would be in very short supply for the next fifteen years.

Twelfth-century chroniclers tend not to be overly interested in the deeds or lives of common people, so the seriousness of the latter's plight may be judged by the fact that their sufferings are a continual theme throughout the conflict. Henry of Huntingdon notes that the trouble began early in Stephen's reign, even before Matilda landed in England: 'There was no peace in the realm, but through murder, burning and pillage everything was destroyed, everywhere the sound of war, with lamentation and terror.' Similarly, John of Worcester – traumatised himself by the raid on Worcester, as we saw earlier in this chapter – tells us that 'the powerful oppress the weak by violence, and obtain exemption from enquiry by the terror of their threats. Death is the lot of him who resists. The wealthy nobles of the land, rolling in affluence, care little to what iniquities the wretched sufferers are exposed; all their concern is for themselves and their own adherents.'

These words are from his entry for 1136, and things were only going to get worse. Of 1140 William of Malmesbury writes: 'The whole year was troubled by the brutalities of war. There were many castles all over England, each defending its own district, or, to be more truthful, plundering it.' Laying waste the land was a normal part of waging war, but it made more sense when it was foreign or enemy territory being attacked. The problem with a civil war was that the participants on both sides were devastating the lands and lives of the very people over whom they sought to rule. As most people lived at a fairly basic subsistence level, the damage done to lands and crops had a significant detrimental effect, to say nothing of the extortion of what little money they might have had saved, as well as the opportunities for general lawlessness which abounded due to the lack of stable government. Between 1130 and 1156 the amount of money collected in tax in England fell by 24 per cent, with the difference being put down to 'waste'; it is not clear whether this term refers to administrative issues or to the devastation of lands and properties, but the result in either case was bad news for the general population. And the devastation would go on, for it was not in the best interests of either party to risk everything on one decisive battle; the war would instead continue to be one of both increment and attrition.

Through 1140 Matilda's domain was consolidated and gradually expanded by her lieutenants. Miles had captured Hereford and was now master of all the lands some 30 miles in every direction from his castle at Gloucester; Wallingford was holding out to the east; Earl Robert attacked Nottingham to the north. Baldwin de Redvers held firm in Dorset and the south. And Matilda's younger half-brother Reginald de Dunstanville made inroads into Cornwall: he somehow (no chronicler is quite clear on the details) came to terms with one William fitzRichard, who was holding the county for Stephen; he married William's daughter and was named by Matilda earl of Cornwall.

Reginald's tenure in Cornwall was not without its problems: the *Deeds of Stephen* tells us that 'on becoming lord of so great an earldom, [Reginald] began to behave with more vigour than discretion to bend all to his will by force of arms'. He managed to alienate the church by plundering its property and imposing a tax, so that he was excommunicated by the bishop of Exeter, and a relieving campaign led by Stephen himself (still indefatigably at the head of his troops) pushed Reginald back and confined him for a while to a single castle, probably Launceston; Stephen then named Alan le Breton, already earl of Richmond, as a rival earl of Cornwall. This duplication of titles and holdings, with both 'monarchs' in England making the same grants to different people, was to be a feature of the war and one that made the lives of the common people, if anything, even worse: they could be harassed for their service or their property by the men of either or both claimants. Stephen shortly performed a similar action when he granted Robert de Beaumont, earl of Leicester, the town and castle of Hereford, even though it was held for Matilda by Miles of Gloucester.

Throughout this time, Matilda remained at Gloucester, receiving reports and making plans. Her chief problem continued to be that her party was not strong enough for all-out attack and needed to continue with guerrilla tactics. While these were on the whole successful, weakening Stephen and forcing him to rush hither and thither to counter them, they actually made little overall progress in advancing her cause, as their small scale meant that they could not make major inroads into his holdings. The inevitable result was devastation and counter-devastation, with England in danger of turning into a wasteland.

By the summer of 1140 it was clear to all that some attempt at peace had to be made before the whole realm descended into chaos and smoking ruin. Enter Henry, bishop of Winchester: his allegiance and his motives might have been a little obscure at this stage but it would appear that he was making a genuine effort to mitigate the horrific effects of the civil war. In his position as papal legate, and therefore the highest-ranking churchman in England, he succeeded in organising negotiations which would bring both parties to the table. Neither Matilda nor Stephen was present in person for the initial round of discussion: she was represented by Robert of Gloucester and he by Queen Matilda, with Henry and Theobald, archbishop of Canterbury, in attendance. This was normal practice: the main protagonists in a negotiation would not meet until their representatives had hammered out a suitable initial agreement. But alas, even that stage was not reached as the talks broke down. In short, there was no compromise available: both parties wanted the crown and the surrender of the other, aims that were mutually incompatible; and neither party was so strong as to be able to force the issue or so weak as to have to give in. Both claimants had sons (Matilda's were Henry, Geoffrey and William, and Stephen's Eustace and William; Stephen also had a surviving daughter, Mary, who was promised to the church) whose rights needed to be taken into consideration, which made them even less likely to back down. William of Malmesbury sums up the feelings of the participants by noting that 'they wasted words and time, to no purpose, and departed without being able to conclude a peace'.

Bishop Henry, who (as William continues) 'knew that it was the particular duty of his office to restore peace', crossed to France and conferred with his brother Theobald, count of Blois, with Louis VII (whose sister Constance was by now betrothed to Stephen's son Eustace) and with various prelates. We do not have exact details of what they discussed, but he returned to England at the end of November with a set of proposals for peace; it is just possible that they included some suggestion of the re-division of England and Normandy, but we will never know for sure as the plans, whatever they were, also came to nothing. 'Upon this,' says William of Malmesbury, 'the legate discontinued his exertions, waiting, like the rest, for the issue of events: for what avails it to swim against the stream?'

As Christmas approached and the trouble-filled year of 1140 wound to a close, stalemate seemed to have set in, with both sides entrenched and unwilling to compromise, and the land crushed underfoot. But unbeknown to all parties during this early part of the winter, 1141 was to be one of the most momentous years in England's history. Many significant events over the centuries have occurred as a result of a seemingly inconsequential incident that then grew, via a snowball effect, into something greater, and this was to be one of them: bizarrely, it all started when the countess of Chester paid a social visit to the wife of the castellan of Lincoln.

≥ CHAPTER SIX ≤

1141: TRIUMPH

MATILDA, COUNTESS OF CHESTER, WAS married to Ranulf de Gernon, who had succeeded his father Ranulf le Meschin as earl of Chester upon his death in 1129. In 1120 the elder Ranulf had surrendered some of his lands in the north of England to Henry I in exchange for recognition as earl of Chester following the death of his cousin in the *White Ship* disaster, but the younger Ranulf had subsequently laid claim to have these lands returned and his rights over them recognised, maintaining that his father had been disinherited. However, much of the area concerned – including Carlisle, Cumberland and the honour of Lancaster – had been granted by Stephen to David, king of Scots, as part of the settlement following David's invasion of 1136, which we discussed in Chapter 4. Ranulf's chances of regaining them had therefore all but disappeared; he had been angry with Stephen at the time, and his dissatisfaction was still rankling in December 1140. However, he had not yet committed himself to either side in the war, as declaring against Stephen would effectively mean allying himself with David, who was firmly in Matilda's camp. Ranulf consequently held aloof; his remaining hope for gain rested on the fact that he believed he had some kind of claim to Lincoln Castle through his mother, who had been an heiress in her own right in that county.

Ranulf was the half-brother (of the same heiress mother by two different marriages) of William de Roumare, who held lands both in Lincolnshire and in Normandy, and who was aggrieved that Stephen, in creating the earldom of Lincoln in 1139, had given it not to him but to William d'Aubigny, the husband of the dowager queen, Adeliza. At some point Stephen would move his earls around, transferring William d'Aubigny to Sussex, where he already held Arundel (indeed, the earldom there was generally referred to as Arundel rather than Sussex), and William de Roumare to Lincoln, but it is not clear from the surviving records exactly when this happened. Given the events we are about to describe, it seems unlikely that the shuffle had taken place by this point.

William de Roumare's wife Hawise was a friend of her sister-in-law Countess Matilda, and shortly before Christmas 1140 they both paid an ostensibly social visit to the wife of the castellan of Lincoln Castle. So far, so straightforward – it was the season for welcoming guests, after all – but there were other factors at work. As married women, the two friends were naturally part of the households of their husbands, but they also had family ties of their own: Hawise was the sister of Baldwin de Redvers, while Matilda was the eldest daughter of Robert, earl of Gloucester.

Lincoln Castle was at the time only sparsely garrisoned – perhaps because of the season or perhaps because no attack on it was expected, given that it was many miles from the main theatre of war. Orderic Vitalis gives the most detailed account of the events that ensued. When the countess's visit was due to finish, Earl Ranulf arrived in person, unarmed and accompanied by just three knights, and sought entry to the castle so he could collect his wife and his sister-in-law and escort them home. There was no reason for suspicion so he was admitted, at which point he and his men managed to overpower the guards, seize weapons and hold the gate long enough for William de Roumare to appear with the armed force he had been keeping out of sight in readiness. Ranulf and William were able to capture the castle, expel the garrison and shut the gates, leaving themselves, their wives and their own men inside. Control of the fortification soon led to control of the town; in a daring heist, a scenario worthy of a feature film, the prosperous city and significant stronghold of Lincoln had been seized from under Stephen's very nose.

Ranulf was at this stage acting entirely in his own interests, and to start with, it appeared to have worked: Stephen was keeping Christmas some 150 miles away at Windsor, which would buy Ranulf some time to consolidate his hold on Lincoln. But, not for the first time, a magnate had underestimated Stephen's willingness and ability to spring into action at speed.

The citizens of Lincoln were supporters of his, and presumably worried about the impact on trade of the present situation; they sent word to the king and asked him to come to their rescue. If he moved quickly, he might catch Ranulf and William unprepared.

Stephen immediately mustered a force, took to the road, and – astonishingly – had reached Lincoln before the end of the Christmas festivities on Twelfth Night. The citizens admitted him and his army into the town; he deployed his forces around the castle and began to prepare for a siege. Ranulf heard of his coming and had to make a quick decision: to stay where he was and settle in for the inevitable siege, or to make a quick getaway and raise reinforcements. He chose the latter, and, leaving William, Hawise and Countess Matilda inside the castle, he slipped away with a few carefully chosen companions, rode for his own lands in Cheshire, and sent a message to Robert of Gloucester. This missive contained two items of note: firstly, the incentive – or threat – that Robert's daughter was trapped and about to be besieged by the king; and, secondly, that if Robert would agree to help him, Ranulf would submit to Matilda and recognise her as queen.

This was perhaps not Matilda's ideal scenario – she might have preferred a declaration of loyalty to her as her father's heir and the rightful occupant of the throne – but she was pragmatic enough to see that having one of England's premier magnates and landholders on her side would be a huge boost to her cause, particularly as the peace negotiations arranged by Bishop Henry had come to nothing; it was clear that the war would continue. And war needed resources, which the earl of Chester had in abundance. Her acceptance of Ranulf's fealty was, says Orderic Vitalis, 'most graciously granted'. Robert was both in agreement with her and concerned about his daughter's safety; we may or may not choose to interpret Ranulf leaving his wife inside Lincoln Castle while he escaped as a cynical ploy to ensure Robert's help.

But, once again, the limitations of her gendered role meant that Matilda would have to stay where she was while the action that might finally put her on the throne would take place elsewhere. She was no doubt kept abreast of the latest news of the recruitment drive and the muster, as Robert and Miles summoned their supporters; these included a number of those 'disinherited' who, as well as having sworn allegiance to Matilda, would be sympathetic to the stand Ranulf had taken and who had a personal grudge against Stephen. She could calculate whether the number of her troops would be enough, and could be told of the lie of the land around Lincoln; but when it came to it towards the end of January, she remained at Gloucester as the men set off, to join forces on the way with Ranulf and the army he had mustered from his own lands. Her hopes were going to stand or fall on the actions of others, and she could have no further influence on the forthcoming engagement. However, her party's logistical operations, for which she must bear overall responsibility, were obviously in good shape: to assemble a force of significant size and get it on the road so quickly, in the middle of the winter, was no mean feat. The consequent speed with which the host was able to reach Lincoln was an influential factor in the result.

Robert, Miles and Ranulf approached Lincoln along the Fosse Way, which would bring them to the bridge over the River Witham at the south end of the city. They arrived late on 1 February 1141. However, for reasons which are unclear – perhaps they decided that the bridge was too narrow, allowing only a few men to cross at once and therefore slowing them down and leaving them vulnerable to arrows from inside the city, or perhaps the citizens had destroyed the structure in anticipation of their arrival – they turned towards the west, where a fording place was to be found about half a mile away.

Stephen, inside the city walls, now found himself in one of the worst possible positions, militarily speaking: trapped between his enemies inside the castle and an approaching army that had arrived much faster than anticipated, and running the risk of being crushed between them. He took advice from those magnates who were with him: their general opinion was that he should make a strategic withdrawal rather than fight; that way he could return at a later date with a much bigger force. But he spurned their advice and decided to fight anyway. Orderic Vitalis criticises this decision, saying that 'the obstinate prince disdained to listen to these prudent counsels, and thought it dishonourable to defer the engagement for any consideration'. However, there are two factors that must be taken into account. The first was personal to Stephen, an episode from his family history that continued to haunt him: in 1098 his father, Stephen, count of Blois, had made just such a 'strategic withdrawal' from Antioch under very similar circumstances (the crusaders had taken the city, were besieging the stronghold within it, and were being approached from behind by a relieving force), deeming the position hopeless; but those left behind had won a great and improbable victory, and Count Stephen had been lambasted across Europe for cowardice, a reputation he never lived down. King Stephen had spent many years emphasising his maternal line, the fact that King Henry was his uncle and William the Conqueror his grandfather; to withdraw in the face of battle might result in the label 'like father, like son' for the rest of his life.

There was also a second, more practical reason for his decision to fight. At this time pitched battles were avoided where possible, due to the gamble they represented – years of careful work could be lost in a day due to any number of variable factors – but in this case it was actually the better option for Stephen: he could move his troops out into the open where they had room to manoeuvre rather than being trapped in between two hostile forces in the narrow streets of the city. It was not ideal, but it was at least the lesser of two evils.

At dawn on 2 February 1141, the church feast known as Candlemas or the Purification of the Blessed Virgin Mary, Stephen heard Mass in Lincoln Cathedral. Mass was conducted by Alexander, bishop of Lincoln (one of the nephews of Roger of Salisbury whom we met in Chapter 5), and several chroniclers make much of the supposed bad omens that occurred both prior to and during the service. Orderic Vitalis says that the night had been broken by great storms, thunder and lightning; the *Deeds of Stephen* tells of how, as the king was given a candle for the feast's procession, it snapped in his hand, fell to the ground and was extinguished. Henry of Huntingdon narrates the same incident and then embellishes it by adding that the pyx, the receptacle containing the host, also crashed to the ground. Hindsight, as ever, was a chronicler's best friend.

The exact details of the remainder of the day are a little hazy, partly due to the various chroniclers not being eyewitnesses and therefore relying on second-hand accounts (which disagree with each other on various points), and partly as they were all clerics rather than soldiers, who may not have had a complete grasp of the military situation or precise terminology. Still, from a close analysis of the accounts of Henry of Huntingdon, William of Malmesbury, Robert de Torigni, Orderic Vitalis, the *Deeds of Stephen* and a few others who mention the events in passing, we can make a reasonable reconstruction of the course of the day.

After Mass Stephen and his army issued forth from the city to a plain to the west, which sloped down from the city walls to the river. The river was swollen (not surprising given the time of year) and the ground around it was marshy. Stephen knew of the fording place and set men to guard it, but Earl Robert and some of his men managed to wade across; William of Malmesbury says they swam, but this is unlikely given the weight of contemporary armour (of which more below) and the fact that they would have been in no fit state to fight had they been immersed for any length of time in freezing water. Robert's men chased away Stephen's guards, enabling the rest of Matilda's army to ford. They then moved a little further away from the river to where the ground was firmer.

At this point Henry of Huntingdon devotes a long passage to a number of pre-battle orations that were given in both armies. These are, of course, not verbatim reports but rather a later rewrite combining what Henry's informants told him of the speeches from memory with what he thought the protagonists ought to have said. It is, nevertheless, worth passing over them briefly in order to get an idea of what was considered appropriate at such a juncture. Let us not forget that for many, indeed most, of the men on the field this was to be their first experience of battle, so a decent leader's speech would have raised morale.

On the king's side, Henry starts with the interesting note that Stephen 'did not have a good speaking voice', so he persuaded one Baldwin fitzGilbert, a more accomplished orator, to deliver it for him. Baldwin produces the sort of speech we might expect: he talks to the troops of their support for the king and the justice of his cause; he encourages them by noting the presence in his host of the many earls 'long practised in warfare', and he insults the opposition leaders. Robert, he says, has 'the mouth of a lion but the heart of a rabbit'; Ranulf 'has designs beyond his powers'; their army is full of 'deserters and vagabonds'.

On the other side, meanwhile, Ranulf thanks the army for coming to his aid, and says that it is only right that since he has brought them into danger, he should place himself at the forefront and strike the first blow against the enemy. He does not mention Matilda. She is, however, the principal subject of Robert's speech. He reminds his listeners that he is old King Henry's son and that the throne rightfully belongs to his sister; also that the opposition are 'every one of them tainted with perjury'. He also indulges in some insults directed at individuals in Stephen's host, and reiterates that Stephen has governed badly and taken away rightful inheritances. He ends with a personal appeal to a specific part of his army: 'And so, you mighty men, whom the great King Henry raised up and this man has thrown down, whom he favoured and this one has ruined, lift up your spirits, relying on your courage, or rather on God's justice, take up God's offer of vengeance . . . if you share a determination to carry out this judgement of God, vow to advance and swear not to take flight, together raising your right hands to heaven.' His army then apparently responded by raising their hands and letting out a 'blood-curdling cry' as they prepared for the engagement.

So we can better visualise the scene before us, it might be useful at this point to give a brief overview of what the combatants looked like, how they were armed and what weapons they carried. In essence, the armour worn by those higher up the social scale had changed little from that of their grand-fathers in 1066. The basic defensive garment was a thick padded gambeson – made up of quilted layers of fabric, wadding and horsehair – worn under a hauberk which was made of thousands of interlinked, riveted links of iron or steel – steel was superior to iron both for armour and for weapons, but it was harder to manufacture and thus more expensive. Both gambeson and hauberk were split back and front from the groin to the knee to allow for easier riding. In the seventy-five years since the Norman Conquest the hauberk had become slightly longer, now reaching to the knee rather than mid-thigh, and it had an integral coif (hood) which could be worn up over the head or folded down when not in use. The hauberk had long sleeves which reached the wrist; mittens with mail on the back could be worn either separately or as an integral part of the sleeve.

On his head the well-armed magnate wore a padded arming cap under his mail and a metal helm over it. Again, this was essentially the same as that of his predecessors, although it was just at this time that the nasal bar of the Norman helm began to expand to form a sort of face-mask which also protected the cheekbones. It was still a long way from the all-enclosing 'great helm' which would develop over the next century, but it was neverthe-less an improvement that reduced the number of serious facial injuries for those able to afford the latest equipment. The more avant-garde combatant might at this stage also have chausses, pieces of mail that covered his lower legs. These had not yet assumed the tubular form of later chausses, which were put on like socks; rather, they were flat pieces placed over the front of the shin and then laced across the back of the calf to hold them in place.

The final piece of defensive equipment was the shield, which remained kite-shaped, something like an inverted teardrop, similar to the ones depicted on the Bayeux tapestry. These were made of wood, perhaps with a leather covering or metal reinforcement, or both; they might display a simple decorative design, but the formal system of heraldry had not yet developed, so shields could not be used to differentiate one combatant from another at a glance.

The fully armed man of this period was a grim figure. The decorated surcoat bearing a coat of arms was still in the future, so he was grey in his metal mail and faceless behind his helmet and shield. He was also ferociously armed with a variety of weapons. The most common sidearm was the sword, worn on a belt and scabbard to the left side; combatants might also have a mace or axe. Each would also have a lance to be used from horseback: these were not the blunt poles of popular imagination but rather something we might now call a spear: a wooden shaft with a sharp, leaf-shaped iron or steel head. Lance technique had developed over the years: a common practice in 1066 (again as depicted on the Bayeux tapestry) was the overarm thrust, but by 1141 the lance was more likely to be couched – that is, tucked under one arm and held steady there. This made the lance a much more effective weapon, as the whole weight of the combatant (and his horse) was behind the sharp point, rather than it being propelled by the strength of the arm alone.

The horse was the symbol of the knight, the better class of combatant: good horses were expensive and both mount and rider needed time to train together, so they were only used by those who had the means to purchase them and the time to train. However, the cavalry charge was not the be-all and end-all of the battle at this time: an effective defensive infantry formation could halt or neutralise it.

Both armies at Lincoln contained more infantry than cavalry. Foot soldiers were of varying quality and experience, as they could be anything from professional mercenaries to local militia. Infantrymen generally carried a spear and whatever sidearms were available (at least one militiaman at Lincoln had an old Norse-style axe, as we shall see), plus whatever pieces of armour they could afford. Archers might also be present in a host at this time, although the bows in use were shorter and less powerful than the 'longbow' proper, which was developed over a century later.

Many factors came into play when a commander drew up his lines for battle. The actual number of troops was obviously important, but so was their function and experience – ten battle-hardened knights were worth more than five times that number of poorly trained, badly equipped local militiamen – and their deployment. Stephen had arrived at Lincoln expecting a siege, not a battle, so he had fewer cavalry, which put him at a disadvantage; however, he was higher up the slope than Matilda's army, which was a plus. He deployed his forces into three sections or 'battles', arranged side by side. He himself would command the centre, which would be made up of infantry and dismounted knights. It might seem odd for a trained cavalry knight to fight on foot, but this was good practice when a party was expecting to receive a cavalry charge. Firstly, a dense formation on foot, with spears facing the charge, could minimise the damage from the horses, perhaps making them shy at the last moment; and having heavily armoured and experienced knights in among the infantry both improved the defensive capabilities of the host and stiffened the resolve of the more lightly armoured foot soldiers. This technique had worked well at both Bourgthéroulde in 1124 and the battle of the Standard in 1138.

To Stephen's right was a mounted force which contained a number of earls. This was a high-profile campaign and the king had with him Waleran, count of Meulan and earl of Worcester; Waleran's half-brother William de Warenne, earl of Surrey; Alan le Breton, earl of Richmond and titular earl of Cornwall; Simon de Senlis, earl of Northampton; and William d'Aumale, earl of York, who had fought at the battle of the Standard. There appears to have been no single overall commander of this wing, with each earl having charge of his own men: this was not ideal, as leadership by committee was a poor tactic in battle, where swift decisions and action were often necessary. On his left Stephen had Flemish and Breton mercenaries commanded by William of Ypres; there were also some men of Lincoln, who were probably positioned at the rear of the host. These were likely to have been the worst trained and most lightly armoured of his troops, but they were defending their homes and they would be useful in guarding against a sortie from the castle.

Matilda's army, further down the slope with the marsh and the river behind them, was composed of a mixture of troops who had never fought together before: Robert's men, Ranulf's men, the 'disinherited' (those whose lands had been confiscated by Stephen so he could reward his followers), and a mass of Welsh mercenaries; both Robert and Ranulf, due to the geographical situation of their lands, had good contacts in Wales. Robert commanded the centre, which was predominantly cavalry; Ranulf took the right with a mixture of cavalry and infantry, possibly also with some archers; and the 'disinherited' were on the left. None of the chroniclers who depict the battle thinks to mention who commanded this wing, but Miles of Gloucester would be a likely candidate. The Welsh were dispersed to the left and the right wings, mainly on the right and probably in front of the other troops as they are the first ones mentioned as the battle got under way.

Matilda's Welsh infantry ('who possessed more daring than military skill', says Henry of Huntingdon, dismissively) were destroyed almost immediately when they were attacked by William of Ypres on one side and Earl Alan on the other; the remaining Welsh broke and fled. But this meant that Stephen's cavalry wings were now more or less dispersed, chasing after the fleeing men – a charge on horseback was an impressive sight but it was very difficult to do it more than once – while the cavalry of Ranulf and of the 'disinherited' remained in place on the wings of Matilda's army. The left wing (possibly led, as mentioned, by Miles) swept forward to engage Alan's troops and those of the other earls; Ranulf's men also moved forward on the right, possibly supported by archers from Cheshire, given that the *Deeds of Stephen* tells us that both William of Ypres and Earl Waleran fled 'before coming to close quarters', which implies a missile attack. Orderic Vitalis says something similar, but in his account William of Ypres and Earl Alan are the first to flee, with the others following. Henry of Huntingdon says of the mercenary captain that 'as an experienced general he perceived the impossibility of supporting the king' and elected to survive to fight another day – he would no doubt have expected less generous treatment than the earls, had he been captured.

Stephen could see his army disintegrating around him, but he fought on. He was on foot in the centre of his host, which was now engaged by Robert of Gloucester's cavalry. Henry of Huntingdon gives a flavour of the combat around him:

You would have seen the dread sight of war all round the royal force, sparks leaping up from the clash of helmets and swords; the fearful hissing [of arrows] and the terrifying shouts re-echoed from the hills and from the city walls. Attacking the royal squadron with a cavalry charge, they killed some, threw others to the ground, and carried off others as captives. No pause or respite was given them, except in the area where the mighty king was standing, his enemies trembling at the incomparable ferocity of the blows he struck.

Stephen demonstrated great personal courage even when he knew the game was up, laying about him with his sword until it broke. He was then passed a battle-axe ('a Norwegian axe', as Orderic describes it, showing that some old-fashioned weapons were still around) by one of the citizens of Lincoln, and he continued to fight on with 'strong and most resolute resistance', as the *Deeds of Stephen* has it. Robert de Torigni says that Stephen 'kept his ground like a lion, standing single-handed in the field'. The one consolation Stephen could take from this day – not that it would be of much comfort – was that nobody could accuse him of lacking courage like his father. In the end he was felled by a stone that hit him on the helmet, stunning him for long enough to be taken into custody by one William de Cahaignes, probably a member of Robert of Gloucester's household. Henry of Huntingdon has him shouting 'Here, everybody! Here! I have the king!'

With Stephen's capture the battle was over. Taken with him were some of his lesser-ranked barons such as Baldwin fitzGilbert (he who had delivered the king's speech because Stephen's voice was unsuitable), Roger de Mowbray, Richard fitzUrse and Gilbert de Gant, who was a nephew of Alan, earl of Richmond and aged only about fifteen. This boy had stayed with his king while all the earls got away, having, according to Orderic Vitalis, 'turned their backs and fled in alarm for their own safety'. Lincoln was sacked by Matilda's army – they deserved it, says William of Malmesbury, as 'they had been the origin and fomenters of this calamity' by summoning the king in the first place – and Stephen was placed in Earl Robert's custody. As might be expected, both from his rank and from Robert's reputation, he was treated with respect and courtesy.

Matilda was in Gloucester Castle awaiting further tidings. The stakes were high: the contents of the next message to reach her would decide whether or not her fight for the throne would continue, whether her future lay as queen, prisoner or exile. She was some 140 miles from Lincoln, so (accounting for a keen rider but one who needed to cope with the short days and bad roads of winter) it was probably around 6 or 7 February that the wonderful news reached her. It was a splendid gift indeed for her thirty-ninth birthday: the kingdom she had coveted and fought for had taken a huge step towards falling into her hands. The messenger was soon followed by Robert of Gloucester in person; he arrived on 9 February with Stephen in his custody.

It is unfortunate for us that we have no eyewitness account of the meeting that took place between Matilda and Stephen. Other than a possible glimpse over the battlements at Arundel in the autumn of 1139, it was the first time they had met face to face for nearly a decade. She now had, in front of her, the man who had publicly sworn allegiance to her and then reneged on his word to have himself crowned, pushing her aside. Whatever words were exchanged, it is probable that Matilda took pains to emphasise her superior position during the conversation: it was unlikely to have been a cosy fireside chat. But Stephen was a crowned king and – whatever Matilda's personal feelings – he must be treated with the dignity of his estate lest monarchy itself should become devalued. Stephen was taken off to a relatively comfortable confinement at Robert's castle of Bristol, to be haunted by the shade of Robert Curthose's lifelong incarceration.

Stephen's imprisonment was, as it transpired, to become less comfort-able. At first he was given some liberty at Bristol, but either he took advan-tage of the situation or Robert became nervous at the responsibility and acted to secure his prize more tightly; the result was that Stephen was put in chains. This was an extraordinary thing to do to an anointed king. William of Malmesbury tries to excuse Robert's action by saying that Stephen 'having either eluded or bribed his keepers, had been found, more than once, beyond his appointed limits, more especially in the night-time': perhaps there was some suspicion that he might charm his gaolers, over-whelmed by the glamour of having a king in their custody, into letting him go, which would be a disaster. Robert took unprecedented action, but these were unprecedented times.

Fortune's wheel had turned. Stephen, weighed down by his chains, was on his way down; Matilda, five years after her father's death, was within tantalising touching distance of the very top. With her rival defeated and in her custody, her claim to the throne could now add conquest to hereditary

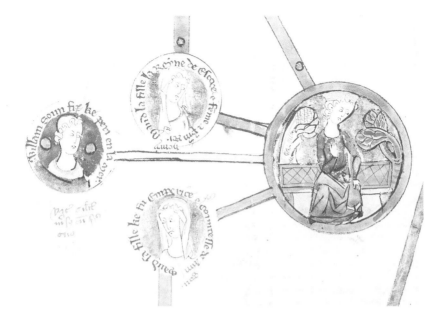

1. Matilda (bottom) is depicted on a genealogical roll, along with her father, Henry I (right), her mother, Edith-Matilda (top), and her only legitimate brother, William Adelin (left).

2. Mainz Cathedral, where Matilda was crowned queen of Germany at the age of eight in 1110, shortly after her arrival in the Empire.

3. The wedding feast of Matilda and Emperor Henry in 1114, as depicted in Ekkehard of Aura's chronicle.

4. Henry I is shown in mourning, above a depiction of his son William Adelin perishing in the *White Ship* disaster of 1120. It was William's death that gave Matilda the opportunity to claim the English throne in her own right.

5 & 6. Reading Abbey, now in ruins, was founded by Henry I; it was both his burial place and the site of a later dispute over the relic of the hand of St James, which Matilda brought back with her from the Empire.

NEAR TO THIS SPOT
WAS BURIED
KING HENRY BEAUCLERC,
WHO FOUNDED
READING ABBEY.
JUNE 18, 1121.

UNVEILED   JUNE 18,1921

7. The tomb effigy of Geoffrey Plantagenet, count of Anjou,
Matilda's second husband.

8. David I of Scotland (left), seen here with his grandson and eventual successor Malcolm IV, was Matilda's uncle and one of her greatest supporters.

9. Arundel Castle, where Matilda took refuge when she landed in England in 1139 to start her campaign for the throne.

10. As an indication that she considered herself the rightful monarch, Matilda had her own silver pennies minted, including this one, struck at the Oxford mint in 1141/2.

11. This fanciful nineteenth-century reimagining of Matilda refusing to release Stephen from captivity shows the stereotypes that have been applied to her over the centuries: she, haughty and imperious, dismisses the feminine and supplicant Matilda of Boulogne, who weeps at her feet. In fact the two women never met in person to discuss the issue.

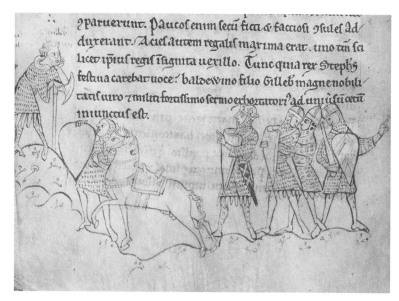

ꝓparuerunt. Paucos enim secū ficti & factiosi insules adduxerant. Acies autem regalis maxima erat. uno tñ scilicet ipsius regis insignita uexillo. Tunc quia rex Stephs festiua carebat uoce: baldewino filio Gilleb magne nobilitatis uiro ⁊ militi fortissimo sermo exhortatorius ad uniusū cetū iniunctus est.

12. A scene prior to the pivotal battle of Lincoln in 1141, from Henry of Huntingdon's chronicle. Stephen (the crowned figure in the centre) needs to give a speech to rally his troops, but his voice is too soft, so he delegates the task to Baldwin fitzGilbert (far left).

13 & 14. Matilda's seal shows her seated in majesty with the symbols of justice, but it is single-sided. Those of her male contemporaries, such as David, king of Scots, have a reverse depicting them as armed warriors – something to which she could never aspire.

15. Westminster Abbey, where Matilda was due to be crowned in the summer of 1141: she came tantalisingly close to being England's first queen regnant, but was driven out of London before the ceremony could take place.

16. The keep at Wolvesey Castle in Winchester. Matilda's troops besieged it during the late summer of 1141, but remained there too long; their retreat from the city proved to be a disaster for her campaign.

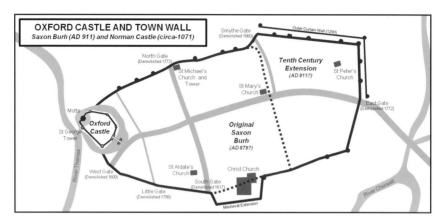

17. Matilda's daring escape from Oxford in December 1142 reputedly took place from a door in St George's Tower. A plan of Oxford at the time of the escape shows that it was indeed very close to the river, corresponding with the chroniclers' descriptions of her crossing the frozen Thames on foot.

18. The remains of Wallingford Castle. Wallingford was held by Brian fitzCount for Matilda, and was the scene of much military action during her campaign. It was also the site of the treaty by which Matilda's son Henry was declared heir to the English throne in 1152.

19. The four Anglo-Norman kings of England: William I, William II, Henry I and Stephen. Matilda, despite all her efforts, is nowhere to be seen.

20. Rouen Cathedral, where Matilda's remains were eventually laid to rest after the destruction of her tomb at Bec Abbey.

21. Matilda's greatest success was in campaigning for
her son Henry's right to be king of England, and she is
mentioned here in the captions both immediately above and
immediately below him. Matilda's line continues through
Henry to her grandchildren, kings of England and queens of
other realms.

right. There were knock-on effects all through the kingdom as magnates adjusted themselves to the new reality. Those who had been against her hastened to act in their own best interests: if Matilda were to be crowned, as now looked likely, she would look least favourably on those who took the longest to declare for her. Meanwhile, those who had supported Matilda since the moment of her arrival might now expect to receive the rewards they had been promised. The pieces on the board rearranged themselves: Roger de Beaumont, earl of Warwick, went over to Matilda voluntarily, while his cousin Hugh the Poor lost his earldom of Bedford to Miles de Beauchamp, who had been disinherited of his lands in that county. Reginald de Dunstanville, Matilda's half-brother, was able to claim sole rights as earl of Cornwall, with Alan le Breton losing both his rights there and also his northern castles to Ranulf of Chester. Ranulf's actions now placed him in Matilda's camp, although that did not necessarily mean that he reconciled himself with David, king of Scots.

As obstacles were removed one by one, the road in front of Matilda was becoming clearer. The main hurdle still in her way was the church, but she was now in a position to deal with this. She left Gloucester on 17 February 1141 to arrange a meeting with Henry, bishop of Winchester.

The path in front of Matilda may have been opening up, but it was one that had not been trodden before. No woman in England had previously been recognised as the holder, in her own right, of kingly sovereignty, and neither the magnates nor the churchmen knew how to deal with the situation. As we noted in Chapter 3, there was no actual law against female succession; if there had been, we can assume that Stephen's delegation to the papal court would have brought it up during the hearing of 1139. But they did not, relying instead on claims that Matilda was illegitimate. Indeed, any hint from Stephen about the validity of female succession in general would have weakened his own position, which was in part based on his relationship with the three previous Anglo-Norman kings via his mother.

There was ample precedent for women wielding power at comital level, both in England and in western Europe, but they had to approach matters differently from their male counterparts. One of the most notable recent examples, of course, was Stephen's mother Adela. But the wording used about her by contemporaries is significant, as in this example from Robert de Torigni: 'After the death of her husband Stephen, count of Blois, Adela, daughter of William, king of the English, ruled the country nobly for some years because her sons were at the time less able to do so.' Adela's name is almost drowned out amid the mentions of her father, husband and sons, which put her firmly in her gendered place: women could exercise authority, but they had to do it on behalf and with the permission of male relatives.

But this was not what Matilda was attempting to do. She wanted to succeed to the throne in her own right, to claim and exercise sovereignty on her own behalf, and this flummoxed her contemporaries. There was some public debate about female succession, which made reference to the Bible: the Book of Numbers depicted God sanctioning female inheritance when there were no sons, as Robert of Gloucester was fond of pointing out. Brian fitzCount went further, engaging in correspondence with both Henry, bishop of Winchester and Gilbert Foliot, abbot of Gloucester, on the subject (and evidently at some length: 'You have written me a book,' writes Gilbert in his reply to a letter of Brian's which is now unfortunately lost). It is worth noting that neither of these men stood to gain anything personally, or for their own families, from supporting female inheritance – Robert had five sons while Brian and his wife were childless, meaning that the matter was not relevant to either of them – so they could make the argument for Matilda's succession without fear of being accused of particular self-interest.

Matilda managed to highlight the confusion over female appropriation of power even further in the way in which she portrayed herself, although it could be argued that the obfuscation was necessary for her purposes. She certainly suppressed her identity as a wife: she did not refer to herself in any official document as the countess of Anjou. This might have hindered her cause in that it left a woman standing alone, a concept alien to the magnates and churchmen around her, but it did also help in that it alleviated the threat of the potential rule of Geoffrey of Anjou over England. Matilda also, at this stage, refused to foreground her status as a mother; she was claiming the throne for herself, not in the name of her son Henry. From a modern perspective it is difficult to blame her for wanting to assert her own rights, but in the context of the twelfth century it did make things rather harder for her. John of Worcester writes that when Henry I designated Matilda as his successor he did so because 'he had as yet no legitimate heir to the kingdom', implying that Matilda should be the one to *provide* that heir rather than *be* one herself. Some magnates may have viewed matters this way; Matilda did not.

The seal that Matilda used in England at this time also illustrates the difficult situation in which she found herself. It was single-sided and depicted her alone – no Geoffrey, no young Henry – seated on a throne in majesty. This was also a common image for men, but kingly seals also generally had a second image on the reverse, one that depicted them as an armed and mounted warrior. Matilda had no such image of her available (and any attempt to add one would have looked ridiculous, making the situation worse), which let slip the weakness of her position in terms of the military nature of kingship, an important consideration at this time. A king also needed to be a knight.

The situation was so alien that there was not really even a word for what Matilda wanted to be. The word 'queen' (Anglo-Saxon *cwen* or Latin *regina*) meant simply 'the wife of the king', and those Anglo-Saxon women who had succeeded in wielding power had done so on behalf of, or at least in the name of, their husbands or sons. Even today, the word 'queen' must be clarified with regard to the relevant surrounding relationships (queen regnant, queen consort, queen mother, and so on), while the word 'king' is unambiguous. In the sense that Matilda was a woman seeking to be crowned, the word 'queen' was appropriate; in the sense that she was seeking to rule in her own right, it was not. She was, in effect, intending to be not a queen but a female king, something that had never happened in England before.

There were, as we mentioned in Chapter 3, two exemplars of female kingship elsewhere: Urraca of León and Castile in the previous generation, and Melisende of Jerusalem in the current one. Melisende's father Baldwin II had taken steps to ensure that she would reign after him, and this seemed to be accepted initially: when Baldwin died, the chronicler William of Tyre wrote that 'the rule of the kingdom remained in the power of the lady queen Melisende, a queen beloved by God, to whom it passed by hereditary right'. For reasons too lengthy to examine here, William may not be considered a strictly neutral source, but his implication is clear. However, Melisende's husband Fulk, who was styled 'king of Jerusalem', gradually assumed more and more authority while dismissing his wife's, and he sought to fill the Jerusalemite court with his own Angevin followers. This led them into conflict as she, with the support of her own nobles, insisted on her rights; she emerged victorious in the dispute and he was forced to capitulate. They were reconciled, and through the late 1130s and early 1140s Fulk issued charters including phrases such as 'with the consent of Melisende his wife' or 'with the assent of Melisende the queen'. Fulk, who was of course Matilda's father-in-law, would die in 1143 leaving Melisende alone on the throne; it was tacitly understood (by the men around her, at least) that she was acting as regent for her son Baldwin III. Bernard of Clairvaux, the influential abbot and doctor of the church, supported her and even went so far as to urge her to be more 'manly' so she could succeed. In a letter to her he wrote: 'Although a woman, you must act as a man by doing everything you have to do "in a spirit prudent and strong". You must arrange all things prudently and discreetly so that all may judge you from your actions to be a king rather than a queen.'

He was, however, to be surprised in 1147; young Baldwin came of age, but Melisende did not resign the throne to him: she saw herself as ruler by right and not merely a regent for him. William of Tyre tells us that Melisende wished 'to emulate the magnificence of the greatest and noblest princes and to show herself in no wise inferior to them', and that 'she ruled the kingdom and administered the government with skilful care'.

The parallels in England were clear, even in the spring of 1141: the daughter and heir of the previous king, who wanted the crown for herself even though she had a son; a husband from the house of Anjou who might prove troublesome if given the chance; the potential for confusion and conflict.

Since the death of Henry I, another queen regnant had succeeded to a European kingdom, news of which had surely reached across the Channel. The circumstances of the accession of Petronilla of Aragon were exceptional: King Alfonso I died in 1134, leaving no children and only one brother, who was a bishop; the brother was given papal dispensation to renounce his vows; he became King Ramiro II (also known, for obvious reasons, as Ramiro the Monk); he married in 1135, fathered a child, Petronilla, in 1136, and then abdicated in her favour in 1137 so he could return to his religious life. The baby Petronilla was betrothed to a man twenty-three years her senior and declared queen. Clearly, this differed from the situation in England, but it is worth noting that Ramiro was not pressured to remain on the throne until he had fathered a son; he considered his progenitorial duties complete at the birth of a daughter, and the nobles of the kingdom accepted her accession. During the long years of her minority her husband ruled in her stead, using the title *princeps Aragonensis*, 'prince of the Aragonese'.

Arguments on the rights and wrongs of the English situation, the available exemplars and female succession generally might be batted back and forth for years. The one way in which Matilda could be sure of her position as queen (or indeed as female king) was to have a crown set upon her head in England, just as she had in Mainz back in 1110 and in Rome in 1117. For this she would need the support of the church, and it was to this matter that she now turned her attention.

Matilda reached the environs of Winchester in late February 1141, having stopped at and accepted the submission of Cirencester on the way. Bishop Henry now found himself in something of a delicate position, and he was trying to juggle a complex set of priorities: 'he was in bewilderment dragged this way and that by different hooks', as the *Deeds of Stephen* puts it. In family terms his allegiance lay more naturally with his brother than with his cousin, but Stephen had shown little fraternal affection himself and had not advanced Henry to the degree which he perhaps expected. As a prelate, Henry's two main concerns were peace in the kingdom and pushing forward with the Cluniac-inspired reforms of the church; both would be better served by accepting the status quo rather than fighting for the incarcerated and possibly doomed king, who had shown little interest in the reforms. On a personal level, Henry was concerned to keep his own position; no monarch, of course, could deprive him of his see or his powers as papal legate but he – or she – could certainly make life more difficult. And, finally, there was the unavoidable fact that Stephen's defeat at Lincoln was not merely a turn of Fortune's wheel: it was a sign of God's disfavour for his kingship.

Bishop Henry agreed to meet Matilda, and they convened on a grey and wet Sunday 2 March on open ground outside Winchester, possibly towards Wherwell. The gist of the negotiations was that she promised to consult him on all important matters of government, and that he would control the appointment of bishops and other senior churchmen; he in return would swear allegiance to her and hand over the royal treasury, which was based in his city. The treasury was not nearly as full as it had been five years previously,

Stephen having depleted it hugely during all the campaigns necessary to keep him on the throne, but it would certainly add to Matilda's available resources and it was a crucial symbolic step: the royal treasury should be in the hands of the source of royal authority. Agreement was reached on these points – witnessed by Earl Robert, Miles of Gloucester and Brian fitzCount, among others – and each party departed temporarily; the following day Matilda entered Winchester Cathedral in a ceremonial procession, to be welcomed by as many bishops and abbots as Henry could assemble at short notice, bulked out with local communities of monks and nuns.

The ceremony was all very well, but something bigger and more formal needed to be done. Bishop Henry used his authority as papal legate to summon a church council; time had to be allowed for the various prelates to travel to Winchester, so it was arranged for 7 April. In the meantime Matilda retired to Oxford, to leave the field clear for her new ally to speak on her behalf. She did not yet have all the highest churchmen of England on her side: Gilbert Foliot, abbot of Gloucester, had been among those to welcome her into Winchester Cathedral, as had Nigel, bishop of Ely, Alexander, bishop of Lincoln and Robert, bishop of Bath, but Theobald, archbishop of Canterbury had not. He now came to Matilda, before the church council (an event at which he would normally expect to preside, by virtue of his office, but at which he would be outranked by Bishop Henry's papal authority), to explain that he could not change sides so easily. In short, he had promised fidelity to Stephen, and he could not change his allegiance until Stephen had released him from his oath. Matilda considered his position, and, perhaps surprisingly, allowed him and a group of other prelates with similar scruples to visit the imprisoned king. Even more unexpectedly, Stephen gave them immediate permission 'to submit to the exigency of the time', as William of Malmesbury puts it, and switch their allegiance. It is difficult to infer exactly what was going on in Stephen's mind at the time, but it is possible that – defeated, captured, enchained, the prospect of life-long imprisonment looming, and feeling that God had deserted him – he had already given up hope. The *Peterborough Chronicle* spells out what was no doubt a common thought: 'When the king was in prison, the earls and the powerful men expected that he would never get out again.' Archbishop Theobald and his companions departed, their errand complete, and prepared to attend the church council.

Henry was going to have to do some fast talking to explain his U-turn, and in particular his apparent desertion of a brother in his hour of need. He did not disappoint, and the speech he gave to the assembled prelates was a superb example of smooth talking that showed him as the consummate politician he was. William of Malmesbury, who was present at the council, has the fullest account. Henry started off strongly with references to the late king and the positive aspects of his reign: 'The clergy of England,' Henry said, 'were assembled at this council, to deliberate on the peace of the country, which was exposed to imminent danger: in the time of King Henry, his uncle, England had been the peculiar abode of peace; so that by the activity, and spirit, and care of that most excellent man, none, of whatever power or dignity, dared make any disturbance.' This would have struck a chord with those present, who had endured in varying degrees the conflict, instability and violence of the preceding five years; Henry I's reign was now recalled as a halcyon time of peace and contentment.

Carrying his audience with him, the bishop next moved on to Matilda's status: 'The king, some years before his death, had caused the whole realm of England, as well as the duchy of Normandy, to be engaged, by the oaths of all the bishops and barons, to his daughter, late the empress, who was his only surviving issue by his former consort.' So far, so good. But Henry's support of Matilda here clearly raised the question of why he had not made this speech five years ago, and why he had backed Stephen in the meantime. He described King Henry's death without male issue and then, skating towards thinner ice, continued:

Therefore, as it seemed long to wait for a sovereign who delayed coming to England, for she resided in Normandy, we provided for the peace of the country, and my brother was allowed to reign. And although I gave myself as surety between him and God, that he would honour and advance the holy Church, and uphold good, but abrogate evil, laws; yet it grieves me to remember, shames me to say, how he conducted himself in the kingdom: how justice ceased to be exerted ... how peace was anni-hilated, almost within the year.

He moved swiftly on to self-justification: 'You know how often I addressed him ... and that I gained for it nothing but odium. Everyone who shall

149

think rightly must be aware that I ought to love my mortal brother, but that I should still more regard the cause of my immortal Father.'

Noting that God had 'exercised his judgement' on Stephen, Henry recovered for a strong finish: 'I have invited you all here by virtue of my legation, lest the kingdom should fall into decay through want of a sovereign ... first, then, as is fitting, invoking God's assistance, we elect the daughter of that peaceful, that glorious, that rich, that good, and, in our times, incomparable king, as lady of England and Normandy, and promise her fidelity and support.'

It was a rousing end to a convincing speech, but it was not met with the universal acclaim he might have hoped: William of Malmesbury goes on to tell us that all present either 'becomingly applauded his sentiments', or that they merely 'by their silence, did not contradict them'. In particular, 'it was a work of great difficulty to soothe the minds of the Londoners', a point to which we will return. But it was enough for now. The magnates and prelates accepted Matilda (who could thus claim to have been elected, adding a third string to her now overwhelming claim to the throne), Bishop Henry pronounced a sentence of excommunication on any who opposed her, and England was to all intents and purposes at peace.

It was Henry, during his oration, who first proclaimed Matilda as *domina Anglorum*, 'lady of the English', a term which is interesting on several levels, especially given our earlier brief discussion on the use and significance of titles. Firstly, it (or, more usually, its masculine form *dominus*) could be used to designate one who had been elected or acclaimed king, but who had not yet been crowned. The three previous Anglo-Norman coronations had been so hurried that there had not really been a need for such terminology, but later generations would make the distinction more explicit. For example, Matilda's grandson John would claim the throne of England as of 6 April 1199, the date of his brother Richard's death, but he was not crowned until 27 May. During the intervening seven weeks he issued charters which referred to him as *dominus Angliae*, that is, 'lord of England'; he did not change his style to *rex Angliae*, 'king of England', until after his coronation. Secondly, the title *domina* (or its Anglo-Saxon equivalent, *hlæfdige*) implied authority. Æthelflæd, the daughter of King Alfred the Great, for example, had been known as 'lady of the Mercians' (*Myrcna hlæfdige*) during her years of rule following the death of her husband. The French Benedictine monk and prolific writer Hugh de Fleury had dedicated his *Historia Ecclesiastica* to

Adela of Blois, addressing it 'to his ruling lady Adela, venerable countess' (*dominae suae Adelae venerabili comitissae*), a 'most serene lady' (*serenissima domina*) at a time when she was widowed and exercising power on behalf of her sons. Thus *domina*, although we do not translate it as 'queen', might actually represent Matilda's position more accurately than the word *regina* itself.

Matilda added it to her list of styles, though it came only third in precedence. She still used *imperatrix* ('empress'), first, together with her status as queen of the Romans; this was followed by 'daughter of King Henry'; only then did she list *domina Anglorum*. This was in contrast to Stephen and Henry I, who both used the simple *rex Anglorum*, 'king of the English', after their coronations. Perhaps her awareness of the lingering insecurity of her position led her to use the combination of styles, to bolster herself against a challenge from any direction. And there was an additional complicating factor for Matilda: if she referred to herself as *regina Anglorum*, 'queen of the English', she would simply be duplicating the title of Matilda of Boulogne, Stephen's wife, who used the same title but based on her marital, rather than personal, status. This might undermine Matilda's position as autonomous representation of royal authority. She could not afford to position herself as a wife; her tripartite royal identity was therefore based on two dead men and on herself alone. The chronicle accounts of the council of Winchester mention neither Geoffrey Plantagenet nor his and Matilda's sons. And Matilda did not send for any of them: she would be crowned alone.

Matilda did not move for London immediately, choosing instead to consolidate her position and presumably hoping to attract more defections as time went on. In early May 1141 she visited Reading Abbey, where she prayed at her father's tomb and accepted more submissions. However, the great magnates in the land were not coming over to her in the numbers or at the speed she would have liked. Waleran de Beaumont, earl of Worcester and count of Meulan, still held for Stephen, as did William de Warenne, earl of Surrey, and Simon de Senlis, earl of Northampton; Stephen's wife Matilda and William of Ypres had a secure base in Kent. Queen Matilda sent entreaties to Matilda asking her to release Stephen from his captivity and restore him to the throne, which Matilda predictably declined to do.

Matilda's most loyal supporters – her brothers Robert and Reginald, Miles of Gloucester, Brian fitzCount and Baldwin de Redvers (now earl of

Devon) remained firmly with her, and she did receive an additional fillip in the late spring when David, king of Scots arrived at her court, which was then in Oxford; this may or may not have been an influential factor in the non-attendance of both Ranulf of Chester and William de Roumare. It was imperative that Matilda gain more high-ranking supporters before she advanced to London, where the citizens were unlikely to welcome her with open arms.

One of the most influential figures in London was Geoffrey de Mandeville, who was castellan of the all-important Tower, the capital's central fortification. Stephen had named him earl of Essex; Matilda did not recognise Stephen's creations but she had an independent charter drawn up which granted the same earldom to Geoffrey and his heirs. She also made him hereditary castellan of the Tower, sheriff and justiciar of the county of Essex, and exempted him from the forest law there, meaning that he could act almost with impunity throughout the county – a dangerous precedent to set for a powerful earl when Matilda should have been trying to consolidate royal power, not dissipate it. Either she was not looking far enough ahead at the potential consequences of her actions or she thought that the immediate gain was of greater importance.

Avoiding Windsor, where a hostile garrison still held the castle in Stephen's name, Matilda reached Westminster (at that time a suburb of London and outside its walls) in mid-June, at which point Geoffrey de Mandeville swore allegiance to her in person. She also accepted the oath of fealty from several others, including Hugh Bigod, he who had once sworn that Matilda's father had on his deathbed disinherited her. It might have been interesting to be a fly on the wall during his submission.

As she settled into the luxurious surroundings, Matilda felt confident. Stephen was in her custody, unlikely ever to emerge; the church was on her side; she held the keys to the royal treasury; she would soon make a ceremonial entry into her capital. And her first act on arriving was a positive one: she nominated one Robert de Sigillo, a monk of Reading and former keeper of the king's seal, as the new bishop of London (a see that had been vacant for some years). She thus publicly exercised her royal authority while resolving a long-standing issue, and she did so in an unexceptionable manner, putting forward a candidate who was acceptable to all parties including Bishop Henry, a fellow Cluniac.

But then trouble started to arise. Bishop Henry, keen to push forward with his agenda of being Matilda's chief advisor, came to her with a proposal. Stephen was in prison and therefore in many crucial respects dead to the world; Matilda would have his crown, but what of his other estates and honours, the ones he held personally? Henry petitioned for them, and specifically the counties of Mortain and Boulogne (which included lands in Essex and Kent), to be conferred on Stephen's elder son Eustace, now around eleven years of age.

Matilda rejected the suggestion out of hand, clearly not paying too much attention to Bishop Henry, or her other advisors, or the way in which this would be interpreted by other magnates. Viewing her action with a charitable eye, it is understandable that she did not want to make Eustace into another William Clito-type character – the son of a dispossessed man who thought he should be king, and who had the resources to mount a challenge to the throne. But this was not the primary concern of her contemporaries. The other barons saw the situation as having the potential to impact on the inheritance of their own estates; Matilda appeared to be ungracious to a blameless child; and, above all, she had humiliated and alienated Bishop Henry, to the extent that he temporarily left her court. As may be inferred from parts of his speech at the council of Winchester, part of the reason Henry had switched his allegiance was that he was dissatisfied with Stephen: Stephen had refused to be ruled by him. Matilda, of course, did not want to be ruled by him either, but she should have been aware that powerful men, particularly powerful churchmen, could unseat a reigning monarch if they were pushed too far. Matilda, as the sole source of royal authority, was entitled to be autocratic to a certain degree, as her father had been before her; but Henry I had matched his autocracy with cunning, and was always one step ahead of the game. If Matilda were to emulate his kingship then she would need to do the same, and she had got off to a bad start.

It was at this stage, however, that Matilda faced an even greater foe: the chroniclers. Monarchs of either sex might be defeated or deposed if they failed at their endeavours, but Matilda now became the target of a barrage of vicious, vituperative criticism from these writers – criticism that was explicitly gendered.

William of Malmesbury, the most sympathetic to her of the contemporary writers, restrains himself. To him the argument with Bishop Henry about

Eustace was a 'misunderstanding', and his criticism is discreet – although he cannot resist the opportunity to praise Robert of Gloucester at Matilda's expense, making an oblique reference to the fact that she would have done better if she 'had trusted to Robert's moderation and wisdom'. John of Worcester contents himself with mentioning Matilda's 'hard heart' and saying that she 'harshly rejected' the petition of the Londoners that we will examine below.

Others, however, are decidedly more severe. Henry of Huntingdon says that once Matilda reached London, 'she was lifted up to an insufferable arrogance . . . and she alienated the hearts of almost everyone'. Interestingly, Henry paints events unfavourable to Matilda as coming about through divine intervention, but does not give the same credit to her positive achievements. For example, it was 'by God's will – indeed, whatever men may have done was by God's will – [that] she was driven out of London', but this comment appears only a few lines after her victory in battle at Lincoln apparently came about only 'because the hazard of war had favoured her supporters'. Roger of Howden, writing later, retained the gendered barbs at Matilda, writing that at this time 'she became elated to an intolerable degree of pride' and acted 'with all the spitefulness of a woman'.

The most venomous comments appear in the partisan *Deeds of Stephen*. Following the council of Winchester, says the author, Matilda 'at once put on an extremely arrogant demeanour instead of the modest gait and bearing proper to the gentle sex, began to walk and speak and do all things more stiffly and haughtily than she had been wont . . . she actually made herself queen of all England and gloried in being so called.' As if calling herself a queen after being acclaimed as one were not provocation enough, the author is shocked that Matilda should want to make her own decisions: 'Then she, on being raised with such splendour and distinction to this pre-eminent position, began to be arbitrary, or rather headstrong, in all that she did.' This recklessness included confiscating lands and honours from those who still supported Stephen, and giving them to her own adherents, a course of action entirely logical in the circumstances, but the *Deeds of Stephen* goes on to lambast her 'extreme haughtiness and insolence' in that she no longer relied on the advice of her closest confidants but instead 'arranged everything as she herself thought fit and according to her own arbitrary will'.

The author of the text is particularly incensed by Matilda's interactions with the citizens of London, who, as already noted, were no more than lukewarm about her acclamation at Winchester. After her entry into the city, when she demanded the financial contribution from the Londoners that was no more than her due, she did so 'not with unassuming gentleness, but with a voice of authority' – a phrase that sounds as if it would be a compliment if aimed at a male king, however inexperienced. The citizens then had the gall to say that they had no money because they had spent it all supporting Stephen against her, so they requested to be excused. We can only imagine what Henry I or William the Conqueror would have made of a such a request, one that would surely be dismissed in short order, possibly with violence. But again, the *Deeds of Stephen* does not like the way Matilda reacted: 'She, with a grim look, her forehead wrinkled into a frown, every trace of a woman's gentleness removed from her face, blazed into unbearable fury.'

If any of these comments about Matilda were to be aimed at Henry I, or even at Stephen, they would sound ludicrous. To criticise a king for arranging matters according to his own will, for walking confidently, or for speaking with a voice of authority, is unthinkable. But double standards abound in the chronicles: what was acceptable in a king was not acceptable in Matilda, who failed to exhibit to the required degree 'the modest gait and bearing proper to the gentle sex'. The hypocrisy in the *Deeds of Stephen* is evident when, just a few lines later, Queen Matilda, Stephen's wife, is praised for being 'a woman . . . of a man's resolution'.

All of the chroniclers we have quoted here, of course, were male and members of the clergy, so they were not representative of society as a whole, but rather of a specific part of it. There were a number of educated and literate women in England in the twelfth century, but they were a small and fairly restricted group, predominantly based in convents and writing about theological concerns rather than contemporary politics. The political commentators were men, men who could not comprehend or accept the idea of a woman in power. They perhaps expected Matilda to act like a *cwen*, a *regina*, a queen consort, a model of gentleness and compassion. But of course, had she done so it is likely she would have been castigated for precisely that, and held up as an example of why women were unfit to rule due to their softness.

Matilda could only take as exemplars the rulers who fell within her own experience. Bernard of Clairvaux would advise Melisende, queen of Jerusalem, to be more like a man in order to succeed, and the stereotypically male traits of Matilda's relations had proven themselves successful over and over again. Affability had signally failed for both Stephen and Robert Curthose; authority and ruthlessness had worked for King Henry and Emperor Henry. Where either of the latter had exhibited mercy or generosity, it was because he could afford to do so. Matilda had seen at first hand the way in which her first husband had wooed the rich and powerful Italians by offering concessions during his stay there in the 1110s, and this could perhaps have served as an exemplar for her to offer similar concessions to the Londoners. But Henry had been a strong and established man and emperor. Had he been an inexperienced boy – the nearest analogous situation to Matilda being a ruling woman – his actions might have been interpreted as weakness and taken advantage of accordingly.

Matilda was also in a situation unfamiliar to a male ruler, in that a king would normally have a queen consort to soften his authoritarianism; she did not. Perhaps some greater effort at combining the elements of male king and female queen might have yielded a better result, but she presumably felt that she could not afford to show any sign of anything that could be perceived as weakness. If she had acted as the chroniclers seem to be implying that she should – that is, using her womanly compassion to set her rival free, relying entirely on her male advisors, releasing the Londoners from their financial obligations – what sort of message would that have sent about the nature of her authority, her kingship? She could not take that risk, and it would have been against her nature to do so. She was in an impossible situation: in short, she was acting like a king, because that was what she believed the circumstances required; but contemporaries did not like and could not accept her acting as a king, because she was a woman.

It is probable that Matilda herself did not subject her position to complex gender analysis. She had a job to do, she needed to do it, and she would blaze her own trail as necessary. She might have alienated Bishop Henry and some of the other magnates, but she still had Stephen in prison, she enjoyed the support of a number of important barons and prelates, and she had been proclaimed 'lady of the English'. On the evening of 24 June 1141, the night before her ceremonial entry into London, she sat down to dinner at Westminster, surrounded by her supporters. Nothing, it seemed, could now stand between her and the crown.

⋟ CHAPTER SEVEN ⋞

1141: DISASTER

UT SOMETHING – OR, RATHER, SOMEONE – did stand in Matilda's
way. And she was about to make her presence felt.

Matilda of Boulogne, Stephen's queen, had not given up hope
when her husband was captured. Instead she had left London in order to
regroup in the south-east of England, along with her principal lieutenant
William of Ypres. William is often referred to as a 'mercenary captain',
which, although technically correct, disguises the fact that he was by now a
powerful and influential man. He was the illegitimate son of a younger
brother of Robert II, count of Flanders, and had been a proposed but not
seriously considered rival candidate to William Clito and Thierry of Alsace
in the competition for the county following the murder of Charles the
Good, as we mentioned in Chapter 3. William had been one of Stephen's
chief military advisors and commanders since the latter's accession, and he
had been rewarded accordingly: he did not hold the title of earl of Kent but
he was in effect just that, with Gervase of Canterbury, a local chronicler,
describing him as having 'all Kent committed to his custody' and 'possessing
the county'. And while other men might have the luxury of changing their
allegiance back and forth, there is no question that William's best interests
would be served by having Stephen returned to the throne. He therefore
threw himself into the task of supporting Stephen's loyal wife.

Queen Matilda attempted briefly to play a feminine, 'queen consort as
intercessor'-type role, but this proved ineffective against her namesake, who
as we have seen refused either to release Stephen or to allow his inheritance

to pass to Eustace; the queen therefore realised that she would have to resort to more direct action. She and William raised a force in Kent and marched towards London, and it is at this point that the *Deeds of Stephen*, in a spectacular manifestation of double standards, notes approvingly that 'forgetting the weakness of her sex and a woman's softness, [she] bore herself with the valour of a man'. On reaching London the Kent forces engaged in a policy of burning and ravaging the surrounding countryside, as the *Deeds of Stephen* describes:

> [the queen] gave orders that they should rage most furiously around the city with plunder and arson, violence and the sword, in sight of the countess [Matilda] and her men. The people of London were in grievous trouble. On the one hand their land was being stripped before their eyes and reduced by the enemy's ravages to a habitation for the hedgehog, and there was no one ready to help them; on the other that new lady of theirs was going beyond the bounds of moderation and sorely oppressing them . . . therefore they judged it worthy of consideration to make a new pact of peace and alliance with the queen and join together with one mind to rescue their king and lord from his chains.

Queen Matilda was able to take something of a carrot-and-stick approach with the Londoners. On the one hand, she was attacking their lands and threatening their livelihoods; but on the other, she was countess of Boulogne in her own right and therefore controlled many of the trade routes between London and the Continent, which could be offered to the citizens if they took her side. They were also aware of Stephen's prior promises of greater self-government for the capital (which Matilda was very unlikely to match, given their initial interactions with her), so it was in the best interests of the burgesses to take the queen's part. They sent representatives to her and agreed on a plan.

As we saw at the end of Chapter 6, Matilda sat down to dinner at Westminster on the evening of 24 June 1141, expecting to make her ceremonial entrance into London the following day. But suddenly, bells began to ring out all across the capital. This was the signal for the citizens to take up arms; they attacked Matilda's followers in the city, opened the gates and poured along the road to Westminster. Matilda had only a very short time to decide what to do, but there was not really any choice in the face of an enraged horde heading straight for her in an unfortified location. She and her immediate advisors mounted horses and fled. They were only just in time: they had barely got away when the mob broke into her apartments and plundered everything they could get their hands on; apparently the dinner was still warm.

It was not an orderly retreat ('ignominious' is the word John of Worcester uses), and Matilda's supporters were scattered. Bishop Henry fled to Winchester; some others headed for their own homes; Matilda, Earl Robert and King David rode back to Oxford to seek the safety of the high walls there. Matilda must have experienced a whirlwind of emotions, from initial terror through humiliation and on to fury. Her plans for a coronation, the one thing which would truly make her queen, were in tatters. She had lost the city of London, and there was little chance of getting it back: the citizens, encouraged by the queen's offers and threats, had made their feelings very plain. Moreover, despite all Matilda's offers to him, Geoffrey de Mandeville took this opportunity to make peace with Queen Matilda, meaning that the stronghold of the Tower was gone as well.

Geoffrey, incidentally, had some explaining to do: when Stephen had set off for Lincoln prior to the battle there, both Queen Matilda and her daughter-in-law Constance (the wife of Eustace and the sister of Louis VII of France, then aged around fifteen) had been installed in the Tower for their own safety. Once news of the defeat reached London, the queen had left for Kent, but Geoffrey refused to allow Constance to accompany her, keeping her in his own custody for reasons that were unspecified but probably as some kind of insurance policy. Queen Matilda, although at the time powerless to prevent this, had not been impressed. But she was now so desperate for allies that she accepted Geoffrey back into the fold.

To add to Matilda's travails, as she considered them on the sixty or so miles to Oxford, the fact that Bishop Henry had chosen to flee in the opposite direction indicated that she might soon also lose her hold both on Winchester and the treasury, and on the church. This, unfortunately for her, proved to be true. Queen Matilda had shrewdly appealed to Henry's ego by repositioning herself to him as a supplicant, and this paid off: the *Deeds of Stephen* notes that he had been moved 'by the woman's tearful supplications, which she pressed on him with great earnestness'. In a feat of doublespeak of truly epic proportions, just two months after proclaiming Matilda 'lady of England' and excommunicating Stephen's supporters, Henry now publicly renounced his allegiance to Matilda and re-declared for Stephen, ordering all England's magnates to do the same. Of course, Matilda's most loyal supporters refused to do any such thing. This prompted Bishop Henry to write a letter to Brian fitzCount, telling him that he was in danger of being 'numbered among the unfaithful men of England' – an accusation that sounds distinctly odd coming from a man who has changed sides and aimed at a man who has not. The irony was not lost on Brian, and his scathing reply, which has fortunately come down to us, is a work of epistolary art.

Brian opens his letter by pointedly refusing to address the bishop as 'the brother of King Stephen', and then goes on to draw attention to Henry's previous instructions:

> To Henry the nephew of King Henry, Brian fitzCount sends greeting . . . you yourself who are a prelate of holy church have ordered me to adhere to the daughter of King Henry your uncle, and to help her to acquire that which is hers by right but has been taken from her by force, and to retain what she already has . . . when I look back to your command to help the daughter of King Henry with all my strength, then I have no fear that I am committing any crime . . . I should be numbered among the faithful men of England, for I have obeyed the lawful command which you gave me.

He mentions the depredations he has endured due to his support for Matilda:

> King Henry gave me land. But it has been taken from me and my men because I am doing what you ordered me to do. As a result, I am in extreme straits and not harvesting one acre of corn from the land which he gave me . . . you should know that neither I nor my men are doing this for money or fief or land, either promised or given, but because of your command and the lawfulness of myself and my men.

He later works himself up to end with a challenge: 'All the faithful men of holy church should therefore know that I, Brian fitzCount, whom good

King Henry brought up and to whom he gave arms and an honour, am ready to prove what I assert in this letter against Henry nephew of King Henry, bishop of Winchester and legate of the Apostolic See, either by combat or by judicial process, though a clerk or a layman.'

It was unusual – to say the least – for a papal legate to be threatened with trial by combat, but the mere mention of it gives us an idea of the extent of Brian's irritation. In order to hammer home his point with even less subtlety, he also provides a list of no fewer than fifty-two named individuals (including, with sarcasm astonishing even in the context of the letter, 'Theobald the so-called archbishop of Canterbury') who he says were witnesses to Bishop Henry's command to serve Matilda. Of course, Brian is being more than a little disingenuous here, as he was serving Matilda long before Henry ordered the magnates to do so at the council of Winchester, but his letter highlights the bishop's startlingly rapid changes of allegiance, and was a valuable contribution to the propaganda war.

Brian, along with Earl Robert, King David and Matilda's other loyal men, needed to collect themselves and advise her as she decided on what to do next. The situation was serious but not fatal: London might be gone, but Matilda's husband Geoffrey of Anjou had been making great gains in Normandy while she had been in England (we will explore this more fully in Chapter 8), so many magnates who held lands on both sides of the Channel were drifting away from Stephen as he could not protect their interests there. Matilda still enjoyed the full support of her original adherents; some notable others – including Waleran and Robert de Beaumont, earls of Worcester and Leicester and previously numbered among Stephen's firmest supporters – were wavering. Indeed, there is some evidence that Waleran defected to Matilda's camp in July 1141 on the basis of the security of his estates in Normandy (where he was count of Meulan, his family's ancestral lands); but he then travelled back to Normandy and so was not part of her court or her army as she planned her next move. And, of course, Matilda still had her trump card: Stephen remained in her custody. While considering her options over the course of the next month, Matilda sent Robert to Winchester to speak to Bishop Henry, but to no avail. She travelled to Gloucester to consult Miles, then returned to Oxford with him and created him earl of Hereford in a charter dated 25 July. By this time she had made her decision: London was too big a nut to crack now that Queen

Matilda held both the city and the Tower, but Winchester, home of the treasury, was of vital and almost equal importance. Matilda and her supporters mustered an army and rode south.

Winchester, unusually, had two castles. The first was the royal one in the west of the city, and this still held for Matilda – the troubles in London had not yet stretched their influence so far. The second was Wolvesey, a splendid castle-cum-palace-cum-residence belonging to Bishop Henry personally (as we saw earlier, he was a noted castle-builder) and situated just inside the south-east corner of the city walls; this meant that it was well protected but also that it benefited from communication and supply access to the open ground outside the city. As Matilda and her army approached Winchester she sent a message demanding that Henry meet her. She may have meant for him simply to attempt to explain himself, but he evidently took it as a threat of arrest; William of Malmesbury tells us that after sending a reply saying ambiguously that he would 'prepare himself', Henry fled, leaving his own castle behind just as she arrived at the royal one on 31 July. He headed at speed for Farnham and then Guildford, where he met Queen Matilda, to whom he had already sent for help as soon as he had heard about Matilda's advance. He left Wolvesey Castle garrisoned against her, and his men there prepared for a fight.

The size of Matilda's army at Winchester is a matter of some debate. The *Deeds of Stephen*, whose author wished to make it seem as large as possible, lists among those present Robert, earl of Gloucester; David, king of Scots; the earls of Cornwall (Matilda's half-brother Reginald de Dunstanville), Devon (Baldwin de Redvers), Somerset (William de Mohun), Hereford (the newly appointed Miles of Gloucester) and Warwick (Roger de Beaumont); and other lesser barons including Brian fitzCount, William of Salisbury (eldest son of the sheriff of Wiltshire), Humphrey de Bohun (son-in-law of Earl Miles) and John Marshal, whom we last encountered in Chapter 5, vacillating in his loyalties. William of Malmesbury, on the other hand, is keen to play down the engagement and therefore to make Matilda's army seem smaller; he mentions only Earl Robert, King David, Miles and 'some barons'.

Matilda installed herself in the royal castle; this time she was at the scene of the military action in person. She would not have been in possession of any armour, so it is unlikely that she would get near enough to the forthcoming siege action to be in any immediate physical danger, but she would certainly have been directing or at least involved in the tactical discussion that went on around the command table: as we will see, one of the most significant decisions of the engagement seems to have been made by her personally. In order to have a base nearer to Wolvesey, Earl Robert established a centre of operations within the town, near the church of Saint Swithin, as soon as he arrived; events moved quickly thereafter. Matilda's forces began the siege of Wolvesey on 1 August, but the garrison there, acting under instructions left by Bishop Henry, caused both a distraction and a potential disaster by throwing out from the castle burning material that, in the summer heat, quickly set the city ablaze. John of Worcester says of the bishop that 'goaded by rage, and to strike terror and dismay into the hearts of the people, he determined to set fire to the city and burn it to the ground'. This seems a strange and potentially desperate thing for Henry to do: while burning and wasting were acknowledged features of warfare, this was his own city, his own flock, who might under more normal circumstances look to him for protection.

The great stone cathedral survived, but much of the town – wooden houses with thatched roofs – was lost. The devastation meant that Matilda's forces were deprived of shelter and provisions, to say nothing of the fate of the unfortunate citizens who lost their homes and livelihoods. But worse was to come when an army led by Queen Matilda and William of Ypres – no doubt with Bishop Henry in tow – arrived. It was an impressive force: they were accompanied by William de Warenne, earl of Surrey; Simon de Senlis, earl of Northampton; Gilbert fitzRichard de Clare, earl of Hertford; and Geoffrey de Mandeville, (still, somehow) earl of Essex, among others. Ranulf de Gernon, earl of Chester, seems to have been wavering in his loyalties at this point: there is some evidence that he made overtures to the queen, but that she and her advisors distrusted him so he returned to Matilda, where he was equally unwelcome for his lack of enthusiasm ('he came late, and to no purpose,' reports William of Malmesbury). Ranulf does not seem to have been involved in the fighting at Winchester at all. The queen's army also included a contingent of Londoners, militia and infantry who would be more use than knights or cavalry in a siege situation.

The queen's army surrounded the town, so Matilda's men found themselves in a dangerous position. They were inside the walls of Winchester – in a close urban environment that had been damaged by fire – besieging Wolvesey, but they were themselves besieged from outside the city, trapping them in the middle of two hostile forces. There was not enough food in Winchester to supply both the citizens and the army (and its horses, voracious consumers of both water and grain), so provisions were needed from outside. Matilda's main supply routes were to the north-west and west of the city – those roads which headed towards her strongholds in the West Country – but the queen's army cut these off so that nothing could get through; those who tried were 'intercepted, and either killed or maimed', according to William of Malmesbury. Queen Matilda's forces themselves, meanwhile, were adequately supplied from the other direction, London and the south-east.

With Matilda trapped, her enemies moved to close the net even more tightly, burning Andover and the surrounding area. The nearby abbey of Wherwell, which Matilda's forces had started to fortify in the hope of creating an outpost – John Marshal had been sent out of the city earlier to oversee this – was also attacked and burned. John was unable to get a relief force back to Winchester; he and the Wherwell garrison were trapped and took shelter in the abbey church, but the queen's soldiers threw burning torches inside. In this they were led by William of Ypres: William of Malmesbury chooses this exact moment to call him 'an abandoned character who feared neither God nor man', but whether this is a specific reference to him burning a church or merely a general comment on him as an enemy of Matilda is unclear. Certainly, the chronicler makes no criticism of the fact that Matilda's forces had attempted to fortify the church in the first place.

The fire took hold. The nuns fled the abbey grounds ('cries and shrieks rang piercingly out from the virgins dedicated to God', notes the *Deeds of Stephen*); and one by one, the knights and men inside staggered out, singed and choking, to surrender. All except one: John Marshal remained inside as the fire roared around him, the flames reaching higher and burning with such intense heat that eventually the church roof melted and collapsed into the inferno. He was blinded, agonisingly, in one eye, by molten lead which cascaded down on to his face; remarkably, he not only survived but also managed to escape, William of Ypres's men having assumed that he was dead when he did not emerge along with the others.

It is not clear exactly how a message about the calamity at Wherwell reached Matilda inside the walls of Winchester, but it is safe to assume that the queen's army broadcast the fact of their victory in order to undermine the morale of Matilda's forces. There was no hope of rescue or reinforcement, so those inside would have to fend for themselves. The question of making a strategic withdrawal may have been raised at this point, but if so it was not acted upon. Meanwhile, the siege of Wolvesey was becoming mired: no chronicler mentions that Matilda's army had brought heavy siege machinery, and such engines would have been needed to break down the walls of the castle. They were expensive, as they required not only large timbers and logistical systems capable of transporting them, but also skilled engineers to construct and operate the machines. We saw earlier how costly Stephen's siege of Exeter in 1136 had been, depleting the royal treasury, and Matilda did not have access to anything approaching that level of finance. But without siege machinery her army was obliged either to starve the garrison out (impractical when those within the castle were better provisioned than those without), or to take it by storm, which would require considerable manpower; and all this while being themselves besieged from outside the city.

The result was both stalemate and the gradual whittling away of resources, human and otherwise. Every day that Matilda's army remained in Winchester, the stocks of supplies grew smaller. And with no coherent plan for, or realistic chance of, taking Wolvesey Castle, they were reduced to skirmishes in the streets, which did little except cost them casualties. Henry of Huntingdon notes that 'conflicts took place every day, not in pitched battles but in the excursions of knightly manoeuvres', while the *Deeds of Stephen* writes of 'knights on one side or the other who were being taken in the daily fighting or were drawn by different fates to meet different deaths'. After a month of steady losses and declining supplies, the situation finally became untenable. Matilda and her army were faced with stark choices: starve, surrender, or try to break out. They decided on the third option, and the withdrawal was planned for Sunday 14 September. But by then it was far too late.

Initially the retreat started in good order: the *Deeds of Stephen* notes that 'as a precaution for the withdrawal they were in close column, all retreating as one body'. The main danger of attack would come from the rear, from the queen's army breaking off its attack on Winchester and chasing them, so Matilda was placed at the front of the column, accompanied by Brian fitzCount and by her half-brother Reginald, earl of Cornwall. The others would follow, keeping an eye out behind them, and Earl Robert would command the rearguard. The disciplined formation did not last long, however; they were attacked almost straight away, resulting in a running and panicked skirmish for about 8 miles. The *Deeds of Stephen* gives some idea of the chaos: 'You could have seen chargers finely shaped and goodly to look upon, here straying about after throwing their riders, there fainting from weariness and at their last gasp; sometimes shields and coats of mail and arms of every kind lying everywhere strewn on the ground; sometimes tempting cloaks and vessels of precious metal, with other valuables, flung in heaps, offering themselves to the finder on every side.' The large body of troops slowed when it reached Stockbridge; there they had to ford the River Test, which caused a bottleneck. The situation became even more alarming as the queen's army closed in, attacking on all sides.

Matilda somehow managed to get away, but it was to be both a close-run thing and an exhausting effort. She and her companions in the vanguard were first across the river; they left the rest behind and galloped off as fast as they could, desperate to put as many miles between them and their enemies as possible, hoping that those still at the ford could delay the pursuers. John of Worcester writes that during this flight, Matilda rode 'like a man': this is often interpreted as meaning that she rode her horse astride, with the implication that this was unusual and therefore a symptom of her desperation, but in fact women riding astride was by no means unheard of at this time. Dedicated side-saddles would not be seen in England until over two hundred years later; before this, if women were sitting pillion behind men or they were travelling at an amble and being led, they could sit sideways on the horse, and there are depictions of this happening in the twelfth century. However, this allows little control of the mount, so in any situation where a woman had to manage her horse by herself at a greater speed – when hawking, for example, which was considered a suitable pastime for ladies – she would have needed to ride astride. It is perhaps this idea of Matilda controlling her own mount out of necessity (sharing a horse or being led would slow the party down), and riding at a soldier's faster and more tiring pace which is being referred to when John of Worcester says she rode 'like a man'.

However she sat her horse, Matilda managed to reach John Marshal's castle at Ludgershall, 20 miles north-west of Winchester, without further incident; if he had also made it there by this time, the sight of his boiled-out eye and the raw, burned skin of his face cannot have cheered her much. It is at this stage of the war that John Marshal, hitherto a minor player, becomes one of the better-documented characters thanks to the beginning of a long Anglo-Norman text entitled the *Histoire de Guillaume le Maréchal* or *History of William Marshal*. As the name implies, this is a biography not of John but of his son William; it was composed in the 1220s after the end of William's long and extraordinary life. It was based on the reminiscences of John of Earley, a man who was William's squire and later his household knight, but John knew his subject only as a grown man; for the earlier part of William's life John based his recollections on the stories William had told him, and for the very beginning of the tale a further layer of confusion was added as William himself could only rely on stories he had been told about the time before he was born, some of which were greatly exaggerated. For example, the text has John Marshal riding with Matilda during her escape from Winchester, presumably to put him at the centre of the action, although one might have thought that the part he actually played at Wherwell was dramatic enough. Thus, although we will refer to this text occasionally from now on, we will treat its assertions with caution.

To return to Matilda, after a brief overnight stop at Ludgershall she, Brian and Reginald set off for Devizes, another 18 miles away. Matilda was tired, downcast, possibly hungry (although we can assume that she had not been the last in the queue for whatever provisions had been available in Winchester), and her feminine upbringing meant that she was not used to travelling at such a pace. She started out riding once more, but eventually reached a point of such exhaustion that she had to be carried in a litter slung between horses. By the time they got past Devizes and on to the safety of Gloucester, another 40 miles, she had had to be tied to it to stop her falling out, and she arrived, according to John of Worcester, 'nearly half dead'.

In order to facilitate Matilda's escape, her supporters had thrown themselves into the thick of the fighting and into danger as they scattered from Winchester; all was chaos as they tried to save themselves. The *Deeds of Stephen* seems to relish their fates:

> What am I to say about the knights, nay, the greatest barons, who cast away all the emblems of their knighthood and going on foot, in sorry

plight, gave false names and denied that they were fugitives? Some fell into the hands of peasants and were most terribly beaten; some concealed themselves in sordid hiding-places, pale and full of dread, and lurked there until they either had a chance to escape or were found at last by their enemies and dragged out in shameful and unseemly fashion.

David, king of Scots, was captured no fewer than three times, but each time he managed to bribe his captors (who must surely have been unaware of the value of their prize) and get away, heading back north to his own lands. Earl Miles also managed to fight his way through, although either in an attempt to be less recognisable or simply for speed, he discarded his armour and accoutrements as he went; John of Worcester says that he was 'half naked' by the time he got back to Gloucester, alone and on foot.

Matilda anxiously counted her friends and retainers as they arrived and congregated at Gloucester. But one of them was destined never to make it, and this was to prove the biggest disaster of the year, if not the whole war. Earl Robert had deliberately remained at the rear of the escaping column, marshalling his men with efficiency and discipline, fighting and stalling for time in order to ensure that his sister could get away. But by the time he reached the congested ford at Stockbridge he was totally surrounded and outnumbered by a force led by William of Ypres. He was cut off from those of Matilda's army who had already crossed, so he turned back to make a last stand. A man of some fifty years of age, he fought on bravely, much as Stephen had done at Lincoln, but it was to no avail. He was, of course, much too valuable a prize to kill, but he was eventually captured. He was taken first before Queen Matilda and then by William of Ypres in person to Rochester in Kent: deep in the heartlands which still held for Stephen, far away from his own estates and influence, and without any hope of rescue.

The engagement had been such a disaster that it became known, with good reason, as the 'Rout of Winchester'. 'Such was the rout ... so terrible and wonderful in the eyes of all that even the oldest man can hardly remember one like it in our age,' says the *Deeds of Stephen*, not without some gloating. The luckless citizens were to suffer once more: they had borne the brunt of the lack of food during the siege (the *Deeds of Stephen* admits that they had been 'grievously tormented' by 'severe famine'); their houses had been burned, and now their city was sacked again by the victorious forces of the queen, who pillaged homes, shops and churches, and 'went away in great joy each to his home with many spoils and countless captives'.

For Matilda, the consequences of the rout were catastrophic. This campaign had been her attempt to atone for losing London, and she had failed. The royal treasury was gone, the support of the church was gone, her army was broken and dispersed, and she had lost the one person she could not manage without. And once more her sex made a bad situation even worse: a king who led his own forces into battle might be incommoded by losing his most influential military commander, but Matilda, who could not, was crippled. The decision to retreat from Winchester should have been taken earlier, before the situation became so desperate – after all, who was going to rescue them, with every one of Matilda's greatest supporters there already? – but it was not. It seems likely that this was due to Matilda herself: that she saw everything she had gained slipping away from her, and so she held on and remained in place far longer than was prudent, stubbornly refusing to accept the reality of the situation. The decision to stay until the last possible moment is certainly more suggestive of the determined and desperate Matilda than the cautious and experienced Robert – who, one suspects, might have been urging a withdrawal for some time but found himself overruled.

Confined as he was in Rochester, Earl Robert continued to do what he could for his sister while his captors took various approaches in their attempts to persuade him to change sides. At first he was cajoled: John of Worcester says that the queen promised that once Stephen was 'restored to his royal dignity', Robert would be 'invested with the dominion of the whole of England under him; both should become just administrators and restorers of the peace'. Queen Matilda may well have been exceeding the bounds of her authority here: there is no way she could have consulted Stephen on this point before making the offer. In any case, Robert refused, principally due to his loyalty to Matilda, but also perhaps in the knowledge that the deal would not be honoured in any case. The queen and her advisors then tried a different tactic. Having first been 'invited by soothing measures', says William of Malmesbury, Earl Robert was 'afterwards assailed by threats'. They threatened to send him across the Channel to lifelong imprisonment in Boulogne, but he was confident that they could not follow through with this; the obvious consequence would be for Matilda to send Stephen in retaliation to Ireland, from where he was highly unlikely ever to return.

The next suggestion was perhaps the obvious one, that Robert and Stephen should be exchanged for one another. This was put forward by both wives in the case – an example of an occasion when it was perfectly acceptable for women to take the lead in such high-level negotiations, because they were acting on behalf of their husbands and keen to get them home. And they were, of course, the reciprocal captors: Queen Matilda might hold Earl Robert, but in his absence from Bristol it was his wife Mabel who had custody of King Stephen.

They had made some headway on the arrangements when Robert himself objected. In another attempt to get the best out of the situation for Matilda, he argued that as an earl, he was not worthy of a straight swap with a king. If Stephen were to be released, it was only fair that he be exchanged for *all* the prisoners who had been taken at Winchester, to make up the difference. Queen Matilda might have been willing to consider this, but her magnates were not: Gilbert fitzRichard de Clare, earl of Hertford, had captured William of Salisbury during the rout, and William of Ypres himself was holding Humphrey de Bohun. Neither was keen to give up on the chance of a lucrative ransom.

The question of the direct exchange was brought forward again, so Robert played his only remaining card. He was not a free agent but rather the sworn liegeman of his sister the empress; therefore it would not be right for him to agree to such terms on his own behalf as it would mean him reneging on his oath to her. The decision would have to be hers, and he would abide by whatever she resolved upon. This was something of a win for him: it presented him as even more honourable, but it also released him from the pressure of having to gamble with such high stakes and then face up to the consequences.

Matilda had to make a decision, and the repercussions would be huge either way. If she agreed to the exchange, she would lose all the ground she had gained during the last two years, and her opponent would be free and restored to his position. She would not give up – of course she would not – and war would rage again, possibly for many years. If she refused, she would keep Stephen and therefore be, in theory at least, the sole royal authority in England. However, theory was a long way from practice, and claiming regal status would not retake Winchester or London. She had other advisors, other tacticians and military generals, but none had the royal blood, the experience, the respect or the vast lands and number of retainers that Robert possessed. She might be able to keep Stephen away from the throne, but she would get no nearer to it herself without Robert. He must be released, and she declared it so.

The exchange was organised. The conditions of each man's liberation were relatively simple: neither had to swear to anything, and each would be free to resume his position and to 'defend his party to the utmost of his abilities, as before' (as William of Malmesbury puts it). The practical arrangements were of necessity much more complex, given the lack of trust that each party had for the other by now. On 1 November 1141, All Saints' Day, Stephen was released from Bristol Castle, leaving there as surety his wife, one of his sons and two unidentified magnates of high rank. He rode for Winchester, where Earl Robert had already been brought under guard in order to shorten the distances and journey times involved in the process. When Stephen arrived on 3 November Robert was freed, leaving behind his eldest son and heir William. When he in turn reached Bristol, Queen Matilda and the others were released; and finally, upon their arrival at Winchester William of Gloucester was liberated. Both Archbishop Theobald and Bishop Henry had offered themselves as additional security for the overall deal, but they were in the end not needed. After a tense week and a half, all had gone according to plan.

Stephen returned to London with his reunited family, presumably suitably grateful to his wife for all her efforts over the previous eight months. It is no exaggeration to say that he might never have been released had it not been for her taking on an active, 'masculine' role; after all, he had done very little during his captivity except to allow the bishops to retract their oaths to him. On reaching the capital, Stephen set about restoring his authority, and the first person to feel the brunt of his ire was his brother Henry. Obliged to summon another council at Westminster on 7 December to overturn the provisions of the previous one at Winchester, Bishop Henry was put in the awkward position (albeit one entirely of his own making) of explaining himself. A legate of the Apostolic See probably refrained from actually squirming in public, but the situation was embarrassing, to say the least. He made an effort to talk his way out of it – or, as William of Malmesbury more memorably puts it in his account of the council, 'by great powers of eloquence, the legate endeavoured to extenuate the odium of his own conduct'.

In front of a stonily silent audience Henry attempted to claim that all his earlier pronouncements had been made under duress, because he had felt under military threat from Matilda; he had supported her 'not from inclination, but necessity'. He concluded by telling the assembled prelates and barons that 'on the part of God and of the pope, they should strenuously assist the king, anointed by the will of the people and with the approbation of the holy see: but that such as disturbed the peace, in favour of the countess of Anjou, should be excommunicated.' This, of course, was the exact opposite of the sentence he had pronounced at the council of Winchester earlier in the year. And his use of nomenclature is revealing: only nine months previously Henry had proclaimed Matilda to be 'lady of the English', but now she was – pointedly – merely the 'countess of Anjou', the least of her titles and the one she never used herself.

Henry had made his point and his peace with Stephen, but he left the council, and ended the year, with his reputation tarnished and his influence diminished. Stephen, meanwhile, went to Canterbury and was symbolically re-crowned by Archbishop Theobald on Christmas Day; Queen Matilda was at his side, wearing her own crown. The list of witnesses on a charter issued by Stephen at his Christmas court (in favour of none other than Geoffrey de Mandeville, who must have been feeling very popular by this stage, courted as he was on all sides) shows that he was attended by at least eight other earls – William de Warenne of Surrey, Gilbert fitzRichard de Clare of Hertford, Gilbert fitzGilbert de Clare of Pembroke (Hertford's uncle), William d'Aumale of York, Simon de Senlis of Northampton, William d'Aubigny of Arundel, Alan le Breton of Richmond and Robert de Ferrers of Derby – as well as William of Ypres, Stephen's steward William Martel, and Baldwin fitzGilbert, brother of the earl of Pembroke, who had given Stephen's speech for him prior to the battle of Lincoln.

Stephen had seemingly regained his position and enjoyed substantial support, but this does not tell the whole story. None of Matilda's earls (as listed by the *Deeds of Stephen* earlier in this chapter) had defected; others were noticeable by their absence. Among those who were not present with either Matilda or Stephen at this juncture were earls Ranulf de Gernon of Chester, William de Roumare of Lincoln, Waleran de Beaumont of

Worcester, Robert de Beaumont of Leicester, and Henry of Huntingdon, the son of David, king of Scots. Their combined influence would be crucial in tipping the balance of the war either way.

Matilda, attended by her loyal men, including those who had by now paid their ransoms and been released, held her own Christmas court at Oxford. This was as near as she could get, in physical and practical terms, to London, and it made a statement of intent: she would not hide away in her West Country strongholds. However, as she took stock of her position she must have realised that it was not favourable. She had survived the military defeat, it was true, but with her position much diminished and, crucially, having lost much ground in the propaganda war. If her victory at Lincoln in February had been seen as a sign of God's favour, the defeat at Winchester in September indicated the reverse. Henry of Huntingdon (the chronicler, not the earl) credits Stephen's recovery to divine intervention, as he draws his account of 1141 to a close: 'Thus the king, taken captive in misery by God's justice, was miraculously freed by God's mercy, and was received by the English nobility with great rejoicing.'

As the cold winter weather took hold and the days grew shorter, the people of England were able to contemplate the ramifications of the situation before them. Although some of them, principally those engaged in trade overseas, may have had a vested interest in the overall victory of one party or another, the majority of the populace just wanted peace and stability. The events of 1141 had briefly offered this, with the prospect of one candidate on the throne and the other out of the way; but the exchange of Stephen for Robert in the late autumn had killed off any hopes of a swift end to the conflict. Even the *Deeds of Stephen*, while rejoicing at its hero's release, sounds a sombre note: 'These indeed were harsh and ill-judged terms and bound to do harm to the entire country, but there could be no other pact of peace and friendship between them for the moment, since the two parties were hotly at variance.' The author goes on to say that 'when the king was at length released from his narrow dungeon, though you would have supposed that an end must now be put to the dreadful wickedness of the kingdom, and thought that both parties must be grieved at such sufferings and unite for the general restoration of peace, the hand of the Lord was once again made heavy over the English.'

This is a common theme in the chronicles at this juncture. These writers had already lived through seven years of upheaval after the death of Henry I and they did not know how much more the realm could take. The portion of John of Worcester's chronicle that survives cuts off abruptly at this point with the depressing words: 'During the whole of the ensuing year, in all parts of the kingdom and country, pillage of the poor, slaughter of men, and violation of churches . . . cruelly—'

The scale of the problem facing the common people is spelled out in a long and famous passage from the *Peterborough Chronicle* that details their sufferings during the war. This text is generally terse in tone (containing such descriptive gems as 'in this year King Henry went across the sea', and similar), but it suddenly explodes into eloquence and lamentation when it tells of the depredations in England throughout the battle for the crown. The passage is lengthy, but it is worth quoting in its entirety so we can get the full emotional effect that the author wished to convey. The barons

were all forsworn and their pledges lost because every powerful man made his castles and held them against him, and filled the land full of castles. They greatly oppressed the wretched men of the land with castle-work; then when the castles were made, they filled them with devils and evil men. Then both by night and by day they seized those men whom they imagined had any wealth, common men and women, and put them in prison to get their gold and silver, and tortured them with unspeakable tortures, for no martyrs were ever tortured as they were. They hung them up by the feet and smoked them with foul smoke. They hung them by the thumbs, or by the head, and hung mail-coats on their feet. They put knotted strings round their heads and twisted until it went to the brains. They put them in dungeons where there were adders and snakes and toads, and destroyed them thus. Some they put into a 'crucet-hus', that is, into a chest that was short and narrow and shallow, and put sharp stones in there and crushed the man in there, so that he had all the limbs broken. In many of the castles was a 'lof and grin', that were chains such that two or three men had enough to do to carry one. It was made thus: it is fastened to a beam, and a sharp iron put around the man's throat and his neck so that he could not move in any direction, neither sit nor lie nor sleep, but carry all that iron. Many thousands they destroyed with hunger.

I do not know nor can I tell all the horrors nor all the tortures that they did to wretched men in this land. And it lasted the nineteen years while Stephen was king, and it always grew worse and worse. They laid a tax upon the villages time and again, and called it *tenserie* [a word sometimes translated as 'protection money']. Then when the wretched men had no more to give, they robbed and burned all the villages, so that you could well go a whole day's journey and never find anyone occupying a village or land tilled. Then corn was dear, and flesh and cheese and butter, because there was none in the land. Wretched men starved with hunger; some who were once powerful men went on alms; some fled out of the land. Never before was there more wretchedness in the land, nor ever did heathen men worse than they did. Too many times they spared neither church nor churchyard, but took everything of value that was in it, and afterwards burned the church and everything together. They did not spare the land of bishops nor of abbots nor of priests, but robbed monks and clerks; and every man who was the stronger [robbed] another. If two or three men came riding to a village, all the villagers fled because of them, imagining that they were robbers. The bishops and the clergy always cursed them but that was nothing to them, because they were all accursed and forsworn and lost.

Wherever men tilled, the earth bore no corn because the land was all done for by such doings; and they said openly that Christ and His saints slept.

Soon there was going to be nothing left to fight for. Matilda might grit her teeth, marshal her forces and carry on her campaign, but any victory was in danger of being pyrrhic. Her resources, without either reinforcement or a significant number of defections, were not going to be sufficient to push for an outright victory; only attrition beckoned. And she also had leisure, during the dark winter days and the long cold nights, to brood on another unpleasant reality: she had discovered during the course of the year just how profound and visceral the opposition to her rule was. The idea that she might act as a female king with her own sovereignty – when it looked like this might actually happen, rather than being just a theoretical possibility – had aroused such a brutal reaction that she had been taken aback. She was probably not ready to face it yet, or to admit it to herself even in private, but the fact was that she was never going to be crowned queen of England in her own right; the male-dominated, self-interested society in which she lived was simply not ready for such a thing. If the war was to be won, she would have to find another way forward.

$$\approx \text{ CHAPTER EIGHT } \ll$$

A FRESH APPROACH

WHEN MATILDA HAD SAILED FOR England in the autumn of 1139, she had left her husband and her sons behind. To modern sensibilities such a course of action might seem callous, but in the context of the time this was not the case. Matilda and Geoffrey's marriage had only ever been one of convenience, arranged for political rather than personal reasons, so as long as they remained married in the eyes of God and the law it did not matter that they lived apart, especially once the business of providing heirs was concluded. And politically it made perfect sense for them to wage a campaign on separate fronts: for her to look after matters in England while he concentrated on Normandy. As for the couple's three sons, they were young, yes, but noble boys were often sent to be raised and educated away from the family home, so the separation was not unusual. Matilda felt that their long-term interests were best served by the safeguarding of their rights and inheritance rather than by her physical maternal presence; she had always subordinated any personal desires to the cause of political gain, and they would have to learn the same lesson.

Since his wife's departure, Geoffrey had been busy. As count of Anjou he had always harboured an acquisitive interest in Normandy, and now he had the justification he needed to claim it by right. If Matilda could take advantage of her married state and status without having her husband next to her in England, so Geoffrey could use his wife's name and claim to the duchy without having her at his side. It was a situation that worked for both of them, and, indeed, he may have had the better of it: in contrast to the unprecedented nature of Matilda's claims in England and the attendant complications, it was taken as perfectly normal and acceptable that Geoffrey should wage war for personal gain in right of his wife.

Geoffrey began with some small incursions, including the siege and destruction of the castle of Fontenay-le-Marmion, near Matilda's stronghold of Exmes. He had a foothold in Normandy already, of course, via the castles Matilda had controlled since her father's death, and also from the gains they had subsequently made in the south of the duchy. But at this early stage of Matilda's campaign in England, the northern part of Normandy was still held and well defended by those who supported Stephen, including Waleran de Beaumont and William de Roumare. This made Geoffrey's situation precarious, as did the alliance between Stephen and Louis VII of France, represented by the marriage of the former's son Eustace and the latter's sister Constance, which meant that Geoffrey could expect hostility from that quarter. He also needed to be careful not to overextend himself. He was unable to spend all of his time and energy in Normandy, as he also had to keep an eye on his existing counties of Anjou (where he had already put down two rebellions) and Maine, where his younger brother Helias was challenging him for control, claiming that their father had left the county to him. Fulk had gained it by marriage – it was not part of his family's patrimony – so the younger son had something of a claim. Geoffrey would eventually defeat and capture Helias, keeping him imprisoned until Helias's death in 1151, but the distraction from that direction meant that his campaign in Normandy was (and would have to remain, for the time being) slow and steady.

The repercussions of the battle of Lincoln in February 1141 were felt across the Channel. Many of the barons believed that Stephen would never be released to resume his reign, so, just as those in England started to make peace with Matilda, so did those in Normandy make overtures to Geoffrey. Indeed, he did not sit back and wait for them to come to him: Orderic Vitalis tells us that 'when Geoffrey, count of Anjou, heard that his wife had won the day, he came at once into Normandy, sent out envoys to the magnates and commanded them as of right to hand over their castles to him'. Among those who came to terms were Waleran de Beaumont, as noted in Chapter 7, and Rotrou, count of Perche. Rotrou, as we saw earlier, was a protégé of Henry I who had once been the husband of Matilda's illegitimate half-sister Matilda, until her death in the *White Ship* disaster; he was now married to Hawise, sister of the William of Salisbury who was captured fighting for Matilda at the Rout of Winchester. A third defector was John, bishop of Lisieux; this was a major coup for Geoffrey, as John had been the head of Stephen's administration in Normandy. Finally, Geoffrey's position was strengthened by the fact that one of the greatest landholders in Normandy was Robert of Gloucester; his declaration of support for Matilda had turned numerous estates from hostile to friendly.

With Stephen in prison, the remaining magnates who held out against Geoffrey in Normandy needed to consider their position. The option they settled on initially was to offer the duchy to Stephen's brother Theobald, as they had done once before in 1135. However, Theobald, as we noted in Chapter 3, was already count of both Blois and Champagne; he had many responsibilities and not a few troubles. He was currently in conflict with Louis VII of France, but would later become one of his closest advisors and his relative by marriage several times over (two of Theobald's sons would go on to marry Louis's daughters by Eleanor of Aquitaine, and Theobald's daughter Adela would later marry Louis himself); his interests were there-fore perhaps best served by looking to Paris rather than Rouen or London. When his own complex situation was added to the combination of his brother Stephen's imprisonment, his brother Henry's sudden espousal of Matilda's cause, and the ongoing conflict in Normandy – he would have to fight for it if he wanted it – Theobald seems to have lost any residual enthu-siasm he may once have had for being duke; he declined the offer. Orderic Vitalis goes as far as to say that 'he declined to burden himself with the weight of such vast cares, but ceded his right . . . to Geoffrey', but this was not a complete abdication of his family responsibilities: Theobald's proposal was that the duchy be offered to Geoffrey, *if* Geoffrey and Matilda would recognise his right to Tours and release Stephen. These terms were declined, but Theobald's suggestion and his refusal of the title, when coupled with the overall turn of Fortune's wheel, meant that more Norman barons were willing to accept the status quo and to acknowledge Geoffrey and Matilda, tacitly, as their overlords.

Unfortunately for us, the great Norman chronicler Orderic Vitalis ceases his work at this point. His final chapter reflects both on the current political situation ('I see the great men of this world crushed by severe disasters and reduced to great adversity') and on his own life. He was sixty-six, 'worn out with age and infirmity', and had been a monk at Saint-Évroul for fifty-six of those years, having been sent across the sea from his native England in childhood. He laid down his pen during a time of great uncertainty in both England and Normandy, with the result that we now lose one of our most incisive contemporary commentators, and the one best informed about events in Normandy.

A cessation of hostilities in Anjou, plus the favourable news from England and the submission of some magnates, meant that Geoffrey could now embark on a more systematic campaign in Normandy. He was a talented and energetic military general – still only in his late twenties, let us not forget – and, although he was campaigning principally in his own interest, his priorities coincided with those of his wife, and so were useful to her. He managed to secure his position in Normandy more thoroughly than Matilda did hers in England via an unremitting determination and the steady accumulation of more castles as he worked his way north and west. Thus the later events of 1141, at Westminster in June and Winchester in September, had less of an effect on his campaign than on Matilda's. Even the release of Stephen at the end of the year did not make too much difference: Stephen concentrated on regaining control of his kingship in England, so Geoffrey was free to continue his efforts in the duchy. By the end of 1142 he had control of all of western Normandy and was turning his attentions on the vital area around Rouen.

Geoffrey and Matilda, between them, had another trump card that they would soon be ready to play – their eldest son Henry. He and his brothers had survived their early infancy and were now becoming valuable pieces in the great game. Henry starts to appear as a figure in his own right at about this time, and Matilda began referring to him in official documents, particularly those that involved magnates who held lands on both sides of the Channel. In the spring of 1141, when he received the previously mentioned charter from Matilda granting him enormous privileges, Geoffrey de Mandeville sent a representative to Normandy, and Henry confirmed all his mother's concessions as 'Henry, son of the daughter of King Henry, rightful heir of England and Normandy'. In the spring of 1142 Henry celebrated his ninth birthday, and Geoffrey of Anjou began the gradual process of switching from fighting in his wife's name to campaigning on behalf of his son. If he succeeded in conquering the whole of Normandy and being named duke, he would remain in that position only until Henry reached his majority; at that point he would resign in his son's favour. And as Henry grew older and stronger, more skilled in arms and with a better awareness of his situation, he would become more of a plausible candidate for the English throne – a factor that now became of increasing importance to Matilda.

In England, the early spring of 1142 was characterised by consolidation and manoeuvring for position rather than direct action; William of Malmesbury says that both sides 'conducted themselves with quiet forbearance from Christmas to Lent'. In truth, the tribulations and exertions of the last year were starting to take a physical toll on the main protagonists, who were both exhausted. The *Deeds of Stephen* says that Matilda 'had been greatly shaken by the rout of Winchester and worn out almost to the point of utter collapse'; her fortieth birthday came and went in a much less positive manner than her thirty-ninth. But something needed to be done, so she roused herself from her torpor. She was at this time based in Oxford, but she travelled to Devizes to meet Robert, earl of Gloucester, and her other advisors. The situation was grim; they did not have sufficient resource to force a convincing result in the war, and with Stephen once more free to pursue his own interests, and the church against her, Matilda's position was as precarious as it had ever been. There was little point in attempting a reconciliation with the church – even Bishop Henry would not turn his coat again so soon – so a military solution must be found. And that meant raising more troops. The outcome of the talks was a plan that must have galled Matilda: she would have to send to her husband for help.

But this was not to prove as simple as it sounds. Envoys were dispatched to Normandy in April 1142; they returned in June with Geoffrey's terse reply that he would negotiate only with Earl Robert in person, as the two men were known to each other. 'Were he to make the voyage,' says William of Malmesbury, Geoffrey 'would, as far as he was able, accede to his wishes: but that all other persons would expend their labour in passing and repassing to no purpose'.

Robert did not want to go; he was unwilling to leave Matilda in England without him now that Stephen was once more at large. But in the meantime, while they had been awaiting Geoffrey's response, events took another turn: Stephen, who was travelling south from York after a visit there to show himself in the north and to raise more troops, had reached Northampton in late April when he fell ill. So serious was his condition that in May and into June rumours spread throughout England that he was dying. We do not have exact details of his collapse, but the stress of his imprisonment – exacerbated by the chains and the consequent lack of exercise – had either caused it or at least not helped. He was no longer a young man and had spent much of the preceding five years in the saddle and in combat as he sought to quell the many rebellions against his rule. Whatever the precise cause of his illness, he certainly did not shake it off easily, lying bedridden for two months from Easter until past Whitsun.

This was both an opportunity to be exploited and an indication that Matilda would be safe without her brother, so Robert agreed, still with some reluctance, to travel to Normandy. He rode for Wareham in Dorset, the only Channel port under Matilda's control (currently in the hands of Robert's eldest son William), and took ship at the end of June, heading for his own city of Caen. Matilda, meanwhile, went back to Oxford. Although this was a little way out of what might be termed her safe zone – only Wallingford lay further east – it was tactically a better place to reside under the current circumstances. The castle was a stone one, recently refortified, and therefore safe from all but the most concerted attacks; and Oxford was much closer to London than Bristol, Gloucester or Devizes. If Stephen were to die, Matilda needed to be in a position to act swiftly.

But then, unexpectedly, Stephen recovered, and he set back to work with his customary energy: the *Deeds of Stephen* says that 'as though he had only just awakened from sleep, [he] vigorously and boldly shook himself out of sluggish inaction'. Soon able to leave his bed and mount his horse, Stephen rode with his forces to Wareham, where he succeeded in taking the castle from the surprised and somewhat ineffectual William of Gloucester, and installed his own garrison. To a certain extent this put Earl Robert out of action; if and when he returned from Normandy, he would have nowhere to land. Stephen, aware that Matilda was at Oxford without Robert or her other closest advisors, planned his strategy with care. Rather than making directly for Oxford, he first swept in a wide arc around it, taking and destroying fortifications that might be used to help, resupply or reinforce her. Cirencester Castle was captured and burned, and he took other, smaller outposts at Bampton and Radcot by storm and surrender respectively. Only then did he turn his attention towards Oxford itself, arriving with a large army at his back on 26 September 1142.

The *Deeds of Stephen*, which depicts the ensuing events in some detail, gives an idea of what he was up against: 'Now Oxford is a city very securely protected, inaccessible because of the very deep water that washes it all around, most carefully encircled by a palisade of an outwork on one side, and on another finely and very strongly fortified by an impregnable castle and tower of great height.' But this was Stephen's best chance for some time of putting an end to the conflict: he threw himself into the task. His troops crossed the river at the ford that gave the city its name – so deep, after much unseasonable rain, that they were almost swimming rather than wading, says the *Deeds of Stephen* – and then 'furiously charged the enemy'. Those men who had come out to try to defend the city were swiftly beaten back and then routed, fleeing towards the open gate; Stephen's men chased in after them before the gate could be closed, and were inside the city itself. Within hours many of the citizens were dead and their homes in flames. The 'impregnable castle', with its separate defences, held out with Matilda inside. She must have felt both terror and a sinking sense of déjà vu as she looked out at the chaos and the flames, and realised there was no way out.

Stephen had let Matilda go from Arundel; she had escaped the mob at Westminster and the queen's forces at Winchester. This time he would not give up, not until she was captured and safely under lock and key. On this point William of Malmesbury and the *Deeds of Stephen* are for once in agreement: the former tells us that Stephen established his siege 'with such determined resolution, that he declared no hope of advantage or fear of loss should induce him to depart until the castle was delivered up, and the empress surrendered to his power', while the latter clarifies that Stephen thought 'he could easily put an end to the strife in the kingdom if he forcibly overcame her through whom it began to be at strife'. Matilda knew she would have to hold out until reinforcements could arrive, but where would they come from? King David was in Scotland and Earl Miles did not have enough men at his disposal to ride to the rescue against such an army. Brian fitzCount was only a few miles away, downstream at his own castle at Wallingford, but this also needed to be defended against the king, so he could not stir. Matilda watched the blockade being established, the siege machinery being built around her position, and knew that her quest, her liberty and even her life might end here.

But, as she had proved many times in her life, Matilda was not of a character to sit back and let events take their course. She was trapped, yes, but she did what she could; she was active. The wording of a passage from the *Deeds of Stephen* evidences her personal involvement:

> After *strengthening and encouraging her garrison* to resist the king *she sent a great many troops* of cavalry to plunder in every direction, earnestly besought, by letter and message, those who were *bound to her* by faith and homage to lend the best support to *her enterprise*, and fortified castles in various places, wherever *she* most conveniently could, some to keep the king's men more effectively in check, some to give *her own* more careful protection [my emphasis].

What would have been most useful to Matilda at this point, of course, was the return of Earl Robert, preferably with a large army at his back. However, Geoffrey of Anjou, finding his brother-in-law a valuable military companion, kept him in Normandy for far longer than would have been necessary just for the negotiations that were originally intended. William of Malmesbury depicts Geoffrey making excuse after excuse, saying that he could not leave Normandy while various castles were held against him there, so perhaps Robert should help him subdue them, so they could get going all the sooner. Robert, unaware of Matilda's perilous situation and perhaps thinking that the best way to get help for her was to go along with Geoffrey's plans, acted with him; between them, they captured no fewer than ten castles over the summer and autumn of 1142.

It was October before the shocking news reached Robert; he immediately set out for England, no doubt cursing all the way. His mission had been advantageous for Geoffrey, but it had failed in its original purpose: the count had not supplied any additional troops. From the available evidence it would seem that Robert's force on his return was a little larger than the one he set out with, but it is possible that this was due to levies from his own lands in Normandy. Geoffrey's reluctance to help his wife was not surprising: by this stage he was well on his way to controlling all of Normandy and no longer really needed her claim to the duchy, other than as theoretical justification for his conquests. And her own campaign in England was of little interest or use to him other than as a distraction that kept some of his own foes on the other side of the Channel. He was already well aware that he was never going to be king of England, whatever happened. If Matilda were to die, it would make little difference to Geoffrey, as he could continue to claim Normandy in the name of his son; such an eventuality might even be advantageous to him as it would allow him to make a new marriage alliance. The one concession Geoffrey did make to Robert was to allow him to take this all-important son, Henry, now nine years old, to England; this is a point to which we will return later in this chapter.

Neither of Robert's options for landing in England was ideal. Heading for Wareham would mean a fight; but sailing all the way along the south coast, around the tip of Cornwall and up to Bristol would take too long. Thus, with fifty-two ships, somewhere between three hundred and four hundred knights, and presumably (although no chronicler gives numbers) other infantry and support troops, he sailed for Wareham on the Dorset coast. This may have been the move least expected by the garrison there, for they could not beat him off: Robert was able to establish a siege and demand terms from them. The garrison, as was usual in cases where they needed to answer to a higher authority, asked for a truce while they sent to Stephen for help. If none were forthcoming, they would surrender. Robert granted their request, partly perhaps on the grounds of honour but also because it was, in the words of William of Malmesbury, 'very agreeable to the earl, as it led him to suppose it might draw Stephen off from besieging his sister'.

But this time Stephen refused to rush into action and would not be lured away from the walls of Oxford Castle. After three weeks at Wareham Robert accepted the garrison's surrender, meaning that he had at least regained a port and therefore a line of communication with Normandy, but he was no nearer his primary objective. Ever the pragmatist, he knew that riding with just his own force would do no good against the king's army; he may also have felt slightly lost without a higher authority to tell him what to do. Robert arranged a general muster of Matilda's supporters to take place at Cirencester (which Stephen had made no attempt to hold – as we saw earlier, he had burned the castle rather than garrisoning it himself), where he met up with Miles and others before setting out on the march in early December. They would still be outnumbered, but the siege had been going on for more than two months, and the situation within Oxford Castle must, by now, be dire.

Matilda was cold, hungry and desperate. Much of Oxford was a smouldering ruin, the bombardment from Stephen's siege engines was incessant, and the blockade was total: no supplies had made their way through, and the food and fuel were running out. She had been completely cut off from the outside world since September and could have no idea that help was on its way, so it is not surprising that she should decide that there was nothing for it but to take matters into her own hands.

The escape took place sometime in the middle of December 1142, certainly before Christmas. The land was white and frozen: heavy snow blanketed castle, city and fields alike. It was no time to be abroad in the countryside, but the dangerous and potentially lethal conditions suited Matilda's purposes, and she could wait no longer. During the silent hours of one night she slipped out of the castle's postern gate, which opened outside the city (some of the more excitable chroniclers say that she was let down by ropes over the walls, but this is unlikely), accompanied by just three or four knights. Henry of Huntingdon notes that they were all 'clothed in white garments, which reflected and resembled the snow', and the camouflage worked: no shouts of alarm sounded as they picked their way down to the river on foot. And this was why the conditions were right: the weather was so cold that the Thames was frozen solid. It must have taken some courage to step out on to it, knowing that swift death by freezing or drowning awaited if the ice did not hold, but Matilda had no choice. She and her knights made it across the river and then, miraculously, managed to slip right through the enemy lines. The *Deeds of Stephen* tells us just how close she was to her enemies, as they tiptoed 'through the king's pickets, which everywhere were breaking the silence of the night with the blaring of trumpeters or the cries of men shouting loudly'. Once past the camp they continued on foot, through the deep snow, some 6 miles to Abingdon. This must have been a wholly unpleasant experience, the cold and wet seeping into their boots and, in Matilda's case, soaking the hem of her long gown and making it heavier as she struggled along. Once at Abingdon they were able to procure some horses, and they rode to nearby Wallingford, there to be welcomed by Brian fitzCount and, we may hope, a roaring fire.

It was an amazing episode, even in the context of Matilda's remarkable life. It is also the last of her escapades to be described by William of Malmesbury; he mentions it in passing, saying that he intends to describe it in full at some later date if 'by God's permission, I shall ever learn the truth of it from those who were present', but he died before he could continue, and we lose another one of our contemporary chroniclers. As we have previously observed, William's narrative is always presented in order to depict Robert of Gloucester in the best light, but his careful descriptions and his insistence on only including events which he had either seen himself or heard directly from an eyewitness make him valuable.

Matilda stayed briefly at Wallingford, but it was too dangerous to be in this isolated easternmost outpost of her territory, and she returned to Devizes, to the strong castle that had once been the home of Roger, bishop of Salisbury. Her escape from Oxford soon became common knowledge and was a tale told by her enemies as well as her friends, even drawing grudging praise from the normally hostile *Deeds of Stephen*: 'In a wondrous fashion she escaped unharmed through so many enemies, so many watchers in the silence of the night . . . I do not know whether it was to heighten the greatness of her fame in time to come, or by God's judgement to increase more vehemently the disturbance of the kingdom, but never have I read of another woman so luckily rescued from so many mortal foes and from the threat of dangers so great.'

Once it became known that Matilda was no longer in Oxford, the castle surrendered. Stephen recognised that he had been outmanoeuvred once more, and let the garrison off with easy terms. News reached Robert and his combined forces before they reached Oxford: he changed course and rode instead for Devizes, where Matilda's joy at being reunited with him was compounded by the unexpected and welcome sight of her eldest son.

Henry was only nine years old, but his arrival in England opened up a whole new dimension in the war for the crown. On the wider political level, Henry was a reminder to the barons of England that Henry I had a direct legitimate royal male descendant. He had never been completely out of the picture: in one of the last entries in his chronicle, William of Malmesbury notes that when envoys had been sent to Geoffrey of Anjou to seek his help, it was because it was his duty 'to defend the inheritance of his wife and sons'; he also says that Robert of Gloucester was urged to undertake the journey 'on account of the inheritance of his sister and his nephews'. But the boy's physical presence in England made his theoretical claim all the stronger. A written agreement of 1142 between Robert and Miles assumes that the war is being fought on behalf of Matilda 'and Henry the son of the Empress'.

Henry's arrival was also a boost to Matilda's campaign on a personal level, and not just because she was glad to see him. If she had not realised it before, she was certainly aware by the end of 1142 that she was never going to sit upon the throne in person. The vicious reaction to her and the attendant backlash, when it had looked as though she would be crowned in her own right eighteen months previously, had been followed by a period of resurgence from Stephen. It would be difficult to replicate the feats of the first half of 1141, and even if she did, what purpose would it serve if the end result were the same? But a new avenue had opened up. She might by now have admitted defeat (to herself, at least) in the battle over who would succeed Henry I – Stephen had occupied the throne for nearly a decade and was unlikely to be unseated – but there was still a war to be fought over who would succeed Stephen, and Matilda would fight to the end to make sure that this was Henry, not Eustace.

Matilda's delight in Henry's presence did not overshadow the necessity of him continuing his education. This meant that he could not be kept at his mother's knee: he needed to join the household of a close and noble male relative in order to receive appropriate training. Thus, while Matilda remained at Devizes, Henry went to Bristol to be placed under the tutelage of the obvious candidate, his uncle Robert. He was educated alongside his cousin Roger, one of Robert's younger sons, who would in later life be bishop of Worcester and a valuable advisor. Henry would remain in Bristol (with regular visits to Devizes, no doubt) until early March 1144, and during this time he began to receive homage in person from English vassals.

The initial boost provided by Henry's arrival reinvigorated Matilda, and she rekindled the spluttering flames of the war. However, she was not in a position to finish it, and another long struggle beckoned. Both parties were entrenched more or less in their original lines, hardly different to the situation in 1139 when Matilda had first invaded: it was as if Lincoln, Winchester and Oxford had never happened. The key factor at this point was that

Geoffrey of Anjou had refused to suspend his own activities in Normandy in order to send an army to his wife that might have swayed the outcome. Matilda was frustrated, and Earl Robert seems to have fallen into something of a holding pattern, keeping the cause alive with caution and waiting until Henry was old enough to be the spearhead rather than Matilda. Robert, we may remember, had been the only voice to speak up for Henry's rights following the death of Henry I in 1135; and, much as he supported his half-sister and was loyal to her, he evidently thought that the only way to win the overall campaign was to replace her at its head.

Other magnates took more direct action, but during this phase of the conflict some of them took the opportunity to act more openly in their own interests rather than declaring themselves under the banner of one royal claimant or the other. One such was the perennially self-interested Geoffrey de Mandeville. As we have seen, he had returned to Stephen's camp during the second half of 1141; he was acting on Stephen's orders when he drove a band of rebels from the Isle of Ely early in 1142. But his amassing of land and titles ('in the extent of his wealth and the splendour of his position he surpassed all of the chief men of the kingdom,' says the *Deeds of Stephen*) did not go down well with other lords, and – in something of a repeat of the arrest of the bishops in 1139 – they persuaded Stephen to seize him when he attended the royal court at St Albans in September 1143. Henry of Huntingdon makes excuses for such unconstitutional behaviour by saying that Stephen did it 'more in retribution for the earl's wickedness than in accordance with the law of peoples, more from force of circumstances than because it was right. For if he had not done this, he would have been deprived of his kingdom through the earl's treachery.' Geoffrey had his lands and castles, including the Tower of London, confiscated, but was then released; 'to the ruin of the whole kingdom', says the *Deeds of Stephen*. He left the court in frustration and fury, gathered his knights and took up arms against Stephen, although without explicitly declaring for Matilda.

Aided and abetted by Hugh Bigod, earl of Norfolk, Geoffrey de Mandeville 'raged everywhere with fire and sword; he devoted himself with insatiable greed to the plundering of flocks and herds' (*Deeds of Stephen*). He sacked Cambridge, looting its churches, and pillaged the Isle of Ely. He then seized and despoiled Ramsey Abbey, expelling the monks and making it his headquarters: it stood on an island, with only one approach over a causeway, and was therefore defensible. This course of action was not particularly unusual – many churches and abbeys were used as bases by both sides throughout the war, as they were generally built of stone – but it did not go down well with the church and Geoffrey was excommunicated. This did not stop him, however, and he terrorised the fenland and laid waste to East Anglia for almost a year, concentrating his attacks on lands belonging to Stephen and his supporters, with the king unable to stop him due to the difficulty of mounting an all-out campaign in the challenging terrain.

Geoffrey's reign of terror came to an abrupt end in August 1144 when he was fatally wounded while attacking the royal stronghold of Burwell: he was shot in the head by an arrow after apparently removing his helmet due to the heat of the day. The wound became infected and he lingered for several weeks before dying on 26 September. 'See how the vengeance of God, of Him who is worthy to be praised, is made known throughout all ages,' gloats the cleric Henry of Huntingdon, although his claim that while Geoffrey held Ramsey Abbey 'blood bubbled out of the walls of the church' is perhaps a little hyperbolic. Geoffrey was still excommunicate, so his body could not be interred; it would remain unburied for nearly twenty years, stored in a lead coffin suspended from the branches of an apple tree, until his son finally gained absolution for him in 1163.

Geoffrey de Mandeville may not have been acting on Matilda's behalf, but his rebellion against Stephen served her cause in that it distracted the king's attention and focused it eastwards, leaving her free to consolidate her hold on the West Country and to seek to expand her domain of influence once more. She remained in Devizes, a castle that was both physically strong and of symbolic significance. The old wooden structure, built around 1080, had burned down in 1113; Roger, bishop of Salisbury had spent seven years and a huge amount of money rebuilding it in stone. As we saw, it had been confiscated by Stephen in 1139, but it had subsequently been recaptured by Matilda's forces. This meant that she could make her plans while benefiting both from substantial stone walls atop a high motte and from being seen to reside in a place of her own, taken by conquest, rather than staying as a guest in someone else's home. Devizes provided her with a centre of power and administration from where she granted charters and received vassals, still acting as rightful monarch; she continued to have coins minted in her name that bore her image.

Stephen did make an abortive foray into the West Country in the summer of 1143; he marched to Wareham – now back in the hands of Robert of Gloucester, as we saw earlier in this chapter – but decided it was too well defended to risk a siege. Then, accompanied by Bishop Henry, he turned towards Wilton, some 37 miles to the north, where their joint forces were soundly defeated by Earl Robert; Stephen and Henry were both forced to flee ignominiously to avoid capture, leaving their lieutenants and men to be killed or caught. Stephen's subsequent sense of guilt, perhaps still over-shadowed by memories of his father, led him to spend a fortune and to surrender the castle of Sherborne in ransom payments for those who had been captured while shielding his retreat.

The loss of William of Malmesbury means that we do not have many personal details of Matilda and her actions during the next couple of years – Henry of Huntingdon's work is more general in scope and the *Deeds of Stephen*, as the title implies, concentrates on the king – but we can piece together other evidence to give an overview of events.

For the principal protagonists, the war resembled ever more the game of chess to which we earlier compared it. Each side had survived a check without being checkmated; each had learned a lesson about the risks inherent in a pitched battle. The focus of attention was therefore the castles around the country, and sieges were common. However, it was mainly the smaller (and therefore less pivotal) fortifications that were taken and retaken: Matilda did not have the strength in depth to be able to besiege any of the larger places that would have been useful to her such as Winchester and Oxford; and equally, Stephen could not get near Bristol, Gloucester or Devizes.

For those lower down the social scale, of course, the conflict looked different. The suffering of the common people, noted all along by the chroniclers, was finally starting to be detected by the magnates – if only because there had been such a thinning of the population due to war and famine that there was now a shortage of available agricultural labour. As the *Deeds of Stephen* notes: 'You could see villages with famous names standing solitary and almost empty because the peasants of both sexes and all ages were dead, fields whitening with a magnificent harvest (for autumn [1143] was at hand) but their cultivators taken away by the agency of the devas-tating famine, and all England wearing a look of sorrow and misfortune.'

Matilda suffered a huge loss on Christmas Eve 1143 when Earl Miles was killed in an accident: he was hunting deer when one of his men shot wildly and the arrow hit him in the chest. This was not just a blow to Matilda's cause but a great personal bereavement; Miles had been one of her three most loyal supporters, a talented general and a valued advisor. Even the *Deeds of Stephen* recognised this, noting that Miles 'was so unquestioning in his loyalty to King Henry's children as not only to have helped them, but likewise to have received the countess of Anjou herself with her men and always behaved to her like a father in deed and counsel'. Miles was succeeded as earl of Hereford by his eldest son Roger, who would continue his family's support of Matilda's cause but with less enthusiasm and more of an eye for the main chance.

Meanwhile, over in Normandy, Geoffrey of Anjou's dogged campaign reached its conclusion. After methodically conquering his way through the duchy over the last five years he was welcomed by the citizens into its capital, Rouen, in January 1144. This, incidentally, was probably the reason for young Henry's recall to Normandy at this point, to prepare him for his future role as duke; he arrived before the end of March. Rouen Castle held out, defended by men of William de Warenne, but Geoffrey was by now supported by both Waleran de Beaumont and by Rotrou, count of Perche – who was killed during the siege – and he prevailed; the castle surrendered on 23 April. Robert de Torigni, the Norman chronicler, starts to refer to Geoffrey as 'duke' from this point, and the official confirmation followed swiftly: he was formally invested in Rouen Cathedral in the summer of 1144 and was acknowledged as duke by Louis VII, his overlord, later that same year. News reached England, where Matilda's emotions presumably veered between relief and joy at the victory and the future prospects of her son, and gall that her husband had succeeded where she had not.

Regardless of her personal feelings, Matilda could reflect upon the fact that Geoffrey's triumph eased her own situation in England. Stephen was still on the throne, still had the upper hand, but he now had no foothold in Normandy at all, and little realistic prospect of getting it back. Therefore those among his supporters who held lands on both sides of the Channel were faced with a stark choice about which estates they were prepared to lose, or which candidate held out the greater possibility of long-term overall success. Matilda might still be stuck in Devizes, with no immediate short-term prospect of extending her influence out of the West Country, but she could prolong the war in England almost infinitely as long as Geoffrey held Normandy.

And infinite the conflict seemed to all concerned, stretching endlessly into the future. The squabbling magnates and lords fell out over private grievances, some even when they were supposedly on the same side, as evidenced by Earl Robert having to step in to mediate in a local dispute in Wiltshire. Matilda had recently raised the family of the sheriffs of Wiltshire to comital rank: both William of Salisbury, whom we met earlier, and his father had died, so William's younger brother Patrick was the one to benefit, being named 1st earl of Salisbury. However, this had created tension between him and other local landowners and rivals, and in 1143 or 1144 Patrick was embroiled in a dispute with John Marshal, the scarred and one-eyed survivor of Wherwell who held three castles at Marlborough, Ludgershall and Hamstead Marshall. John, whom the *Deeds of Stephen* describes unapologetically as 'the offspring of hell and root of all evil', was not a man to back down from a fight even when outranked by his opponent, and the spat threatened Matilda's relatively stable peace in her heartlands. In the end an agreement was reached whereby John would put aside his wife and marry Patrick's sister Sybil, thus providing any future children with noble kin and the associated prospects for advancement.

Fractures in Matilda's camp became even more apparent in 1145 when Philip, the most volatile of Earl Robert of Gloucester's sons (the *Deeds of Stephen* describes him variously as 'a man of strife', 'supreme in savagery', 'a perfect master of every kind of wickedness', 'fierce and full of wrath', and depicts him 'raging most furiously' and 'extend[ing] by violence his arbitrary power'), defected to Stephen for reasons that are unclear. Faringdon, which had been garrisoned by Philip to control the road between Oxford and Malmesbury, was lost to Stephen, thus leaving Wallingford even more exposed. Stephen sensed an opportunity to rid himself of this thorn in his side and moved into the Thames valley, building an entire siege castle to oppose Wallingford, but the ever-loyal Brian fitzCount and his wife held out.

In the summer of 1146 an attempt at peace negotiations was made, led on Matilda's behalf by her half-brother Reginald, earl of Cornwall. On his way to meet Stephen's representatives he was captured and threatened by his turncoat nephew Philip of Gloucester, but an outraged Stephen ordered his immediate release as he was travelling under safe conduct. As it happened, the talks came to nothing – this was no surprise, as the demands of both parties remained the same as they had been since 1139. Each wanted the crown, so there was no compromise position. The *Deeds of Stephen* sums up the pointlessness of it all: 'The countess's adherents, claiming the sovereignty for her by right, were trying to deprive the king of the royal title and the king's honour; he on his side stated that he would not make them any concession at all with regard to anything he had got in any way whatsoever; and as there was this difference of opinion between the two parties they went back again to their former condition of hostility.'

Other magnates continued to pursue their own interests, including the powerful earl of Chester, Ranulf de Gernon. After Geoffrey de Mandeville's death the principal theatre of war had moved from the fenlands to the north Midlands, where Ranulf held sway. Ranulf, as we will remember, had a particular issue with David, king of Scots, one of Matilda's firmest supporters, although David was now ageing and venturing no further south than Carlisle. Now Ranulf hesitated, vacillated, and finally defected back to Stephen in 1146. But Stephen did not trust him and took him prisoner; Ranulf was forced to surrender some castles (including the one he had taken by subterfuge at Lincoln) to gain his freedom, at which point he immediately returned to Matilda's camp, where he would remain until his death in 1153.

In the course of Ranulf's rebellion his nephew Gilbert fitzRichard de Clare, earl of Hertford (whose mother was Ranulf's sister), was seized as a hostage: in a now-familiar move Stephen demanded the forfeiture of his castles as the price of his freedom, and in an equally familiar move, Gilbert agreed and then rebelled as soon as he was at liberty. To complicate matters further, his paternal uncle Gilbert fitzGilbert de Clare, earl of Pembroke, tried to claim the castles from Stephen as his own rightful inheritance (which was optimistic, to say the least, as Gilbert fitzRichard, although childless, had a younger brother who would be a nearer heir); Pembroke, too, withdrew from Stephen's court when this request was refused. None of this was sensible on the part of the king, and is perhaps an indication of his growing suspicion of the motives of the magnates and his unwillingness to trust anyone other than his wife and William of Ypres. The de Clares had not been acting on behalf of Matilda but were rather seeking to protect their own family inheritance; Stephen's actions threw them, *de facto*, into the opposition party.

The other major figure among the earls, Waleran de Beaumont, finally grew tired of the whole situation and set out instead to fight a war where the sides were more starkly divided into what he perceived as right and wrong: in 1147 he joined the expedition to the Holy Land that would later be known as the Second Crusade. With him went his half-brother William de Warenne, and also Philip of Gloucester, renegade son of Earl Robert. Stephen, of course, was in no position to go anywhere, so the English contingent joined the forces led by Louis VII, king of France.

In March 1147 Matilda's son Henry turned fourteen. He had been in Normandy with his father for three years, but sometime that spring, for unknown reasons, he decided of his own accord that it was time to take a more active role in events in England: he gathered together a small band of friends and mercenaries and set sail.

When he landed a brief panic ensued, as word spread that the son of the empress had invaded with a huge force, intent on conquest. The *Deeds of Stephen* says that Henry 'came to England from overseas with a fine company of knights. At his arrival the kingdom was straight away shaken and set in a turmoil, because the report of his arrival, to spread more widely in its accustomed way, stated falsely that he was at the head of many thousand troops, soon to be very many thousand, and had brought with him a countless quantity of treasure.' It seems unlikely that these rumours were spread deliberately, for they would serve no purpose other than raising the possibility of Stephen arriving with a large army of his own. On the contrary, Henry would be best served by remaining undetected as long as possible in the hope that his small force could pull off some swift and unexpected victories. But England had been in a state of war for so long that the sight of ships and troops approaching was enough to send panicked rumours flying.

The whole enterprise was foolhardy and badly planned, the brainchild of an overactive and ambitious teenager who seemingly had no idea that he might be jeopardising everything that his mother had worked for over the course of many years. The one hint of sanity was that Henry did not attempt to attack any major fortifications; instead he headed for the smaller castles of Cricklade and Purton, which were some 12 miles east of Malmesbury and about 25 miles north of Matilda's position in Devizes. But even there he had little chance of success: he had no siege machinery to speak of – essential when attacking a fortification if huge losses of men were not to be endured – and his force was small and consisted principally of mercenaries who had been hired on credit. Yes: Henry had somehow managed to persuade the group to join his escapade without paying them, promising only payment from their victories and the booty he expected to gain in England. When they were easily beaten back at Cricklade and Purton, and left at a loose end, the mercenaries began to drift away. The *Deeds of Stephen* tells of the result: 'When it was certain and plainly noised abroad to the knowledge of all that he had brought a small party of knights, not an army, and they, having been hired not for ready money but for money promised in the future, accomplished nothing of note, but were always sluggish and remiss in all their doings, then the king's party took heart again and resisted them everywhere with courage and resolution.'

The potential arrival of a well-armed royal host was dangerous, and Henry soon realised that he needed help. He sent appeals to Matilda and to Earl Robert, but neither of them came to his rescue. This seems hard to understand. The *Deeds of Stephen* rather spitefully says of Robert that he was 'brooding like a miser over his moneybags' and adds that Matilda 'was in want of money and powerless to relieve his great need'. But Matilda could surely have found some way to assist Henry if she had wanted to; this was, after all, her eldest son and heir. It is more likely that she could have helped but refused to do so, having no sympathy for his reckless adolescent actions – taken without her advice or permission – which might put at risk the position she was still trying to build, and wanting him to face the conse-. quences of his foolishness. She had learned her lessons in the school of hard knocks; so should he. And she could gamble on the fact that the ever-merciful (to the point of folly) Stephen would not really hurt him. The best thing for Henry to do at this juncture was to get back across the Channel as soon as possible, and Matilda evidently thought that denying him resources was the best way to achieve this. However, it turns out that Henry had not even planned that far ahead, and he was too broke to arrange his passage. So he took the obvious course of action: in an act of almost fantastical audacity, he asked Stephen for money. And, true to form, Stephen obliged; Henry was back in Normandy by the end of May, little more than two months after setting out on his great adventure.

This whole episode has the air of a storm in a teacup. So insignificant did it seem at the time that Henry of Huntingdon does not even mention it in his chronicle, dedicating most of his 1147 section to the crusade. Thus the *Deeds of Stephen* is our only contemporary source, so we must draw our conclusions both from and between the lines of that narrative. Not surprisingly, the author attempts to portray Stephen's actions in a sympathetic light: 'And though the king was blamed by some for acting not only unwisely, but even childishly, in giving money and so much support to one to whom he should have been implacably hostile, I think that what he did was more profound and more prudent, because the more kindly and humanely a man behaves to an enemy the feebler he makes him and the more he weakens him.'

At first glance there may be a shred of truth in this. Stephen might simply have wished to get Henry out of his way as quickly as he could. There were also shades of the 1139 situation at Arundel: Stephen might be damned for unchivalrous behaviour if he attacked a boy. But this was a boy who had knowingly taken up arms against him, who was trying to unseat him from the throne; he should have dealt with the situation more firmly. Showing clemency and generosity to his enemies had been a tactic that had failed over and over again for Stephen. He was at war, and had been for the best part of a decade; he could have ended it all at a stroke if he had captured and imprisoned young Henry. Instead he was storing up problems for himself in the same way Henry I had done when he showed uncharacteristic mercy to the young William Clito in 1106. Stephen had not learned from this lesson, or indeed the many others of his reign. Even if he considered himself personally safe on the throne, he should have had the foresight to see that Henry was going to cause huge problems for the succession and for Eustace.

Indeed, this is demonstrated by just three words from the *Deeds of Stephen* during its description of Henry's escapade. Previously, the text referred simply to 'the countess of Anjou and her son', but the author chooses this precise point in his narrative to begin referring to Henry as 'the lawful heir' to England, an epithet he will go on to use over and over again as time passes. Even more interestingly, Henry is also now 'the son of the count of Anjou', the progeny of his father, not his mother. The mention above of Matilda's unwillingness or incapacity to give financial support to Henry at this juncture is in fact the very last mention of her in the *Deeds of Stephen*, so irrelevant has she become to its narrative of events. Henry is now Stephen's primary antagonist, and the author, perhaps tired of the never-ending conflict, softens towards him in an attitude that he just cannot bring himself to take towards Matilda.

Others were also starting to see Henry in a new light, in an unforeseen consequence of his exploit. He had been rash, he had been reckless, yes; but he had also demonstrated a particular combination of bravado and effrontery that happened to appeal to a certain section of the English nobility. That is to say, such behaviour appealed to them when it was exhibited by a young man of their own ilk; if Matilda had done something similar either at this time or in her youth, the reaction would have been very different. But Henry was not his mother: he was male, a young man of royal blood who was perfectly entitled to make claims on his own behalf in a way that the magnates could not accept from her. Thus Henry became the focus of attention as Henry I's 'true' heir.

As we have noted, Matilda had been coming to the conclusion for some time that she needed to concentrate her efforts on her son rather than herself, and now the unhappy realisation dawned that the best way to do this was to get completely out of his way. She had fought long and hard, but the personal antagonism towards her was now a hindrance to Henry and the overall dynastic struggle. She would need to remove herself from the scene; as ever, her personal desires must be subjugated to the cause. And a sad event was the catalyst that made up her mind.

In the autumn of 1147 Robert, earl of Gloucester, was gathering together a small campaign force, perhaps in an attempt to capitalise on Stephen's failure to take action against Henry, when he fell ill with a fever. At first the illness seemed relatively minor, but his condition deteriorated rapidly and he died on 31 October, his wife Mabel by his side. He was in his late fifties and had been active in one campaign or another for most of his life. He may have been a distant figure during Matilda's early childhood, and an absent one during her years in the Empire, but he had been her most faithful supporter and believer in her cause in all the years since, the steady rock on whom she could lean when her father and husband let her down.

We should also note, however, an important point that is often overlooked: Robert needed Matilda as much as she needed him. What would his life have been, had she not decided to stand up for her rights? Stephen would always have been suspicious and jealous of him, and Robert could have spent years watching his influence, earned through sterling service to Henry I, slip away – accompanied perhaps by the chipping away of his lands and titles, the confiscation of his castles. He would have been an irrelevance at best, and in danger at worst, and it is worth reminding ourselves that it was only when his own interests were seriously threatened in 1138 that he declared for Matilda at all. But after that date, fighting for Matilda gave meaning to his life, gave him a cause. Robert was admired by his contemporaries for his values, and rightly so, but he was a natural follower, not a leader: praise for him generally centres around words such as steadfast, reliable and loyal.

Robert took the correct decision not to claim the throne in his own name in 1135, as he probably would not have enjoyed any more success than Stephen. He too was gracious and amiable, qualities that were attributes in a friend but failings in a king. Matilda gave her half-brother the opportunity to demonstrate publicly his talent in those matters in which he excelled – single-minded devotion to a cause, military tactics, personal engagement in combat – while relieving him of the necessity of engaging in activities and behaviours at which he was less adept: political strategy, decisiveness, harsh authoritarianism. Together they made a fine team, one that could have excelled in leading England; but a sibling pair comprising a woman and a bastard was just too unorthodox for their contemporaries to contemplate as a ruling authority.

Robert's unexpected and untimely death left Matilda with only one of her three original loyal supporters, and he too was ageing and not long for the world. Brian fitzCount had been utterly dependable throughout his life, first to his patron Henry I and then to Matilda as Henry's heir; he had doggedly defended Wallingford against everything Stephen could throw at it for the best part of a decade, but now he, too, started to fade from the picture. Mentions of him in contemporary chronicles become sparse and then disappear altogether, so it is difficult to work out exactly what happened to him. He was certainly dead by 1151, but the evidence suggests that he had retired from active life some time in 1147 or 1148, the most likely scenario being that he and his wife, both childless, had withdrawn to join religious orders. It was a quiet end for a remarkable man, and Matilda now stood alone.

It was time for a new generation to take up the fight. In early 1148 Matilda took ship for Normandy; she was never to return to England, but her struggles were far from over.

CHAPTER NINE

THE NEW GENERATION

ATILDA ARRIVED SAFELY IN NORMANDY, travelling first to
Falaise for the summer of 1148 and then on to the capital,
Rouen, where she would settle more permanently. There she
re-encountered her husband ('was reunited with' is perhaps not the most
accurate term, given the nature of their relationship); she was also able to
see her younger sons again for the first time in nine years. The wording of a
charter in favour of the abbey of Mortemer, a Cistercian foundation about
20 miles to the south-east, makes it clear that the whole family of five,
exceptionally, were together in Rouen in October 1148. Henry I had built a
royal residence in the city near to the priory of Notre-Dame-du-Pré, a
subsidiary house of Matilda's favoured abbey of Bec (about 30 miles distant),
and it is likely that she took up residence there. She would remain in Rouen
for many years, becoming involved in local projects – for example, she
financed the replacement of the old wooden bridge across the river with a
fine new one in stone, which became known as the Pont-Mathilde – but
this does not mean that she had decided to retire to a quiet life. Rather, she
entered a period of consolidation while she came to terms with the new
placement of pieces on the board.

It might be useful here to step back for a few moments and summarise
the overall position at this time, the autumn of 1148, so that we can consider
Matilda's activities in their proper context. She was forty-six and Stephen
some ten years older; they had been in dispute for thirteen years and at war
for nine. They had three children each: Matilda's were Henry (aged fifteen),

Geoffrey (fourteen) and William (twelve); while Stephen's were Eustace (eighteen and recently knighted, marking his entry into manhood), William (thirteen) and also a daughter of around twenty, Mary, who was a cloistered nun. In Scotland, King David was in his sixties; he was still proclaiming his support for Matilda but he now relied to a much greater extent on his grown son and heir Henry, earl of Huntingdon and Northumbria.

In France, King Louis VII was twenty-eight and had been on the throne for eleven years; his marriage to the heiress Eleanor of Aquitaine had produced a single infant daughter, Marie, and they would soon have a second, Alix. Both Louis and Eleanor were away on crusade, with France left in the capable hands of Suger, abbot of Saint-Denis. Stephen's brother Theobald, approaching sixty, remained count of both Blois and Champagne, and had a family of four sons (the eldest twenty-one) and five daughters. Matilda's husband Geoffrey of Anjou had for the previous four years been recognised as duke of Normandy, while still holding the counties of Anjou and Maine.

Over in the Empire, Lothar II had died a decade previously and Conrad III had been elected to succeed him. Conrad was the nephew of Matilda's first husband, Emperor Henry, and brother to the late Frederick, duke of Swabia, who as we will remember had been a candidate for the throne in the election of 1125 following Emperor Henry's death. Conrad was at this time king of Germany and Italy, but he had not yet been crowned emperor (in fact he never would be, styling himself 'king of the Romans' until his death in 1152). He was in his mid-fifties and had known Matilda personally in her youth.

In England, Stephen might have counted himself more secure now that Matilda was on the other side of the Channel, but he still had the earls of Cornwall, Devon, Gloucester, Salisbury, Hereford, Chester, Worcester and Norfolk to contend with. To recap, they were respectively: Reginald de Dunstanville, Matilda's younger half-brother; Baldwin de Redvers, who had still never acknowledged Stephen as king; William of Gloucester, not as effective as his late father Robert but still a major landholder whose interests were entwined with Matilda's; Patrick of Salisbury, now brother-in-law of John Marshal; Roger, son of Matilda's faithful supporter Miles of Gloucester; Ranulf de Gernon, who had left Stephen's party after his arrest and the forfeiture of his castles; Waleran de Beaumont; and Hugh Bigod.

Waleran was on his way to the Holy Land by this point, but his lords and knights adhered to Matilda's cause on his orders. Gilbert fitzGilbert de Clare, earl of Pembroke, had died at the end of 1147 or the beginning of 1148 – at any rate before Matilda sailed for Normandy – and the accession to the earldom of his teenage son gave Stephen a respite from trouble in that quarter.

Normandy was to be Matilda's home for the foreseeable future. Here at least she was secure: the duchy was held by her husband Geoffrey, his authority unquestioned, so she could not be unseated. Whether or not Matilda was recognised by her subjects as duchess in her own name by hereditary right or simply by virtue of her marriage to Geoffrey as conqueror, was a moot point, but in practical terms this made little difference to her situation: the power was firmly in male hands in either case. Perhaps the relief of being 'duchess of Normandy', no questions asked and no further battles to be fought, meant that she was less interested in the details. Matilda had certainly become more resigned to her marital situation, making no further attempt to dissolve the union, and with no discord becoming evident enough for chroniclers to mention it. She and Geoffrey had common cause in supporting their son Henry, and that must have been enough. Normandy, of course, was geographically well situated for their purposes; it could welcome and shelter exiles from England, and act as a base from which further invasions could be planned or launched. There was little danger of Stephen attempting to reassert any authority there, so Matilda could safely concentrate her efforts on her son's plans.

Matilda and Henry now worked as a team, dividing tasks between them. Naturally, given their relative ages, genders and circumstances, the bulk of the military aspects of their campaign would fall to him, and he wasted little time in organising the next phase; he sailed for England again in the spring of 1149, probably around Easter. Once there he headed for Devizes, where he met up with a number of staunch adherents to the cause: his uncle Reginald, earl of Cornwall; Patrick, earl of Salisbury; John Marshal; and the two earls of his own generation, William of Gloucester and Roger of Hereford. Henry began positioning himself as a lawful claimant to the throne almost immediately, accepting homage and making a grant that mentioned both 'the lady empress my mother' and 'King Henry my grandfather'.

His next step was to deal with any lingering perceptions that he was, at sixteen, still an untried boy. He would not be taken seriously as a magnate and the holder of lands in his own right until he had been knighted; this would be simple enough to arrange in itself, but the identity of the man bestowing the honour and the location of the ceremony would both have a symbolic significance. Here Henry scored a masterstroke on both counts, and it is not difficult to see Matilda's hand in the plan as it was being formulated. Rather than being dubbed a knight in Normandy, Henry would receive the honour over the Channel, in order to highlight his claims there. But there was nobody in England of sufficiently high status to outrank a young man who was both a duke in waiting and a claimant to the throne itself. For this he needed a reigning king, and he could find one further north; a well-established and well-regarded monarch who also happened to be Henry's great-uncle and one of Matilda's most fervent supporters.

It was at Carlisle on 22 May 1149, the feast of Whitsun, that 'David, king of Scots, bestowed the arms of manhood upon his nephew Henry', in the words of the chronicler Henry of Huntingdon. Henry had also brought with him 'the sons of some men of birth, that they might receive the honour of a knight's arms at the same time as himself' (*Deeds of Stephen*), which was another shrewd move. In the immediate short term Henry needed the support of wise, powerful and established figures, but when – as he seems to have had no doubt would eventually happen – he had gained his crown, he would need to move forward with men of his own age whom he could trust to be loyal. The camaraderie engendered by a shared knighting experience would bind them to him more closely than almost anything else. Ranulf, earl of Chester, was also present at the ceremony; he made his peace at long last with King David, and was rewarded with the return of the honour of Lancaster.

With the sword of a knight at his side, enthusiastic young companions around him and a great earl brought more closely into the fold, Henry must have been satisfied with his position as he rode south once more. And Fortune smiled on him: the way was beset with danger but he avoided capture by Stephen, who was at York, and then evaded no fewer than three separate ambushes set by Stephen's son Eustace through Herefordshire and Gloucestershire. Eustace, enraged at his failure to capture Henry and no doubt feeling the pressure piling up on his own position, resorted to a different tactic. The *Deeds of Stephen* tells us that Eustace's men 'took and plundered everything they came upon, set fire to houses and churches, and, what was a more cruel and brutal sight, fired the crops that had been reaped and stacked all over the fields, consumed and brought to nothing everything edible they found'.

This depiction of Eustace and the negative view of his activities differs noticeably from the same text's portrayal of Stephen, and there are a couple of possible explanations for this. The first is that the post-1147 part of the chronicle may have been written by a different author from the main part of the text, with the second author being slightly less pro-Stephen and more pro-Henry than his predecessor. However, the text does refer to Henry as 'the lawful heir' to England well before this section starts, so this cannot account for it entirely. More likely is that the author(s) were weary of the war and its depredations, and additionally that they felt that Eustace was a different and less sympathetic figure than his father. Devastating land was a normal and accepted part of war, as we noted earlier, but the burning of already harvested and stacked crops in the fields at this crucial time of year smacks of a particular cruelty, leaving the workers to wonder how they would survive through the winter and spring. It was also, in this case, not a particularly effective tactic, as it would be the common people who would starve, not the military garrisons of Malmesbury and Devizes who were safely shut up in their well-stocked castles, and who were Eustace's real opponents.

Henry made a brief foray into Devon, capturing Bridport, but he was called back to Devizes as Eustace had now adopted a more logical tactic and assailed the castle there, killing those in the surrounding houses and buildings, and even managing to get past the outer defences of the castle itself. But Henry's response was swift, and his reinforcements turned the tide, as the *Deeds of Stephen* tells us: 'They began to make violent assaults on the enemy and resolutely and irresistibly drive them back with the edge of the sword, furiously bringing down men and horses with whirling weapons and flights of arrows.' The two younger men, rather than the mother of one and the father of the other, were now generally considered to be the principal protagonists in the war; this is illustrated by John of Hexham (successor to Richard, whom we met earlier, as prior of that foundation), who writes that 'there was between [Henry] and Eustace, the son of King Stephen, a contest of arms, for they were rivals for the same crown'.

Although he had succeeded in driving Eustace away from Devizes, Henry was not in a position to push for further gain, having insufficient troops with him in England to do anything other than launch occasional guerrilla raids. He would not make the final push for the throne until he could be more certain of success; for the present he withdrew, and he was back in Normandy at the beginning of 1150. This was not a negative move, however, as promotion awaited him there: now that he was a man and a knight, his father Geoffrey held to his original promise and resigned Normandy in his favour. Matilda's son was now a duke.

As we might expect, Matilda had been active on her son's behalf during his absence, and she continued after his return, using her diplomatic experience and skills to push for official confirmation of his new status. The French king Louis VII had returned from his crusade in November 1149, and throughout 1150 Matilda negotiated with him, with the intention of securing his recognition for Henry's accession as duke of Normandy – and also of transferring his support for the English succession from Eustace to Henry. This was no simple challenge as Eustace was Louis's own brother-in-law, and Matilda was once again in direct conflict with Stephen, who was attempting, with the help of his brother Bishop Henry, to keep Louis on side. Suger, the abbot of Saint-Denis and an influential figure in France who had acted as regent in Louis's absence, was approached by both sides for help: Stephen and Bishop Henry wrote to him to plead their cause, and Matilda and her ally Arnulf, bishop of Lisieux, did the same. Arnulf had succeeded his uncle John to that see following the latter's death; interestingly, he is the same Arnulf who as archdeacon of Sées had argued to the papal court of 1139 that Matilda was illegitimate. How he managed to recover from this in her eyes is anyone's guess, but it does further demonstrate the fact that she did not allow past personal grudges to override current political necessity.

Matilda and Arnulf were successful. The septuagenarian Suger was an astute politician who could see which way the wind was blowing; he had also, in his youth, known and admired Henry I (he had written of him that 'he was a very courageous man, excellent in peace and war, whose great reputation had spread almost throughout the world'). In one of his last acts before dying in January 1151 he sided with King Henry's daughter and grandson, had a word in Louis's ear, and urged Matilda and Geoffrey to approach the French king directly.

Henry and his father travelled to Paris in the early summer of 1151. It is not clear whether Matilda accompanied them, but as no source mentions her presence we may assume that she did not. Count Geoffrey 'the Handsome', still only thirty-eight, and his energetic eighteen-year-old son appear to have cut quite a dash at the royal court, and they met not only the increasingly ascetic Louis but also his queen, Eleanor, who was about halfway between them in age and quite taken with them both. The political negotiations were a matter for the men, however, and they hammered out an agreement between them. In short, Henry agreed to surrender the Norman Vexin to Louis, did homage, and was then recognised by the king – the Norman overlord – as duke of Normandy.

'Rejoicing' at their progress, as Robert de Torigni tells us, Henry and Geoffrey left Paris and headed south. But Geoffrey was never to reach home; he fell ill with a fever during the journey and died in September 1151. This, naturally, caused a hiatus in events as the body was transported to Le Mans for burial and everyone accustomed themselves to the new state of affairs. Henry's status was increased once more: at eighteen he found himself count of Anjou and Maine as well as duke of Normandy, his title in Maine being now undisputed as his uncle Helias had died in prison earlier that year. Henry would, however, later experience trouble in the patrimonial domains from his younger brother Geoffrey, a point to which we will return.

Geoffrey Plantagenet's death also changed Matilda's situation. On a personal level the loss of her husband was not an overly devastating blow; although they had reached some sort of agreement on working together during the latter part of their marriage, they had never truly reconciled and were not a close couple. Following this, her second widowhood, Matilda had no thoughts of remarrying. Firstly, she was approaching fifty years of age; secondly, she could enjoy the status of noble widow and the (relative) freedoms that this entailed; and, thirdly, without a husband she could focus exclusively on the career of her son, and this is the task to which she continued to apply herself. At first they issued some charters jointly; two extant grants that can be dated to around this time both begin with the words 'Empress Matilda, daughter of King Henry and her son Henry, duke of Normandy'. For these Norman-focused documents, at least, Matilda had dropped 'lady of the English' from her styles, but she was by no means finished with the kingdom across the sea.

* * *

1152 was not to be quite such a pivotal year as 1141 had been in the struggle for the English crown, but its events certainly escalated matters in a number of different and sometimes unexpected ways. It started fairly quietly with the death in January of Theobald, Stephen's older brother. His two separate titles and lands were inherited by different sons: the eldest, Henry, became count of Champagne, and the second, another Theobald, count of Blois. They were ambitious young men who were in a position to stir up trouble for Matilda and her family.

In March 1152 Louis VII of France divorced his wife Eleanor of Aquitaine. Their marriage had produced only two daughters in fifteen years; the lordship of Aquitaine was important to the French crown, but not as important as providing a male heir to the throne, so nobody raised any particular eyebrows when the union was dissolved on the expedient grounds of consanguinity. This technically meant that the marriage had never been valid in the first place, but the couple's daughters were declared by the church to be legitimate because both parties had entered into the union in good faith, conveniently only realising that they were too closely related once it became clear they were unlikely to have a son. Eleanor, newly single, began to make her way back to her own lands in Poitou, but the journey was fraught with danger: the extensive lands of France's richest heiress could be claimed by any man who could take and marry her. Theobald, the new count of Blois, attempted to kidnap her, as did Matilda's ambitious teenage second son Geoffrey. But Eleanor evaded them, having a different and more eligible husband in mind, one much more suitable for an ex-queen and better positioned to protect her inheritance; when she reached Poitiers she met ('either suddenly or by design,' says Robert de Torigni, although an arrangement seems likely) Henry, duke of Normandy, and they were married there on 18 May 1152.

No source records whether Matilda was consulted on the marriage or what her opinion of it was. She must have seen the political advantages of the match, although whether she thought her son reckless in his disregard of the possible negative consequences must remain a matter for speculation. Although Henry did not immediately include 'duke of Aquitaine' among his styles, he did add the lands of Aquitaine to his holdings in Normandy, Anjou and Maine, thus securing the southern border of Anjou and holding sway over the whole of western France as far south as the natural barrier of the Pyrenees.

In so doing, Henry made a powerful enemy, as Henry of Huntingdon notes: 'This marriage brought about great enmity and discord between the French king and the duke.' Louis VII had, of course, reconciled himself to the loss of direct control of Aquitaine as the consequence of his divorce, but the subsequent events had taken him by surprise and were very much to his disadvantage. Although the control of vassals' marriages was not strictly a privilege of French overlordship (as was accepted practice in England), as overlord of both Normandy and Aquitaine he might have expected at least to be consulted on the marriage alliances of their respective duke and duchess. Even if this were not the case, he certainly would not have wanted them to marry each other, thus creating the huge agglomeration of lands that meant Henry controlled more of France than he did. And his own daughters, who remained in his custody (Eleanor would never see either of them again), would lose their status as heirs to Aquitaine if Eleanor were to bear her new husband a son. An enraged Louis therefore reacted almost immediately upon hearing the unwelcome tidings. Within months Marie and Alix – then aged seven and two – were betrothed respectively to the brothers Henry, count of Champagne, and Theobald, count of Blois. Louis then formed a military coalition with both of these young men, and with others whose lands or positions were threatened by Duke Henry's dramatic rise: his own younger brother Robert, count of Dreux; Henry's younger brother Geoffrey; and King Stephen's son Eustace.

Matilda, living in Rouen, was only some 35 miles from the French border, but she was in no position to ride with troops to counter the new threat. The only thing to do was to summon Henry himself, but he was more than 150 miles in the other direction, at Barfleur and about to sail for England. The news reached him in July, fortunately before he had embarked: young Geoffrey was on his way to Anjou, having pledged to raise a revolt there against his brother, and the others had crossed the border into Normandy and were assailing one of his castles there, which Robert de Torigni identifies as Neuf Marché. In Henry's favour was the fact that he had troops already assembled; he performed an abrupt about-turn from Barfleur and marched eastwards with speed. Robert de Torigni thought that the coalition would be too hard to overcome – 'nearly all of the Normans now thought that Henry would rapidly lose all of his possessions' – but in fact the whole enterprise turned out to be something of a non-event. As

Henry closed in on the alliance's army, they retreated; he then marched into Anjou, where the lords, faced with their angry and powerful count on the one hand, and the prospect of his under-resourced younger brother on the other, made the wise and correct choice. Given that his campaign in England had been postponed anyway, Henry spent the rest of the autumn of 1152 on a circuit of Aquitaine with his wife, showing himself to their vassals and marking his authority there. England would wait until the new year.

Although she had remained in Rouen during the troubles on the Norman–French border, Matilda was kept informed of events in England (we know, for example, that her half-brother Reginald, earl of Cornwall, sailed to Normandy for a visit in the spring of 1152) and she was well aware that 1152 had been a year of significance there also.

Stephen, although not constantly in arms as he had been for much of the previous decade, was nevertheless only too aware of the continuing opposition to his own reign and the precariousness of his son's position; situations that were exacerbated given the spectacular rise of Matilda's son. Stephen's claim to kingship, as we explored in Chapter 4, was based on the fact of his coronation, not on the principle of hereditary succession. Therefore he was in personal possession of the throne, but it was not at all certain that Eustace would be the one to succeed him, for any arguments he put forward based on primogeniture would undermine his own position. He could also not make any use of the principle of porphyrogeniture, for Eustace had been born while he was merely count of Boulogne. Thus, for several years, he had been trying to secure Eustace's succession in the best (and perhaps only) way that he could: by having the boy crowned during his own lifetime. This was a well-established custom in France, where the Capetians had been practising it since the late tenth century, but it was unprecedented in England. The stakes were high: if Stephen succeeded in his aim then Eustace and the Blois dynasty would be all but unassailable, so Matilda's party needed to put every effort into preventing it.

In this they were helped both by the scruples of the archbishop of Canterbury and by Stephen's ongoing conflict with the church in the persons of various bishops. Archbishop Theobald was a man of principle: as we saw in Chapter 6, when Matilda had been proclaimed lady of the English he had insisted on being released in person from his oath to Stephen before he would accept her. At the time this had not been to Matilda's liking, but now his integrity worked in her favour and Henry's; Theobald would not depart from precedent and perform the ceremony until he had explicit permission to do so from the pope.

Innocent II, who had been pope when Stephen took the English crown and who had recognised his kingship at the council of 1139, had died in 1143; following the two very short reigns of Celestine II and Lucius II, Eugenius III had ascended the papal throne in 1145 and was the current incumbent. In 1151 the archbishop of York, Henry Murdac, was sent to Rome; partly on church business and partly, in the words of John of Hexham, 'on the business of the king and the realm, of which the chief matter was that the king's son Eustace might be established by papal authority as heir to the throne'. But the answer, when it came, was in the negative. During his brief six-month reign Celestine II had written to Archbishop Theobald, and according to the papal memoirs of John of Salisbury, had 'forbid[den] him to allow any change to be made in the English kingdom in the matter of the crown, for that matter was in dispute and so any claim for the transfer of right was to be refused'.

After considering his options for several months, Stephen took the matter up once more at a council held on 6 April 1152, during his Easter court. He formally designated Eustace as his successor, and oaths were sworn to the young man by a number of the lay magnates present. However, Stephen knew as well as anybody that oaths sworn in front of a king in favour of his designated heir could later be disavowed, so he needed to push for the coronation to be sure. He asked the bishops to recognise his son's rights, and demanded that Archbishop Theobald carry out the ceremony; the prelates all refused to comply, citing precedent and the papal instructions. This angered Stephen, who, of course, had form when it came to mistreating bishops who stood against him. Henry of Huntingdon tells us of his reaction to their negative response: 'Boiling with rage at this crushing humiliation, father and son [Stephen and Eustace] ordered them all to be shut up in a particular building, and subjecting them to powerful intimidation, urged them to do what they demanded. They were filled with greatest dread, for King Stephen had certainly never loved the clergy . . . they maintained their resistance, even though in fear of their lives.'

Stephen, however, did not carry through with his threats, as Henry of Huntingdon goes on to reveal: 'They came away unscathed, though robbed of their possessions, which they received back later from the penitent king.' Archbishop Theobald, meanwhile, had fled to Flanders, which thwarted Stephen's plans completely: the coronation would not be seen as valid if it were carried out by anyone other than the archbishop of Canterbury, and that was now even less likely than it was before. He had also lost any influence he might have had with the papal court: one of Pope Eugenius's other acts was to decline to renew his brother Bishop Henry's status as papal legate.

Stephen suffered a terrible loss just a month after the council, on 3 May 1152, when his beloved wife Matilda died following a short illness. They had been married for twenty-seven years and produced a family of five children, losing two of them in infancy. She had been his greatest supporter, refusing to surrender when he was captured and imprisoned, and taking up arms on his behalf; moreover, following his release she had done the expected womanly thing and dropped back seamlessly into the role of consort, peacemaker and mother. She had agreed to pass on her patrimony of Boulogne to her son Eustace when he came of age, in order to further his prospects. Despite her lack of a front-line role after 1141, Stephen had relied on her constantly for advice and encouragement. Queen Matilda was buried at Faversham Abbey in Kent, which she and Stephen had founded four years previously.

Stephen, who had, as we noted above, lost his brother Theobald just a few months earlier, was reeling from the loss of his wife, but he was not to be allowed to grieve in peace. Matilda's supporters were still agitating on her behalf and Henry's, and Stephen had to rouse himself to respond. June 1152 found him outside the walls of a new castle built by John Marshal somewhere between Hamstead Marshall and Newbury, establishing a siege camp. In the context of the war this was a relatively minor incident, not even mentioned by Henry of Huntingdon, but it subsequently found fame due to the later career of an innocent participant.

Hearing that his lightly garrisoned outpost was under siege, John Marshal sought a truce with Stephen, offering up his son William as hostage for his good faith. William was the fourth of his sons and the second by his second wife Sybil; at this point he was around five years old. Stephen agreed to the terms and temporarily withdrew his forces to allow John to approach the castle, ostensibly to speak to the castellan about surrender. The *History of William Marshal*, although still not entirely reliable for this period, based as it was on the second-hand reminiscences of an old man sixty years later, is nevertheless vivid in its depiction of the episode: 'What occurred was that the siege forces withdrew and the Marshal refortified his castle; he had found it very much lacking in defensive forces, so he installed there valiant knights, sergeants and archers, determined to put up a good defence and unwilling to surrender the castle; the Marshal had no time for the idea of peace.'

This re-garrisoning was in direct contravention of the agreement that John had made with Stephen, so the king needed to retaliate or at least make some kind of statement of intent. He sent a message to John saying that his young son – a hostage for his word, which had clearly and publicly been broken – would be executed unless he surrendered. This would be a serious threat in any other circumstances; Henry I had permitted the mutilation of children for less. But John, whose scarred face and missing eye from the incident at Wherwell eleven years previously were testament to the fact that he was not a man to give up easily, sent back the famous reply that 'he did not care about the child, since he still had the anvil and hammers to produce even finer ones'. Little William seemed doomed, but Stephen could not bring himself to execute the child; instead he kept the boy as a hostage in his custody.

William Marshal would, of course, go on to have a stellar career in which he would serve not only Henry II but also three of his sons and eventually even his grandson, the future Henry III. But nobody in the environs of Newbury, or indeed elsewhere in England, could possibly have predicted that in the summer of 1152. All they saw was Stephen, king for seventeen years, still making threats he would not carry through, still failing to stamp out rebellion, still exhibiting his weakness before magnates who were tiring of the endless war and staring at the bleak prospect of it continuing for another generation.

In early January 1153, before the conclusion of the Christmas festivities, Matilda waved her son off once more. Was she frustrated at remaining in one place for so long, at being so far from the centre of the action? Perhaps. But duty was – as ever – distinct from personal inclination, and she had plenty of other responsibilities, tasks that were crucial to the overall cause but nevertheless more conventionally 'feminine' in nature. Firstly, she had to rule and keep the peace in Normandy. This was a role she had long coveted in her own right, and one that had been denied her – but now she was wielding power in the name of a male relative, her authority became acceptable to contemporaries. Secondly, and on a more personal level, she needed to safeguard the future of the dynasty. While Henry was in England, Duchess Eleanor would join Matilda's household, and, eight months after her wedding, she was in the early stages of pregnancy. Along with prayers that mother and baby would stay safe for the duration, Matilda no doubt added a request to the Almighty that the child would be a boy. She was already, as it happened, a grandmother – Henry had an illegitimate son named Geoffrey who had been born shortly before his marriage to Eleanor – but, as her own bitter experience had taught her, there was no substitute for a legitimate male heir, and the lack of one could cause untold trouble.

Despite the winter weather and a ferocious gale in the Channel, Henry arrived safely in England on or around 6 January 1153, the feast of the Epiphany. He had with him some 140 knights and 3,000 infantry, probably hired on credit, and was relying on his supporters already in England to rally to him. We should not forget that these men remained loyal to his cause due in great part to the unflinching determination of his mother: Matilda might be overlooked and almost forgotten in England now, five years after her departure from its shores, but she had laid the groundwork for his fight. If she had not, if she had given up during all the hard times in the 1130s and 1140s, Henry would by now be no more than count of Anjou and Maine, and seen as something of an irrelevance across the Channel. He, therefore, started this campaign for the crown in a much more favourable position than she had herself in 1139. And, of course, he enjoyed the colossal stroke of luck of having been born male: he had every right (and expectation) of acting in ways that Matilda had been criticised for, and, crucially, his maleness made it much less problematic for the English magnates to support him.

These magnates were, as we mentioned previously, increasingly disillusioned with the never-ending war. Although many of them were nominally still entrenched in opposing camps, they were veering towards the view that any option that provided a lasting peaceful solution, and provided it soon, would be preferable to the status quo. Some also made private arrangements among themselves: for example, Ranulf de Gernon, earl of Chester (and a supporter of Matilda and Henry), made an agreement with Robert de

Beaumont, earl of Leicester (still in Stephen's camp), that they would try not to go to war with each other; if they were forced to do so by their respective overlords, neither would take more than twenty knights into battle, and any property captured by the other would be returned. Similar arrangements were made by others, with those who held lands on both sides of the Channel also tending to the opinion that the best long-term solution would be to reunite England and Normandy under one ruler, so they had only one overlord – and for this there was only one realistic candidate.

Eustace thought differently. His father had been king of England almost as long as he could remember, he had been brought up in the expectation of the crown, and he was prepared to fight for it. But his position was becoming ever more untenable. When his main rival had been a mere ageing female he could see himself as the obvious choice to succeed his father, but now, still uncrowned, with an adult male cousin on the horizon – one who was both the grandson and obvious hereditary heir of Henry I, and also the holder of a great deal of power and resource in his own right – Eustace's status as heir to the throne was under threat. The tide was turning: the church had refused to crown him, the barons were drifting away, and the chroniclers picked up on the undercurrents. Henry of Huntingdon, who had never been a particular admirer of Matilda, nevertheless now starts referring to Henry as an 'illustrious young man ... distinguished by arms worthy of so great a leader', while news of his invasion 'distressed' Stephen, whose 'face changed from grandeur to wrinkled grief'. The *Deeds of Stephen*, meanwhile, depicts the king becoming 'gloomy and downcast' while Henry, 'the lawful heir', gains in popularity; all Eustace can do is 'rapidly follow him [back from France] to resist him in England'. But Henry had made contact with his supporters before sailing, so they were ready and waiting; the barons were 'flocking in eagerly to join him'.

For the first time in many years, an Angevin incursion into England was not supported by the Scots. King David was old and ailing; he remained in the north after Henry's arrival and died at Carlisle in May 1153. Unfortunately for Scotland his only son Henry, earl of Huntingdon and Northumbria, had predeceased him in 1152, so David was succeeded on the Scottish throne by his grandson Malcolm, who had just turned twelve; the family's English interests were represented by Malcolm's ten-year-old brother William, later named earl of Huntingdon. Thus Scotland, under a child king and a regency, was concentrating on its own affairs and took no further part (for now) in the struggle for the English throne.

As it happened, Henry did not need the assistance of the Scottish king in his current campaign, managing the task with the resources already at his disposal. After all the years of war and devastation, there was to be no great final battle, but rather a series of smaller events which, as they built up, meant that everyone agreed that enough was finally enough.

In February there was a stand-off between Henry's forces and Stephen's in shockingly bad weather at Malmesbury. This was well out of what would normally be considered the campaigning season, and Henry of Huntingdon gives a flavour of the unsuitability of the conditions: God 'sent such squalls into their faces, submitting them to such rigours of harsh cold and such a battering by tempestuous gales . . . the storm was in the faces of the king and his men, with the result that they could neither hold up their weapons nor handle their spears, which were dripping with water.' The torrential rain and snow had rendered the River Avon 'so fast-moving and swollen that it was terrifying to attempt to ford and impossible to get out of'; neither side dared risk the crossing, and eventually Stephen withdrew. Several of his hitherto loyal magnates, including Robert de Beaumont, earl of Leicester, realised the game was up and offered homage to Henry. These new adherents, with their widely spread lands, opened up a path for him through the Midlands; Henry set his troops to march north and then east, accepting the surrender of Warwick and Bedford castles and enlarging his army as he went. Then he turned again, to where Stephen was besieging Wallingford, arriving in late July or early August 1153.

Initially there was some tension: the *Deeds of Stephen* tells us that 'as the two armies, in all their warlike array, stood close to each other, with only a river between them, it was terrible and very dreadful to see so many thousands of armed men eager to join battle with drawn swords, determined, to the general prejudice of the kingdom, to kill their own relatives and kin.' But Wallingford, held doggedly for Matilda since 1139 and emblematic of so many of the war's troubles, was not to be the scene of a climactic engagement: the magnates on both sides simply refused to fight. As the *Deeds of Stephen* continues: 'The leading men of each army . . . shrank, on both sides, from a conflict that was not merely between fellow countrymen but meant the desolation of the whole kingdom, thinking it wise . . . to join all together for the establishment of peace.'

Stephen and Henry were forced into negotiations, in which they were aided by Archbishop Theobald (now returned to England having made peace with the king) and also Henry, bishop of Winchester. According to Henry of Huntingdon, Bishop Henry had 'earlier thrown the realm into grievous disorder' but now 'seeing everything destroyed by robbery, fire and slaughter, was moved to repentance and worked towards the ending of such evils through concord between the princes'. A draft agreement was reached whereby Stephen would remain king for the rest of his life, but that Henry would be his heir.

This arrangement makes it seem as if the two parties were equally balanced, but the phraseology used by Robert de Torigni to describe the situation indicates that he, at least, saw Henry as very much in the ascendant: 'The duke gave full permission to the king to hold the realm during the whole of his lifetime.' In any case the treaty suited the magnates and it would presumably be welcomed by the rest of the population of England if it entailed an immediate cessation of hostilities; however, it did mean that Stephen had agreed to disinherit his son. Eustace, 'greatly vexed and angry' says the *Deeds of Stephen*, as well he might be, withdrew from his father's court in a rage. He had a band of friends, but no supporter of great rank or power, as they were all in favour of the agreement made at Wallingford, so there was little he could do in practice other than to express his frustration by violence – and this he did. He headed for Cambridgeshire, where he furiously sacked the abbey at Bury St Edmunds, burning crops and devastating the countryside for miles around.

Eustace was an able, albeit headstrong, young man, and the prospect of another conflict beckoned. But Henry's extraordinary luck held once more: Eustace died very suddenly just weeks later, in late August 1153, apparently of a seizure. The clerical chroniclers Gervase of Canterbury and Henry of Huntingdon both attributed his demise to God and Saint Edmund's retribution for sacking the abbey; possibly it was some kind of extreme reaction to stress. But whatever the cause, it was certainly fortuitous for Henry: Eustace was only in his early twenties and could have been a thorn in his side for years to come.

Eustace's epitaphs were nowhere near as positive of those of the long-dead William Adelin or William Clito, also cut off in or approaching their prime: Henry of Huntingdon manages to say he was 'a man proven in military skill',

217

but then goes on to add that he was 'obdurate against the things of God, very harsh towards the incumbents of churches, very loyal towards those who persecute the Church', and that in removing Eustace from the earth, God 'was already, in His great kindness, preparing the tranquillity of His realm'. The *Peterborough Chronicle* notes merely that 'he was an evil man, because wheresoever he came he did more evil than good'. Eustace and his wife Constance had produced no children – another boon for Henry, as this meant that the struggle could not be continued for a third generation. The widow returned to France, where her brother King Louis swiftly arranged a second alliance for her; she married Raymond, count of Toulouse, in 1154. Stephen buried his son at Faversham, next to his wife, and gave up.

The Treaty of Winchester, formally ratifying the details of the agreement reached at Wallingford, was sealed on 6 November 1153. 'Justice,' says Robert de Torigni, was 'looking down from heaven', while Henry of Huntingdon seems on the verge of bursting into song: 'O what boundless joy! What a blessed day!' He continues with a heartfelt statement: 'Thus the mercy of God brought to the broken realm of England a dawn of peace at the end of a night of misery.' By the terms of the treaty, all lands would return to the control of whoever owned them 'on the day that King Henry was both alive and dead', that is, 1 December 1135. All castles (several hundred of them, including temporary fortifications) constructed during the nineteen years since Henry I's death were to be demolished. All hostages taken during the conflict were to be released – including little William Marshal, who had remained in Stephen's custody since the incident at Newbury over a year previously. 'So it was arranged and firmly settled,' says the *Deeds of Stephen* as it enters its final section, 'that arms should finally be laid down and peace restored everywhere in the kingdom.'

Nobody was particularly interested in putting forward any claim on behalf of Stephen's younger son, William, a youth of eighteen who comes across in all the available evidence as something of a nonentity. Totally overshadowed by Eustace, he had not been brought up to expect a crown and did not want to fight for one. He would be count of Boulogne, succeeding his mother and brother; it was confirmed that he was also free to inherit those honours, including the county of Mortain, that Stephen had held before ascending the throne. William had also previously been favoured by his father with the hand in marriage of the heiress Isabel de Warenne, only child of Earl William de Warenne (who had died on crusade in 1148), and the huge tracts of lands that came with her. He would be the foremost Anglo-Norman magnate and he saw no point, and no future, in making a bid for the crown.

News of the treaty made its way to Rouen. Matilda would never sit on the throne of England, but her son would: she could tell herself that she had lost the battle in order to win the war. However, she was to receive one last metaphorical slap in the face at Stephen's hands.

The details of the future transfer of power in England and of Henry becoming Stephen's heir had to be legally justified, somehow. If the hereditary right to the throne was to stem from Stephen, then why was his son William not to be king next? But, conversely, if the right were derived directly from Henry I, why was his grandson not on the throne already in place of Stephen – or, indeed, why was Matilda not in possession of the crown? In order to smooth over these issues a compromise had been reached, one which was proclaimed at Westminster at Christmas 1153: the essence of it was that Stephen, in his position as crowned king, would officially 'adopt' Henry, swearing in the terms of the settlement to maintain him as 'my son and heir in all things'. Matilda was mentioned only insofar as she was 'the mother of the duke', bound – along with Henry's wife and brothers – to keep the provisions of the treaty.

This all seemed logical at the time, especially to the male parties involved in the drawing up of the treaty. But in hindsight – and no doubt to Matilda at the time – it was an outrageous sidelining of all that she had achieved. She had fought for her own rights and never reached the throne. Despite her own crushing disappointment and frustration she had continued to fight on behalf of her son, and now he was being publicly portrayed, even if only technically, as *Stephen's* son, *Stephen's* heir; Matilda was written out of her own story.

Duke Henry, as we noted earlier, did retain his style as 'Henry fitz-Empress', and would continue to do so for the rest of his life. Possibly an argument could be made that this was due more to the grandeur of the imperial title than to any specific recognition of Matilda's achievements, but it is clear from the way that he relied on her for advice and regency (we will explore this in greater depth in Chapter 10) that he appreciated her continuing wisdom and experience. In the autumn of 1153 Matilda was able to send some welcome dynastic news to him: his wife Eleanor had given birth to a son, William, in August. The child was now directly in line for the English throne as well as being the heir to territories comprising most of the western half of France.

Matilda, we should reiterate, was by no means putting her feet up and retiring to a life of domesticity in Normandy, despite the arrival of her grandson. Louis VII was still aggrieved at Henry's marriage to Eleanor and might attack at any time, and the counts of Dreux, Champagne and Blois remained unfriendly; if Matilda was less than vigilant and let Henry's position slip, the French could make gains, and those Anglo-Norman magnates who still wavered or those with an eye to the main chance might turn against them. In the meantime she also dealt with more routine administrative matters such as grants and appointments. For example, in the spring of 1154 she is recorded as confirming the appointment of the prior of Bec (and chronicler) Robert de Torigni as abbot of Mont-Saint-Michel.

Henry returned to Normandy at Easter 1154, to be welcomed by his mother, wife and son, and also by his youngest brother William, who had not joined Geoffrey in his abortive rebellion. The twenty-one-year-old duke was in an exceptionally favourable position. He had Normandy, Anjou, Maine and Aquitaine to rule, with capable female relatives to act for him while he could not be everywhere at once; he had a son and heir, and could hope for more children now that he was reunited with Eleanor; he had the prospect of the English crown to look forward to. He was probably not expecting that particular title to come to him until he was a little older, but this favourite of Fortune was smiled upon once more when Stephen fell ill less than a year after the treaty was sealed; he died on 25 October 1154, in his early sixties, and was buried at Faversham Abbey next to his wife Matilda and his son Eustace.

Stephen had made one snap decision at a crucial time, December 1135, and he had spent the rest of his life trying to live up to it and to deal with the consequences – tasks for which he was hopelessly unprepared and unqualified. He was, like his cousin Robert of Gloucester, a natural follower rather than a leader, and this was his downfall. He was a very able soldier who reacted swiftly to any given military situation (it could well be argued that it was his undoubted courage, his willingness to take up arms and his skill in combat that kept his kingship going as long as it did), but he was not a great long-term strategist or a visionary inspiration to his followers. He relied on his younger brother Bishop Henry for political acumen, his son Eustace (in later years) for backbone, and his wife Queen Matilda for everything. He was not helped by finding himself in a position that was always going to be all but impossible to maintain, but the decision to seize the crown in 1135 had been his own and he should have given more thought to how he was going to keep it on his head once it was put there. He was well liked as a man – a good comrade and companion who could be kind and generous, but he lacked the necessary authority and ruthlessness to make an effective king by the standards of the twelfth century.

By the time Stephen died he was a broken man. He had lost the two people closest to him and was fully, blindingly aware of his own limitations and failures. This must have been a crumb of comfort to Matilda, who seems not to have overtly revelled in his death but who must have been at least relieved and possibly even overjoyed in private. Stephen had usurped her position; he had derailed the whole course of her life and put it on a path of struggle, conflict and war; he had done it because he felt that his rights as a man trumped hers as a woman, regardless of their individual suitability (or lack thereof) for the throne. He had forfeited any right to her sympathy. But now he was gone, his son was gone, his dynasty was all but gone; Matilda lived and could glory in the prospects of her own heir, born of her own body.

For the first time since the demise of Edward the Confessor, the death of a king of England did not result in an immediate scramble for the crown. Henry was in Normandy with Matilda when the news reached them; while he waited for the weather to improve enough for him to make the Channel crossing, they took the opportunity to put their affairs in order. The administration of the duchy would be left in her capable hands; he expected his absence to be a long one while he asserted his authority in England. It was six weeks until conditions were favourable enough for him to sail – six weeks during which peace held in England. The *Peterborough Chronicle* says that this was because 'no man dared do other than good because of great awe of him' – the sign of an authoritative monarch – and Robert de Torigni reiterates the sentiment: 'England was perfectly tranquil, out of the love and fear which it bore towards Duke Henry, whose accession to the throne no one called in question.' Henry sailed on 7 December, and was crowned at Westminster Abbey on 19 December 1154. The *Deeds of Stephen*, which began in chaos with the death of one King Henry, ends in splendour with the coronation of another: 'The duke, returning gloriously to England, was crowned for sovereignty with all honour and the applause of all.'

Matilda was not there. After all the years of struggle, she did not witness the final triumph. She had the excuse that she needed to remain in Normandy in order to act as Henry's regent, but the fact was that her presence at the coronation would have been problematic in all sorts of ways; she thus absented herself from what should have been the greatest moment of her life in the name of family duty. Henry, however, did ensure that she was represented symbolically: the crown that was placed upon his head by Archbishop Theobald was one of the two that Matilda had brought away from Germany three decades previously.

⋟ CHAPTER TEN ⋞

'THE GOOD MATILDA'

MATILDA WAS NOT THE QUEEN of England, but she was the politically active mother of the king. This was a new situation for the
Anglo-Norman dynasty: the mothers of William I, William II
and Henry I had not lived to see their respective sons' accessions, and
although Adela of Blois survived for two years after Stephen's, she had
already been in a convent for over a decade. The lack of precedent gave
Matilda the opportunity to carve out a new and personalised role for herself.

As a matriarch of extensive international experience, it was natural for
Matilda to act as one of her son's advisors: he was, after all, only twenty-one
years old at the time of his coronation. And – unlike many other headstrong
young men thrust into positions of power – it seems that he was, at least at
first, amenable to accepting her advice and guidance. This appears to have
been well known at court in later years; the author Walter Map, writing
towards the end of the twelfth century with an in-depth knowledge of
Henry's household, gives the following anecdote in his *De nugis curialium*
(*On Courtiers' Trifles*):

> I have heard that his mother's teaching was to this effect, that he should
> spin out the affairs of everyone, hold long in his own hand all posts that
> fell in, take the revenues of them, and keep the aspirants to them hanging
> on in hope; and she supported this advice by an unkind analogy: an
> unruly hawk, if meat is often offered to it and then snatched away or hid,

223

becomes keener and more inclined to be obedient and attentive. He ought also to be much in his own chamber and little in public: he should never confer anything on anyone at the recommendation of any person, unless he had seen and learned about it himself.

It is possible that Walter Map meant this as criticism of Matilda – her supposed harshness of character coming to the fore in her dealings with the men around her – but in fact it comes across as both sensible and cautious, and also authoritarian in a way that both Henry I and Emperor Henry might have recognised and approved.

Indeed, having spent many years being characterised as wilful, Matilda now found that, as her son was even more so (although, naturally, this was seen as less of a fault in him), she was cast in the role of being the voice of reason and caution that stopped him charging headlong into ill-thought-out exploits. As an example, in the summer of 1155 Henry considered invading Ireland in order to conquer it and give it to his younger brother William – who as the third son had no share in the family patrimony – and the question was discussed at a council in September 1155. However, the plans were shelved, and Robert de Torigni is clear that this was because Matilda was opposed to the idea.

There are several possible reasons for Matilda's disapproval of the scheme. We can dismiss straight away any thought that it was because she did not want her youngest son William far away in a hostile land to the west: he might have been only nineteen, but we know enough of Matilda to be sure that she did not expect or wish for her boys to be cosseted. More likely is that she was aware of the huge expanse of land under Henry's control, with its many attendant responsibilities, and she did not want him to spread himself too thinly. Henry's success or otherwise in keeping a firm grasp on all his territories would be predicated on his travelling frequently to visit each one; the journey across the choppy Irish Sea was only really feasible in good weather, and the prospect of him being stuck at the western edge of the world for weeks or months by adverse conditions could be very detrimental to his interests. Moreover, both the political situation and the terrain in Ireland meant that any attempted invasion would require a huge amount of energy, time and resource. Henry was as yet in the very early stages of his reign, and the spectre of the recent and long civil war still loomed over England and Normandy; he would therefore be better advised to concentrate in the short term on stamping his authority on the lands he already held rather than seeking new ones. William fitzEmpress was compensated with lands in England, although the distribution was canny: he was given estates scattered across fifteen counties, which made him rich but did not give him a particular power base on which to build. He showed no signs of disaffection and was content with his lot.

The same could not be said of the middle brother, Geoffrey. He was a mere fourteen months younger than Henry, but this was all-important in an age when primogeniture was gaining ground as the preferred method of passing on estates and titles. Henry had inherited the whole of England, Normandy, Anjou and Maine, and all the revenues that came with them; Geoffrey had three castles left to him by his father. He was frustrated and ambitious, but had so far been unsuccessful in his attempts to better his situation. He had failed to capture Eleanor of Aquitaine after her divorce in 1152 – and had subsequently seen her marry his brother, thus not only depriving Geoffrey of Aquitaine but also adding it to Henry's domains – and he had been swiftly defeated when he tried to form a coalition with Louis VII of France and his sons-in-law later that same year.

Following this failure he and Henry had apparently been reconciled; the details are not clear, but we can assume that Matilda was consulted during the process. Geoffrey is next heard of for certain in early 1154, at which point he was the prisoner of Theobald, count of Blois, his erstwhile ally (which adds credence to the idea that he was now on good terms with Henry). It is possible that Henry might have been happy to have his brother out of the way for a while, but Matilda stepped in. The conditions in which Geoffrey and others were being kept were harsh: a companion of his, a nobleman named Sulpicius of Amboise, died while in Theobald's custody. Matilda may well have supported her eldest son in all things, including family rivalries – she had, after all, been fighting for his rights for many years – and believed in the school of hard knocks, but this did not extend to seeing her second son die in captivity. She persuaded Henry to negotiate with Theobald, and Geoffrey was released. Of course, there was a further political imperative here, which the far-sighted Matilda would have spotted, in that being on good terms with Theobald would lessen any danger on the eastern borders of Maine and Anjou while Henry was elsewhere.

Once Geoffrey was released he initially remained on good terms with the family unit, and Robert de Torigni places him at Rouen with his mother and brothers when Henry stopped there to make plans ahead of his journey to England for the coronation, late in 1154. But by 1156 he was in revolt again. He now claimed that his father Geoffrey of Anjou had decreed, on his deathbed, that Henry was to cede Anjou to the younger Geoffrey if ever he succeeded in becoming king of England, so that he should have some share in the family inheritance. On the face of it, this would be possible: although Henry held England, Normandy, Anjou, Maine and Aquitaine this did not mean that they were all one unified block – rather they were separate titles that happened to be held by the same man, so in theory they could be split up again.

However, the story itself is unlikely and was probably fabricated by Geoffrey. If it were true, then why had he waited five years since his father's death to publicise it? Furthermore, if Geoffrey had known of this supposed plan since 1151, then it would have made more sense for him to side with Henry, rather than Louis and Eustace, in the conflict of 1152. But for now the pretence served as justification for his rebellion. Unfortunately this set him against both his brother and his mother, neither of whom would countenance the loss of any part of Henry's accumulated empire; Henry lost no time in assembling troops and laying siege to Geoffrey's castles of Chinon, Mirebeau and Loudun. Earlier that same year, in February 1156, Henry had done homage to Louis VII for Normandy, Anjou and Aquitaine, and been reconfirmed in the first two holdings and formally recognised as duke of the third. He therefore approached Geoffrey's castles not only in possession of substantial military resource but also in an unassailable legal position and on the moral high ground. Few of Geoffrey's friends and potential allies risked joining him, and he was forced to yield all three castles.

After a second revolt against his overlord, any other rebel might expect to face harsh consequences, but once more the brothers were reconciled; and once more, although we have no definitive evidence either way, we can assume that Matilda was involved in the process. Geoffrey was allowed to keep Loudun and was bought off with an annuity of £1,000 sterling and £2,000 Angevin (thus around £1,500 sterling in total, something like two to three times the annual income of an earl in England) for the other castles; Henry summoned his wife from England and they went on a tour of Aquitaine; Matilda remained in Normandy exercising her son's authority there.

Matilda, now in her mid-fifties, was by this point considered something of a staid and conventional older aristocratic woman – a far cry from what she had been before, and perhaps not entirely accurate even now, as we shall see. Possibly there was some element of her mellowing with age or in the light of the gratification of seeing her son on the throne of England, but she still had the energy to undertake the tiring day-to-day business of governance. Henry, of course, could not be in all his domains at once, and he was happy to leave Normandy in Matilda's capable hands; she acted as regent for her son there as she had once done for her husband in Italy.

The fact that Matilda now exercised authority by proxy was one of the principal factors behind another sea change in the way she was portrayed by contemporaries. During her time as empress in Germany, when she had played a familiar, intercessory, non-threatening queen-consort role, she had been loved by her subjects and known as *die gute Methilt* ('the good Matilda'). During the war in England, when she had attempted to seize power for herself and rule in her own right, she was criticised and decried for her presumption, her confidence, for transgressing the traditional 'feminine' role. But now that she was once more officially playing a supporting role to a man, she gained in popularity. These developments can hardly be coincidental.

The new image was helped by the fact that the principal sources from which we can glean details of Matilda at this stage of her life are the writings of two men who knew her personally and who had reason to be sympathetic: Robert de Torigni and his younger compatriot Stephen of Rouen, both of them monks of Bec, a foundation that continued to benefit from Matilda's generosity. Indeed, during these years in Normandy Matilda became increasingly concerned with spiritual matters. She had always been as pious as a queen or aristocratic woman was expected to be, and it was not unusual for a noble of either sex to become more devout as they aged. Some, like Adela of Blois and possibly Brian fitzCount, retired to religious houses. Others went further and actually took holy orders: Waleran de Beaumont, for example, would end his days as a monk in 1166. Matilda did not retire; her interest in religion was more active, and she both established new foundations and donated to existing ones. Moreover, she retained her royal dignity in her dealings with the various orders: she was a benefactor and a patron, not someone who washed the feet of beggars or lepers as her mother might have done. An interesting aside to Matilda's activities at this stage is that she was able to rekindle her childhood acquaintance with one of her namesake illegitimate half-sisters: Matilda, abbess of Montvilliers, a Benedictine house near Le Havre on the Norman coast. Indeed, the sisters worked together to support the Cistercian house of La Valasse, the foundation of which had originally been envisaged by their father Henry I, and the process revealed a flash of the Matilda of old. The details are complex and we will not examine them here, but in essence there arose a dispute among the Cistercian hierarchy concerning the transfer of a community of monks to La Valasse from another house, at which point Matilda briskly informed the abbots that she would give her donation and support to another order if they did not go along with her wishes. They gave in.

Her continued donations and almsgiving were not restricted to any one particular order: Benedictines, Cistercians, Cluniacs, Augustinians and Premonstratensians all benefited from Matilda's generosity. In this activity she was exercising the freedom to manage her own affairs that was granted to a noble widow. The funds did not come from Henry or from his duchy's income; rather they were Matilda's own personal wealth, made up of the movable cash and jewels from her days in the Empire and income from her dower lands.

During these years in Normandy Matilda continued to exercise her diplomatic expertise at an international level, as evidenced by a disagreement that arose in 1157 between Henry II and Emperor Frederick Barbarossa, who was the son of Frederick, duke of Swabia, and therefore great-nephew of Matilda's first husband Emperor Henry, and who had succeeded his uncle Conrad on the imperial throne. The squabble concerned the mummified hand of Saint James the Apostle: as we will recall, Matilda had brought this relic with her when she left Germany in 1125; it had subsequently found a home at Reading Abbey, Henry I's flagship foundation. Now, some three decades later, the hand was a prized possession of the abbey and the centre of a growing cult that attracted many pilgrims and patrons. Henry II naturally wanted to hold on to it, and Matilda would no doubt have supported him, keen to sustain and increase the prestige of the abbey where Henry I, source of their justification for royal power, was buried.

The emperor, meanwhile, was eager to have a relic of such significance back within his own borders, and he sent envoys to Henry II with a letter requesting him to send the hand. The exact text of this letter has not come down to us, but we do have Henry's reply, a fine example of the way in which he extricated himself from a difficult position. The letter starts in a style which, although perhaps not quite obsequious, is certainly fulsome:

> To his cordial friend Frederick, by the Grace of God unconquerable Emperor of the Romans, Henry King of England, Duke of Normandy and Aquitaine and Count of Anjou [sends] greetings and the harmony of true affection. We thank your excellency and best of rulers as much as we are able for that you have graced us with your envoys, greeted us in your letters, and were the first to send us gifts and, what we cherish even more, that you began to forge compacts of peace and love between us.

There follows a reasonably lengthy passage rejoicing in their amity and fellowship, and looking forward to continued unity and peace. The actual subject of the reply only squeezes in at the very end, immediately before the sign-off: 'As to the hand of St James about which you wrote to us, we have charged master Heribert and our clerk William to reply for us by word of mouth.' Henry was not prepared to put it in writing, but his answer was a firm 'no', and the hand remained at Reading.

However, there was another issue: regardless of how secure in his position and how powerful Henry might have been at this stage, it was still not a shrewd move to antagonise the emperor. He needed to placate him somehow, so it would be a good idea to send him some other rich gifts in lieu of the hand. Who did Henry know who had experience of the Empire and might be able to advise?

We cannot be absolutely sure that it was Matilda who chose the gifts to send to Frederick Barbarossa, but it would have been foolish not to ask her, and Henry was not foolish. Moreover, the selection of presents certainly implies that she had a hand (no pun intended . . .) in the decision. Among the predictable jewels and falcons was a magnificent pavilion, made of the finest materials and so large that it could only be raised mechanically. Given that Frederick was shortly to travel to Italy, it was just about the most useful thing he could have received, as Matilda, with her own personal experience of crossing the Alps, would have been well aware. There is a record of the pavilion being erected outside Milan once Frederick reached Italy, where it was much admired and used as the venue for a Mass celebrated by the archbishop of Milan.

Amid the pomp of international diplomacy Matilda was careful to maintain family relationships, but she suffered a personal loss in 1158 when her middle son Geoffrey died unexpectedly. Since his rebellion two years previously he had remained loyal to his brother, and had finally seen an improvement in his position. The citizens of Nantes in Brittany had deposed their count, and had applied to Henry II for advice on whom to install as a replacement. He had suggested Geoffrey – a useful way of enriching his brother at someone else's expense – and Geoffrey had been offered the title in 1157. He was not to live to enjoy it, however, dying unmarried and childless just a year later at the age of twenty-four. While Matilda grieved, Henry took Nantes into his own hands and used it to further his own interests in Brittany.

A year after losing her own son, Matilda was to see the final fall of Stephen's dynasty. His surviving son, William, died childless in 1159, thus putting paid to any lingering suspicions that the house of Blois might make a renewed bid for the throne, or that William might be used as a puppet by anyone discontented with Henry. Indeed, Henry went one better, arranging a marriage between William's widow, the heiress Isabel de Warenne, and his own half-brother, Hamelin of Anjou (the illegitimate son of Geoffrey Plantagenet, born during Geoffrey's separation from Matilda), who took the name Warenne and who bound those estates more closely to Angevin interests for years to come.

King Stephen's sole surviving child, Mary, had been a nun since childhood; she was by now abbess of Romsey. As both of her brothers had died childless she was heiress to the rich county of Boulogne, and with this wealth and position at stake she was abducted from the convent by Matthew, a younger son of Thierry of Alsace, count of Flanders (whom we last saw in Chapter 3 bringing stability to that region), who married her and claimed the comital lands and title *jure uxoris*. After bearing him two daughters Mary eventually succeeded in having her marriage annulled, at which point she re-entered religious life, where she remained until her death in 1182. Her little girls were King Stephen's only legitimate grandchildren, but they could never be considered as having a serious claim to the throne of England. Firstly, they were merely the daughters of his daughter; secondly, their mother was a professed nun, kidnapped from the cloister, so doubts could always be raised about their legitimacy; and, thirdly, they belonged to the houses of Flanders and Boulogne. Neither of them ever set foot in England, which was by now ever more firmly in the grasp of the king, Henry fitzEmpress.

In 1160 Matilda fell gravely ill. The situation was serious enough for Henry to rush to her side and for her to make further bequests to churches, monasteries and the poor in anticipation of her demise – all unnecessary, as it happened, as she survived. We do not know exactly what she was suffering from, but it would seem that she was permanently weakened by the experience and never enjoyed a return to full health. It also appears that it was at about this time that Henry began to pay less attention to his mother's advice, although it is debatable whether this was due to her illness or to the growing confidence of a man who had now been king for six years.

In 1161 Theobald, the archbishop of Canterbury, died. He had held the position for twenty-two years, braving difficult circumstances to work towards peace throughout the realm and within the church; careful thought needed to be given to his successor. The new archbishop would be elected by the monks of Canterbury, but in practice the wishes of the king would weigh heavily in the equation, and Henry's favoured candidate was his friend, close advisor and chancellor Thomas Becket – an unexpected choice to be head of the church in England, given that he was a layman. Matilda was adamantly opposed to his appointment, an opinion in which she was joined by Gilbert Foliot, formerly abbot of Gloucester (and correspondent of Brian fitzCount), and now bishop of Hereford. Henry ignored them, and in 1162 the monks duly voted according to their king's wishes and elected Thomas Becket. Becket was ordained a priest on 2 June 1162 and enthroned as archbishop the day afterwards.

It is not the purpose of this book to analyse in detail Henry's subsequent relationship with Becket; suffice it to say that he might have wished he had listened to his mother. It is evident from surviving correspondence that she was later entreated at a very high level to intervene in the disputes that arose between them. Thomas wrote to ask her to intercede, making reference to her influence, her hereditary right in the kingdom and her past actions: 'You ought, if you please, employ the diligence of a mother and the authority of a lady to recall him to duty, you who acquired the kingdom and duchy for him with much effort and transmitted hereditary rights to him in succession.'

He got short shrift in reply:

To Thomas, archbishop of Canterbury, Empress Matilda. The lord pope [Alexander III] charged and enjoined me for the remission of my sins to intervene to re-establish peace between my son the king and you and attempt to reconcile you with him. Then, as you know, you also asked me, wherefore with greater dedication, as much for the honour of God as for the honour of holy church, I took pains to begin and manage the matter. But it seemed very grave to the king and his barons and council, since he asserts that though he loved and honoured you and made you lord of his whole kingdom and all his lands, and raised you to greater honour than anyone in his land, so that he should believe more securely in you than in any other, you disturbed his whole kingdom against him as much as you could so that little was left for you to do but to disinherit him by force ... One thing more I tell you truly, that you cannot recover the grace of the king except by great humility and most evident moderation.

This is the real Matilda, her character continuing to shine through in the evening of her life: the woman who is not afraid to intervene in affairs of the highest order, and who has no qualms about giving even so lofty a personage as the archbishop of Canterbury a thorough dressing-down ... and no doubts about her right to do so. If Becket dared to make a reply to this missive, it has not survived.

Amid the travails of the Henry–Becket relationship, Matilda was grieved in January 1164 by the death of her youngest son, William. He had remained loyal to Henry and enjoyed the income of his many lands in England, but he had sailed to Normandy to retire to the abbey of Bec in 1163, perhaps indicating that he was already ill. As with so many of the other young men in our story, he died before his time and childless; Matilda had him buried in Rouen Cathedral.

All her hopes for the future were now invested in her one surviving son, Henry. Fortunately, thanks to him she had a growing brood of grandchildren: again in an echo of events elsewhere, Eleanor had cast off previous accusations of difficulty in conceiving to give birth to six children in the first twelve years of her second marriage. The couple's eldest son William had died in infancy, but they had since produced three more sons and two daughters (the elder, naturally, named Matilda) who all survived; they would shortly have a third daughter and a fourth surviving son, the last born when Eleanor was forty-four. Matilda could be confident that her grandsons would continue the dynasty of English kings she had founded, and that her granddaughters would contribute to the family honour in due course by making favourable marriage alliances. One union had already been arranged, intended to forge a more lasting peace between France and Normandy: the eldest surviving son of the marriage of Henry and Eleanor, another Henry, had been betrothed to Margaret, daughter of King Louis of France by his second wife, when he was five and she was just two years old.

Events in France were of course of great interest and importance to Matilda, and she had been keeping herself informed of developments. Louis VII had remarried in 1154, two years after his divorce, to Constance, the daughter of Alfonso VII of León and Castile (who was himself the son of the former queen regnant Urraca, whose career we discussed in Chapter 3). Constance bore him two daughters but died in childbirth with the second in 1160. By that time Louis was in his mid-thirties and desperate for a son, so he married again just five weeks later, this time to the teenage Adela, sister of the counts of Champagne and Blois, and daughter of Matilda's cousin Theobald. Initially this decision looked to have backfired, for Adela did not become pregnant and Louis grew anxious once again, unable this time to play the consanguinity card to rid himself of a wife. But after an agonising five-year wait Adela conceived, and in 1165 she gave birth to the future Philip II, known to posterity as Philip Augustus.

With the relief of finally having a male heir to plan for, Louis was emboldened. Tensions arose between him and Henry II, and once more Matilda – now the elder stateswoman of western Europe – was called in to try to defuse the situation. In the summer of 1167 war was threatening in the Vexin, the long-disputed area on the Norman–French border; Matilda was by now too infirm to travel far, but she engaged in correspondence with Louis. As ever, her style was forthright, as can be seen in this excerpt from one of her letters:

To Louis, by the grace of God excellent king of the Franks and her natural lord, Matilda, empress and daughter of a king, [sends] greetings and loyal service with love. May your excellency recall that I have often asked you about the quarrel between you and my son, the king of England, but you have made no response which satisfies or informs me. Therefore I am sending Remigius of St Valery to implore your highness: do not delay, if it please you, to send me the details about the quarrel. For unless you do so, such may happen between you that I will not be able to amend.

A truce was agreed between the two kings in August 1167, partly due to Matilda's intervention. Henry took the opportunity to travel to Brittany to press his claims there; it was the only part of western France not under his direct control. The Breton succession had been murky for some years, involving deathbed claims of illegitimacy, disinheritance and family in-fighting, and Henry was poised to take advantage of the chaos – he had a foothold already, as he held the city of Nantes. He would eventually succeed in his aims in Brittany, forcing the duke to step aside in favour of his only child, a daughter named Constance, whom Henry betrothed to his third son Geoffrey. But his mother the empress would not live to see it.

Matilda had been in failing health for some time and she died at Rouen on 10 September 1167, at the age of sixty-five, surrounded by the brothers of Bec; the monk and chronicler Stephen of Rouen travelled to Brittany in person to break the news to Henry. Matilda had little to bequeath to her son; he had already received everything she had spent her life fighting for. She was buried before the high altar at the abbey of Bec, to which most of her remaining riches were donated, including both the crowns she had brought from Germany and a golden cross, two gospel books bound in gold and studded with gems, and other precious items including the ornaments and vestments from her private household chapel.

The funeral was conducted by Hugh, archbishop of Rouen, assisted by Matilda's associate of many years, Arnulf, bishop of Lisieux, and in the presence of many monks and clergy. The epitaph on her tomb was the one we quoted in our introduction:

> Great by birth, greater by marriage, greatest in her offspring
> Here lies the daughter, wife and mother of Henry.

* * *

Matilda's body was, in death, to enjoy as little rest as she had had in life. The abbey of Bec was sacked in both 1418 and 1421 during the later stages of the Hundred Years' War, and Matilda's tomb was destroyed during one incident or the other, probably the second; the pillaging English troops of Henry V were presumably unaware that they were desecrating the remains of his seven-times great-grandmother. When restoration work was undertaken in 1684 some of Matilda's bones were found and reburied at Bec, but her tomb was destroyed again in the 1790s during the French Revolution, as part of the rejection of all things royal. Her remains were finally re-interred in Rouen Cathedral in 1846, though one can only speculate on how Matilda might have felt about ultimately losing her centuries-old argument with her father about where she should be buried.

There are not as many extant epitaphs of Matilda as we might have expected, given her pivotal role in the affairs of England and Normandy. A later writer, Ralph of Diss, was aiming to praise Henry II's daughters when he said that they shared 'the nobility of their grandmother the empress, and her masculine courage in a female body ... an example of fortitude and patience'. Robert de Torigni and Stephen of Rouen, as might be expected, left thoughts of their own. Robert is fairly circumspect at the actual moment of Matilda's death; it occurs while he is in the middle of a narration of Henry's campaign in Brittany, so he merely says that 'the intelligence of the death of his mother, the empress Matilda, reached him ... her affectionate son distributed countless treasures among churches, monasteries, lepers, and others of the poor, for the good of her soul'. But at an earlier point in his work, where he writes more specifically of Matilda while she was still alive, he is more forthcoming: 'She was truly a woman of excellent disposition, kind to all, bountiful in her almsgiving, the friend of religion, of honest life, one who loved the church, by the abundance of whose gifts the church of Bec has attained no small degree of splendour.'

Stephen of Rouen describes how he travelled to Brittany to break the sad news to Henry, unable to resist the opportunity to note of himself in the third person that 'the monk was well known to the king, and was as beloved as he was faithful'. But he returns swiftly to the proper subject of his narrative, indicating just how much Matilda meant to Henry and to what extent this great king relied on his mother:

Hence the monk intimates to the king that his mother had died.

Beyond the measure of what is believable, he [the king] weeps and
    laments.

Not surprisingly; nothing in the world is more beloved than her
    to him.

For she gave him the crown, and she was his mother.

This was his father's legacy, who ordered him always to love his mother.

And to be obedient to his own counsels.

Mindful of this, he subjected three things to his mother's rule:

Himself, his own behaviour, and his rulership too.

Stephen adds that Henry losing his mother is like a ship losing its anchor, and he later refers to her as *magna Mathildis*, 'the great Matilda'.

Stephen of Rouen knew Matilda only towards the end of her life, when she was considered a benign matriarchal influence; his eulogy after her death is therefore not particularly unexpected. But the great warrior Matilda should not be allowed to fade away in such a conventional manner. A more fitting way to end this chapter is to quote the words of Gilbert Foliot, the eminent bishop who knew Matilda when she was in England, when she was fighting for her rights, and when she was at the very height of her unpopularity. His assessment of her at that crucial time was markedly different from that of others:

> She crossed the sea, passed over mountains, penetrated into unknown regions, married there at her father's command, and remained there carrying out the duties of imperial rule virtuously and piously ... and though she had attained such high rank that, it is reported, she had the title and status of queen of the Romans, she was in no way puffed up with pride, but meekly submitted in all things to her father's will ... in all this you will not find any cause why she should have been disinherited.

CONCLUSION

WILLIAM THE CONQUEROR'S FAMED IRON will was inherited by some of his children and grandchildren, but not others. This resulted in conflict, death and destruction across large parts of England and Normandy for more than six decades after his death, struggles that were further complicated by two additional factors: that no strictly defined procedure for the (Anglo-Norman) transmission of the English crown had yet been established, and that his ruthless determination to succeed was not transmitted along gendered lines. Most notably, it passed his eldest son Robert Curthose by; it also failed to instil itself to any great extent in either Stephen or Theobald of Blois or Robert of Gloucester. William Clito showed signs of it and, had he lived longer, the succession in Normandy and potentially even in England might have looked very different. But the Conqueror's steel was certainly inherited by three of his children – William Rufus, Henry I and Adela of Blois – and two of his grandchildren, Bishop Henry and Matilda.

The men of this rarefied group were able to pursue their own paths, whether secular or clerical, with varying degrees of success but with nobody doubting their right to do so. Adela and Matilda, on the other hand, had to make their way through a world filled with gendered expectations. Adela did so in the approved manner: she married a nobleman chosen by her father and exerted authority in his name rather than her own, managing his affairs while he was away; after his death she took advantage of her widowed status appropriately by arranging suitable marriages for her daughters and

237

careers for her sons, unsentimentally putting the eldest aside when he failed to live up to her expectations; and once she had seen them all settled on their paths she again conformed to societal expectations by retiring to a convent.

Matilda, like her aunt, had grit and determination in abundance, but she was destined for a different path. Initially it did not seem so, and a more conventional existence beckoned: sidelined by the birth of a brother and sent away to marry a foreign ruler, she had the life of a queen consort mapped out for her. And she made a success of this, despite the terrifying beginnings. Many girls of eight might have been overwhelmed at being shipped off alone to a foreign land – especially when they were then married to an older man and expected to consummate the union at the age of twelve – but the evidence demonstrates that Matilda did not merely survive; she thrived. She made a favourable impression both on Emperor Henry and on his subjects; she immersed herself in their world and learned all she could of its language, politics and governance. By the time she was sixteen she was ruling northern Italy on her husband's behalf, a position of daunting responsibility to which he would not have appointed her if he had not thought her capable, and with which she coped admirably and easily.

But then two incidents beyond her control changed the course of Matilda's life and raised her expectations: the deaths in 1120 of William Adelin and in 1125 of Emperor Henry. If we examine her actions in the decade between 1125 and 1135, trying to see her simply as a person, we might conclude that her conduct was not exceptional, as the eldest and only surviving legitimate child of the reigning monarch, 'born in the purple' and descended on both sides from royalty, to whom the magnates had sworn allegiance, and who expected to succeed to the throne. But it was impossible at the time not to view her situation through the lens of gender; she was not a person but a woman, and thus her ambitions became both unusual and unacceptable.

It has been said on numerous occasions, to the point where it is almost generally accepted, that it was in the summer of 1141, when she began acting 'haughtily', that Matilda's 'true character' came to light – normally in an attempt to justify an argument that she would not have made a good monarch, and that England had a narrow escape from the horror of rule by a self-important woman. We will return to the incidents of 1141 shortly, but this author would argue quite forcefully that it was actually the events of 1135–39 that show us the real Matilda. Stephen was in England, crowned, accepted and with the whole English treasury at his disposal. Matilda was stuck at Argentan, immobilised by pregnancy, in possession of limited funds and written out of the story. It would have been all too easy for her to give up at that point, to accept her lot and her future as the countess of Anjou. But she did not. Instead, she marshalled all the resources she could while keeping a firm eye on the future, and when she was rewarded with the one piece of luck that came her way, the defection of Robert of Gloucester to her cause, she was in a position to make the most of it. As we noted in Chapter 5, depictions of Matilda's entry on to the English stage in 1139 tend towards the passive, but it might just be the case that, in realising that Stephen would act in the predictable way that he did and planning accordingly, she was in fact the author of a brilliant strategic coup.

Throughout her career, and in subsequent interpretations of it, Matilda has not been given the credit she deserves for her actions. We have at least managed to move away from the view that prevailed up until the middle of the twentieth century, that she was merely the puppet or passive figurehead for her half-brother (one noted historian of the era even referred to her faction as 'Robert's party', as if Matilda had nothing to do with it), or indeed barely mentioning her at all. This, as noted in the introduction, may stem from the prominence given in historical writing at that time to men and men's actions. From a more modern viewpoint, and in the light of more recent studies in queenship and on individual women in the Middle Ages, we should no longer accept this interpretation; indeed, we should go further, recognising her not just as an equal partner in the enterprise but as its undoubted leader.

One of the words used to describe Matilda in the title of this book is 'warrior'. This term can, of course, be interpreted in several ways. Matilda did not don armour or set out to participate in battle personally – although the evidence of the Anonymous of Béthune indicates that she was later remembered as having done so – but she was directly involved in several military engagements, such as those at Le Sap in 1136, Winchester in 1141 and Oxford in 1142, as well as the stand-off at Arundel in 1139, and she was certainly at the head of the table while the overall strategy of her English campaign was being formulated. She might therefore be considered more as a general than a soldier, planning her battles although not executing them in person; but then, the same could be said of many male generals, whose status as 'warrior' is not questioned or dismissed as Matilda's has been.

What is now clear is that Matilda took action and the initiative on her own behalf to a greater extent than has previously been believed. A woman like her – crowned queen of one realm at eight and another at fifteen, sole imperial regent in Italy at sixteen, who had fought past every obstacle thrown in her path since – when presented with the opportunity to invade England and take the crown that she saw as hers by right, did not suddenly ignore a lifetime of political and strategic experience, sit back and leave everything to Robert of Gloucester. The idea is implausible, if not down-right laughable. Indeed, as noted in Chapter 8, what we really need to do is turn the accepted narrative on its head and recognise that it was *he* who was indebted to *her* for giving him the opportunity to make more of his life than he might otherwise have done.

Matilda was an active participant in the military aspects of her campaign, not merely a figurehead. And, as any text on the subject will tell us, war is not just about the battles themselves. The logistical systems that Matilda and her advisors had put in place to ensure that troops could be raised quickly and efficiently when needed were major factors in the victory at Lincoln, enabling Robert and the army to arrive earlier than Stephen was expecting and thus forcing him to rush his own plans.

Matilda's lack of direct combat experience did count against her at Winchester in September 1141: she should certainly have taken the decision to withdraw from the impossible situation much earlier, a course of action that might have avoided Robert's capture and the consequent necessity of releasing Stephen from his prison. But, to balance this mistake, she did single-handedly engineer her own intrepid escape from the siege of Oxford in the depths of winter in 1142, saving herself from capture and ensuring that the war could go on.

A woman at war was a problem for some twelfth-century contemporaries. Or rather, to be more precise: the issue was not that Matilda went to war, but that she did it *on her own behalf*. At this time, men frequently expected women to be able to cope in supposedly 'masculine' fields, managing and defending estates in their husbands' absence (perhaps for years on end if they had travelled overseas), negotiating for their ransom and release if they were captured, and protecting family rights. But, crucially, female action and female agency were acceptable and laudable only when the female in question was acting – even if only nominally – on behalf of a male. This is why Matilda of Boulogne can be praised in the *Deeds of Stephen* for 'forgetting the weakness of her sex and a woman's softness' and bearing herself 'like a man', while the same author, in the same part of the text, criticises Matilda for 'put[ting] on an extremely arrogant demeanour instead of the modest gait and bearing proper to the gentle sex'.

This new and more nuanced interpretation can help to shed light on the seemingly contradictory portrayals of women at war and women in positions of authority that abound in the chronicles we have examined, where some of them – in marked contrast to Matilda and others who sought power in their own right – are praised for taking an active political or military role on behalf of male relatives of all ages. Writing of the latter half of Queen Melisende's reign in Jerusalem, William of Tyre declares that she had 'clearly overcome the status assigned to women', ruling well '*since her son was as yet under age*'; William of Malmesbury says of Æthelflæd, lady of the Mercians, that 'this most powerful woman *assisted her brother greatly*'; Orderic Vitalis tells his readers of a young noblewoman who, in the absence of her husband, kept watch over their castle, wearing a hauberk and patrolling the walls: 'how greatly the young countess deserves praise for *serving her husband* with such loyalty' (my emphasis in all three cases). In no case does a chronicler express surprise that a woman should be capable of taking such action; the reaction to her depends entirely on the context.

There are, of course, some modern parallels to this sort of depiction of women, and we may perhaps be justified in expressing surprise at such marked similarities despite eight centuries having elapsed. It is not difficult to find disparities in the portrayal of those women who, in their position as politicians' wives, are lauded for their community or charity work in traditionally feminine areas, and those who seek office on their own behalf.

A brief analysis of Matilda's character may help to explain why she was able to keep her campaign going for as long as she did. One key factor here is that she inspired a remarkable loyalty and devotion in her followers; it is unlikely that they would have remained by her side through thick and thin (and especially thin) if they had not believed in her cause and in her personally. They fought for their liege lady with the same determination and skill that they appreciated in her. This may in part be attributed to residual loyalty to Henry I, particularly in the cases of Robert of Gloucester, Miles of Hereford and Brian fitzCount, who all had cause to be grateful to the old king. But as the years went by this became less of a factor, so we must look to Matilda herself for an explanation.

Of importance here is that Matilda never seems to have engaged in the sort of double-dealing that was a factor in Stephen's lessening popularity: she might have had trouble attracting magnates to her cause, but once they were there she dealt fairly with them. Stephen, on the other hand, could be recklessly generous only to turn around and suspect his favourites of acting against him – as could be attested by Geoffrey de Mandeville, Ranulf de Gernon, the de Clare family and various bishops over the years. He was erratic in his patronage, his politics and his martial dealings: he made threats he failed to carry out and promises on which he failed to deliver, neither of which was what the magnates needed from a military leader or a monarch. Matilda, meanwhile, observed the rules of war as closely as any knight, and this was appreciated by her supporters. She may not have had as many long-term adherents as Stephen, but what she lacked in quantity she made up for in quality – which is one of the principal reasons why the war lasted so long despite the vast disparity in resource between the two parties. Robert, Miles and Brian were three powerful and influential men who never wavered from her service for an instant once they had sworn allegiance to her in 1139, so they must have seen something in her besides being merely her father's daughter. Similarly, the dowager queen Adeliza took quite a risk in offering shelter to Matilda at Arundel, and this cannot be entirely attributed to a residual loyalty to Henry I.

On the subject of Brian fitzCount, here is perhaps the place to reiterate that any assertions that he and Matilda had some kind of affair (as proposed by at least one of Matilda's less scholarly biographers, as well as various writers of fiction) are false. There is a logical basis for this statement, which can be drawn from contemporary evidence. Those chroniclers of the war in England who opposed Matilda presented her negatively, as we have seen on multiple occasions. For any twelfth-century writer, the easiest way to denigrate a woman or destroy her reputation was to accuse her of promiscuity (rumours of unchaste behaviour were certainly circulated about Eleanor of

Aquitaine while she was on crusade, for example, and there are many other cases including both Melisende of Jerusalem and Urraca of León and Castile). Therefore, if there had been even the slightest hint of Matilda having an adulterous relationship with Brian – or, indeed, with anyone else – the hostile writers would have pounced on it, made much of it and used it to illustrate why Matilda was unfit to rule. But they did not: the fact that they were reduced to criticising her merely for supposed 'masculine' behaviour shows that they had nothing else to accuse her of.

Two facets of Matilda's character also make it extremely unlikely that she would undertake such a liaison. Firstly, she was known to be pious and she would certainly have been aware of the church's rules on marital fidelity, and unlikely to contemplate breaking them so scandalously. And, secondly, it would have been political suicide: such a relationship could never be maintained in absolute secrecy, and as soon as it became common knowledge – or even common rumour – it would have sounded the death knell to any hopes of her acceding to the throne. Matilda has been accused of many things over the years, but stupidity is not one of them, and the woman who had given up so much in pursuit of her goal would not have acted in so foolhardy a manner.

To return to the subject of Matilda's portrayal by chroniclers, it is worth noting that even those more favourably disposed towards her struggled to find appropriate terms to describe her. By far the most common positive epithets used about women in twelfth-century literature are 'noble' and 'beautiful'; if the woman in question is married then praise relating to fertility comes in third. This gives us a very good idea of the attributes for which women were valued, and of how far outside that paradigm Matilda sat. Chroniclers therefore had great difficulty in finding positive epithets for such an active woman without resorting to male adjectives, which tied them in narrative knots: we are relying on the testimony of men who did not even have a vocabulary to describe what they were seeing.

Something on which a number of hostile writers (and even some of the more neutral ones) agree is Matilda's so-called arrogance and haughtiness when she was named lady of the English in 1141; this requires closer investigation as part of our analysis of her character. As we noted in Chapter 6, the same behaviour exhibited by a man who had just been proclaimed king and who was awaiting coronation would be at worst unremarkable and more probably praiseworthy: comporting himself with suitable dignity, speaking with authority, acting decisively and arranging matters to his own satisfaction. Such behaviour was only considered 'arrogant' because it was being displayed by a woman who was acting in a manner which male magnates, churchmen and chroniclers considered unsuitable. Their fear of the unknown, of the upsetting of the gendered status quo, caused them to lash out.

Let us also consider the situation from Matilda's own point of view. Despite her exalted rank she had always been, in personal matters at least, powerless. She had been sent away from her home as a child, never to see her affectionate mother again; she was forced to marry a stranger, a much older man; she had to adapt to a new country and a new language. All this happened during her childhood, but even as an adult – and an adult of sense, intelligence and experience, at that – she was forced into the humiliating position of having to marry a boy more than a decade her junior, against her will. After attempting to leave him, she was sent back, control of the situation belonging to her father and her husband rather than to her. Who, having endured a lifetime of such indignities and abuses, would not relish the sudden rush of freedom, the realisation that nobody could tell them what to do any longer? Matilda's descendant Queen Victoria, on succeeding to the British throne in 1837, valued the personal freedom and agency she would thenceforth enjoy after a stifling childhood; how much greater must the release have seemed to a mature woman seven centuries earlier? This is something no twelfth-century nobleman, the head of his household and the agent of his own destiny, could possibly have understood.

The evidence of Matilda's later actions also argues against charges of arrogance. If she was as stubborn as has sometimes been implied, she would have kept on the same path, grimly clinging to the belief of her own superiority and sure that it would be recognised eventually. But she did not: she was sufficiently self-aware, after the disaster of mid-1141, to realise that she was never going to be crowned and that therefore she should change her approach. After the crushing defeat at Winchester in September and the subsequent loss of Stephen from her custody, she rethought, reorganised her priorities and made Henry her focus. What it must have cost her in personal terms to sideline herself in favour of a male relative, even one as dear as her son, can only be imagined, but the actions she took were the very opposite of arrogance. Matilda fought on and on in Henry's name, in

England and in Normandy, tackling not just the English king but the French one as well, and eventually received the 'reward' of her son's recognition and coronation – which she did not even witness, in order to avoid detriment to his cause. She then acted in a subordinate position to her son, sacrificing her own ambitions to the overall dynastic objective as she kept a firm grip on Normandy on his behalf, and still interacting with kings, emperors and archbishops to the end of her life.

Matilda never became queen of England. But could she have done anything differently that might have improved her chances of success?

To a certain extent the answer must be 'yes': she did not by any means mount a perfect campaign or act without fault, and it is important that we acknowledge her weaknesses in this regard. Matilda could have made a bolder bid for the crown of England as soon as she heard of her father's death late in 1135; she was not aware at that time of her uncle David's support from Scotland, but she could perhaps have anticipated it and acted accordingly. Her pregnancy was undoubtedly a major factor in her not making an immediate physical move, but she could have been bolder in her statements and in seeking support from those men who had previously sworn to uphold her rights in the English succession.

Matilda and Geoffrey's conflict with Henry I towards the end of the old king's life put Matilda in a difficult position. Overall she had done the right thing in accepting – however reluctantly – the match with Geoffrey: her position as heir depended on it, as we discussed in Chapter 3. She could, therefore, not really be blamed for siding with her husband against her father when they were at odds, although once again it might have been possible to handle the situation better; she does not appear to have been a particularly effective peacemaker. It was unfortunate that Henry died when he did, but given his age it could hardly be considered unexpected so a few more overtures at reconciliation, perhaps involving his adored grandsons, might not have gone amiss.

When Robert of Gloucester came over to Matilda's side in the early summer of 1138 they could have moved more quickly to invade England. They might not have had the element of surprise – Robert's decision to renounce his homage to Stephen publicly and formally had put paid to that – but they could have taken advantage of the rebellions that were already springing up in Herefordshire and Shropshire, and the continuing incursions from Scotland, all of which were taking up a great deal of Stephen's time and attention. But in the event it was a year and a half before they actually sailed, meaning that the rebellions had been quashed or had petered out, and they had to start from scratch in a position of relative weakness. Once established, Matilda's party did have a great deal of success in proportion to their resources, and she approached her claim to the throne in the appropriate manner by acting as if she were the rightful monarch, issuing grants, minting coins and lodging in a royal residence. Her party enjoyed success at Lincoln in February 1141 and endured disaster at Winchester just seven months later, but the crux of the whole campaign came in between the two, and far away from any battlefield.

Stephen was a good knight and a loyal follower – of his uncle, if not his cousin – who exhibited both personal bravery and tactical acumen. He also appears to have been a pleasant man who cared for his immediate family. But more than this was needed in order to be an effective king in the context of the twelfth century, and here Stephen failed. He was too much in the habit of relying on his advisors, thus building a reputation for indecision, and he could be easily influenced by whoever held sway over him at the time, examples of his favourites including (but not being limited to) Bishop Henry and Waleran de Beaumont. He failed to retain the support of the aristocracy, despite creating more earldoms than all his Anglo-Norman predecessors put together. Various magnates used Stephen's flaws as an excuse to rebel. Some did this on Matilda's behalf, either actually or nominally, and others for their own benefit; but in either case Matilda's cause was a convenient excuse. However, it was only useful while she was, as it were, the leader of the opposition; as soon as it looked as though she had really succeeded, as soon as it looked like a woman might *actually* be crowned in her own right, there was insecurity and panic.

Matilda was almost the opposite of Stephen. Had she been a man, her conduct and actions would have been seen for what they were: decisive, firm and autocratic, in the mould of Henry I, who was universally considered a good king – if sometimes not a particularly likeable man. But, crucially, she was not a man, and she could have made more of an effort to mitigate this disadvantage. Matilda believed that she should not be treated any differently from a male contender for the throne, but this was unrealistic in the contemporary context and she should have realised that she needed to play a different game. However much it galled her to play the feminine role, to act in a way that the barons would see as 'womanly', she could have swallowed her pride and her instincts and tried harder, for political gain.

But, having said that, we must equally recognise that had she acted in a more conventionally feminine way, she would have been rejected for kingship anyway on the basis that she was too soft. She was trapped in a no-win situation. Power in the twelfth century was inherently male and, as we noted above, the only effective way for a woman to exercise authority was to do it in the name of a man. Nobody questioned Matilda's right to act as regent in Italy when it was on behalf of her husband. Nobody questioned Queen Edith-Matilda's proxy rule over England when Henry I was absent. Stephen's wife Matilda of Boulogne was praised for her exploits in support of her husband, despite them being very similar to the actions for which Matilda was censured.

Therefore, it would seem that the only possible way in which Matilda could have done better in her English quest would have been to declare from the start that she was campaigning to put her son Henry on the throne, to fight for *his* rights as the old king's grandson. Had she been trying to convince the magnates that she could make an effective regent – supported by Robert of Gloucester, who was both highly regarded by his peers and not seen as a threat – then she might just have succeeded, or at least might have been better received than she actually was. She might have retained some personal royal status: as her sons were only aged two and one at the time, and given high rates of infant mortality, it could have been emphasised that if they died then any future sons of hers would be next in line to inherit.

But Matilda's own pride would not allow her to take such a course of action, and justifiably so: it was *she* who was the king's daughter, *she* who had been 'born in the purple', and *she* who had been named heir to the English throne. She wanted it for herself, and why should she not? However, fighting for her own rights in such a patriarchal society was doomed to failure, a fact that she did eventually realise, but only after a bloody decade during which England had been worn to rags by the attritional nature of the conflict – a decade during which both she and Stephen were more preoccupied with the question of who was to reign than with the state of the realm that would be left for the victor to rule over.

So much for the twelfth-century interpretation of events. From our twenty-first-century perspective we must have some sympathy for Matilda's position and ask why she should not have put forward her own claims when she had the blood right to inherit the crown and the political skill and military support to keep it. With the benefit of hindsight, we can see that her chances of being crowned queen in her own right all but disappeared in the summer of 1141. If Matilda could not get the crown put on her head even with the king in her custody, even with the evidence of God's support in battle to add to her hereditary claims, then she was never going to. Her triumph at Lincoln was not the catalyst for a mass defection to her; some magnates came over to her only when they thought she was actually on the point of coronation, and others not at all. And once her fortunes were reversed many of them melted away, leaving her with only those loyalists who were hers to start with, those who thought that she as a woman was capable of ruling – and there were simply not enough of these to force a result.

The conclusion we must come to is this: Matilda could have done better, but whatever she did she was never going to win, because of the simple fact that she was a woman. If Matilda had acceded to the English throne in her own right, her reign would have been beset by troubles. To begin with, she would have needed to rely on someone else to lead her armies; this might also have been the case for a male king who was young, old or incapacitated, but it would have been used against her in a way that simply would not have applied to them. No monarch is perfect, but Matilda's every slip would have been jumped on as being representative of her entire sex. When Stephen did something his magnates did not like, they might have complained, they might have rebelled; but they did not generally use it as the basis for an argument that men were temperamentally unsuited to rule.

Medieval England countenanced the reign of several underage boys and at least one lunatic – to say nothing of various men who were alleged to have been murderers, rapists, or both – but never of a woman. There would not be a queen regnant until Mary I in 1553, and even then we might qualify her accession by noting that there was no viable male candidate available: all the other half-dozen possibles were also women. So what chance did Matilda have, four hundred years earlier? The answer is, without a doubt, none.

* * *

By her own, perhaps rather black-and-white, standards, Matilda's campaign in England was a failure. She did not overthrow Stephen, she was not crowned and she was never recognised as queen regnant. However, eminent figures from history need to be judged over a longer term, greater than the span of their own lifetimes, and by these measures Matilda's influence was much more significant than it might have seemed to her on her deathbed. Having discussed what she did not achieve, let us conclude by examining what she did.

If Matilda had not doggedly pursued and fought for her rights, the subsequent royal line of England would have looked very different, with the throne passing to the ineffectual William of Blois (or, indeed, the erratic Eustace of Boulogne, who might not have died in 1153 had he not been disinherited) instead of the energetic Henry fitzEmpress. There would have been no royal Plantagenet dynasty. Every subsequent monarch of England, and later Great Britain, has been a direct descendant of Matilda – although, as she might have been pleased to note from the turmoil surrounding the inheritance of the various dynasties of York, Lancaster, Tudor, Stuart and Hanover, not necessarily by direct male primogeniture. Matilda will never be listed among the monarchs of England, as she was uncrowned in an era when coronation was the paramount signifier of kingship, but her influence on the royal line was profound.

As the blazer of a new trail, Matilda was also the setter of precedents that influenced later events. She was the first Anglo-Norman to carve out a role as a politically active queen mother, a baton that was picked up enthusiastically and effectively by her daughter-in-law Eleanor of Aquitaine, as well as other future dowagers. She was the first to prove that the crown could at least be transmitted through the female line: Henry II sat on the throne but – his treaty of 1153 with Stephen notwithstanding – he derived his right to do so from Matilda as the daughter of Henry I. A similar situation would arise in 1485 when Henry VII, who claimed the throne via his maternal line, would be crowned himself even though his mother was still alive.

Matilda's precedent of transmission via the female line was an important step on the path towards female sovereignty, and later queens regnant would benefit from her pioneering activities. As we noted above, the first woman to rule over England in her own right was Mary I, elder daughter of Henry VIII. When she acceded the prevailing thought was that she could or should act as queen regnant only until such time as she married, upon which her husband would become king; however, the idea was addressed and rebuffed in the 1554 *Acte declaring that the Regall Power of this Realme is in the Quenes Majestie as fully and absolutely as ever it was in any of her moste noble Progenitours Kinges of this Realme*, which established biblical and historical precedents – and referenced Matilda. The question of subordination to a husband has not arisen in relation to any queen regnant in England since that time.

Matilda was, as her epitaph stated, a daughter, wife and mother. But she was much more than that. She was a twice-crowned queen, an empress, and 'lady of the English'; she was a well-travelled, politically astute woman of the world; she was an able strategist who could understand and take advantage of complex military situations; she was someone who had a cause to believe in and who never gave up on it. Given the gendered constraints within which she was forced to operate, she achieved much more than might feasibly have been expected. She did not meet with unalloyed success or appreciation during her lifetime, but her great achievement was her legacy – and also that both her triumphs and her failures were her own. In a world that expected her to be an accessory, an adjunct, a cipher, Matilda was the master of her fate and the agent of her own destiny, and it is thus that she deserves to be remembered.

SOURCES AND TRANSLATIONS

Primary sources

THE *ANGLO-SAXON CHRONICLE*, INCLUDING the version of it known as the *Peterborough Chronicle*, is widely available in translation in print (Michael Swanton's 1996 edition is both comprehensive and accessible) and online. The full text of the Peterborough manuscript is available from, among other sites, Project Gutenberg at http://www.gutenberg.org/ebooks/657 (accessed 30 August 2018). Those who relish the challenge of reading from the original manuscripts in Old English may do so at the Luna website, at http://bodley30.bodley.ox.ac.uk:8180/luna/servlet/view/all/what/MS.+Laud+Misc.+636 (accessed 30 August 2018).

Wace's *Roman de Rou* and Benoît de Sainte-Maure's *Chronique des ducs de Normandie* were both originally written in the Anglo-Norman dialect of Old French, and they are both available in French editions. Wace's text is also available in English, in the excellent 2004 translation of Glyn Burgess; Benoît's, alas, is not.

Five of the German chronicles, as noted in the introduction, have been the subject of different authorial attributions and mis-attributions over the years; editions and translations dating from the nineteenth century and the first half of the twentieth may list authors and texts in various combinations. The work of Franz-Josef Schmale and Irene Schmale-Ott in the 1960s and 1970s began the disambiguation; further detailed research was carried out by T.J.H. McCarthy, and it is his 2014 edition, collectively entitled *Chronicles of the Investiture Contest*, that I have followed here. Otto of Freising's chronicle has been translated into both German and English, the latter most widely available in the 1928 translation of Charles Mierow, which was revised by Karl Morrison in 2002.

The major series that collates the medieval Latin historical writing of England is the Rolls Series, which comprises 99 works in 253 volumes published between 1858 and 1911, although nearly all of them are available only in the original Latin – it being assumed in those days that anyone with an interest in reading such things would not require a translation. Since that time, many new editions and translations of the works cited in this book have become available.

The Oxford Medieval Texts series, started in the 1950s, continues to produce a number of excellent facing-page editions and translations of twelfth-century Latin chronicles, including the *Gesta Stephani* (edited and translated by K.R. Potter, 1976) and the works of Orderic Vitalis (Marjorie Chibnall, six volumes, 1968–80), John of Worcester (Reginald Darlington, Patrick McGurk and Jennifer Bray, three volumes, 1995–98), Henry of Huntingdon (Diana Greenway, 1996), William of Malmesbury's *Gesta regum Anglorum* (K.R. Potter, R.A.B. Mynors, R.M. Thomson and M. Winterbottom, two volumes, 1998–99) and his *Historia novella* (K.R. Potter and Edmund King, 1998). Most of these books are now, unfortunately, relatively difficult to get hold of, so readers who do not have access to an institutional library may like to consult those translations that are more readily accessible: Henry of Huntingdon now has an Oxford World's Classics paperback, for example, and nineteenth-century translations of the other works are available either in hard-copy facsimile reprints or online (on which subject, see below at the end of this section).

The chronicles of Robert de Torigni and Stephen of Rouen are among the most difficult to consult. Both are available via the archive.org website, but only in the original Latin; anyone searching for an English translation of either text will find that Stephen's is not available at all, and Robert's can only be found by being aware (as I wasn't, to start with) that he is occasion-ally also known as Robert de Monte. Joseph Stevenson's 1855 translation was made available in facsimile reprint in 1991 and copies of this are extant, if not exactly easy to find.

All of these primary sources, plus others consulted, are listed in the bibliography; further details on the English texts and their authors can also be found in Antonia Gransden's *Historical Writing in England, Vol. I: c. 550–c. 1307* (1974). In each case, while the more modern editions listed in the bibliography for each work are generally to be preferred, I have also listed the older editions, as those from the nineteenth century are now generally freely available via various online libraries and archive sites. The most comprehensive of these are archive.org, Gallica and Monumenta Germaniae Historica, for works published in Britain, France and Germany respectively; web addresses for these and other online resources may be found at the end of the bibliography.

Secondary sources

The major academic biography of Matilda, as mentioned in the introduction, is Marjorie Chibnall's *The Empress Matilda: Queen Consort, Queen Mother and Lady of the English* (1991), without which any subsequent work would be much the poorer. She is also the subject of the less scholarly *Empress Matilda: Uncrowned Queen of England* (1978) by Nesta Pain; more recently she features as a case study both in Helen Castor's *She-Wolves: The Women Who Ruled England before Elizabeth* (2010) and in Charles Beem's *The Lioness Roared: The Problems of Female Rule in English History* (2006), both of which feature clear and in-depth analysis of the problems Matilda faced due to her sex.

Numerous biographies of Stephen are available, all providing indispensable information on Matilda and her activities, albeit from a different point of view. Chief among these are Edmund King's *King Stephen* (2010) in the Yale English Monarchs series and R.H.C. Davis's *King Stephen* (1967; 1990). Valuable accounts of Stephen's reign, as well as his life, are John Appleby's *The Troubled Reign of King Stephen* (1970), H.A. Cronne's *The Reign of Stephen: Anarchy in England 1135–54* (1970) and David Crouch's *The Reign of King Stephen: 1135–1154* (2000; 2013).

Information on Matilda may also be gleaned from biographies of her father and her son; here I have found Judith A. Green's *Henry I: King of England and Duke of Normandy* (2006; 2009) of particular interest, along with C. Warren Hollister's *Henry I* (2001) and W.L. Warren's *Henry II*

(1973; 1991; 2000), both in the Yale English Monarchs series. Chris Given-Wilson and Alice Curteis include a very useful chapter on Robert of Gloucester in their *The Royal Bastards of Medieval England* (1984).

A great deal of scholarship on medieval queenship has been produced during the past two decades, and I have benefited enormously from reading the many different articles in *Medieval Queenship*, edited by John Carmi Parsons (1994); *Queens and Queenship in Medieval Europe*, edited by Anne Duggan (1997); *Queens and Power in Medieval and Early Modern England*, edited by Carole Levin and Robert Bucholz (2009); and Elizabeth Norton's *England's Queens: The Biography* (2012). Lindy Grant's *Blanche of Castile: Queen of France* (2016), a biography of Matilda's great-granddaughter, contains both discussions on women in positions of power generally and a number of references to Matilda herself; Ralph Turner's *Eleanor of Aquitaine* (2009) is a wonderful study of a woman who was obliged to wield power through the men in her life.

On Matilda's war in England, the best specific source is Jim Bradbury's *Stephen and Matilda: The Civil War of 1139–53* (1996; 2005). There are numerous works on warfare of this period more generally; some that include the study of Matilda and the Anglo-Normans are John Beeler, *Warfare in England 1066–1189* (1966); Stephen Morillo, *Warfare under the Anglo-Norman Kings 1066–1135* (1994); Michael Prestwich, *Armies and Warfare in the Middle Ages: the English Experience* (1996); and J.O. Prestwich, *The Place of War in English History 1066–1214* (2004). On the more specific subjects of women and war, and war's effects on the common people, see Sophie Cassagnes-Brouquet, *Chevaleresses: Une chevalerie au féminin* (2013) and Sean McGlynn, *By Sword and Fire: Cruelty and Atrocity in Medieval Warfare* (2008) respectively.

Full references for these and all other secondary works cited may be found in the bibliography.

Translations

Translations of quotations from chronicles and letters that appear in this book are taken from the published English editions of the relevant works where available (as listed in the bibliography), and are my own where not, other than those acknowledged below:

The translation of the letter from William Clito to Louis VI, which appears in Chapter 3 (p. 66), is reproduced from Edmund King, *King Stephen* (2010), p. 34.

The translation of the letter from Brian fitzCount to Bishop Henry, in Chapter 7 (p. 160–1), is reproduced from Edmund King, 'The Memory of Brian fitzCount', *Haskins Society Journal*, 13 (1999), pp. 75–98 (at pp. 89–90); King notes that the letters were first translated into English by H.W.C. Davis in *English Historical Review*, 25 (1910), at pp. 300–3.

The translation of the passage from Henry II's letter to Emperor Frederick Barbarossa, in Chapter 10 (p. 229), is reproduced from Karl Leyser, *Medieval Germany and Its Neighbours, 900–1250* (Hambledon Press, 1982), pp. 216–17.

The translation of Matilda's letters to Thomas Becket and to Louis VII, in Chapter 10 (pp. 232 and 234), are reproduced from the online project 'Epistolae: Medieval Women's Latin Letters'; both the original Latin text and the translations may be found at https://epistolae.ccnmtl.columbia.edu/woman/27.html (accessed 16 August 2018).

The translation of the passage from Stephen of Rouen's *Draco Normannicus* dealing with Matilda's death, in Chapter 10 (p. 236), is unpublished and was carried out by PhD researcher Minji Lee; it is reproduced here by her kind permission.

BIBLIOGRAPHY

Primary sources

Anglo-Saxon Chronicle, trans. James Ingram (London: Everyman, 1912)

Anglo-Saxon Chronicle, ed. D. Whitelock, D.C. Douglas and S.I. Tucker (London: Eyre & Spottiswoode, 1961)

The Anglo-Saxon Chronicle, trans. Michael Swanton (London: J.M. Dent, 1996)

Annales monastici, ed. Henry R. Luard, 5 vols (London: Rolls Series, 1864–69)

The Anonymous of Béthune, *Histoire des ducs de Normandie et des rois d'Angleterre*, ed. F. Michelet (Paris, 1840)

Benoît de Sainte-Maure, *Chronique des ducs de Normandie*, ed. Francisque Michel, 3 vols (Paris: Imprimerie Royale, 1836–44)

— *Chronique des ducs de Normandie, par Benoît, publié d'après le manuscrit de Tours avec les variantes du manuscrit de Londres*, ed. Carin Fahlin, 3 vols (Uppsala: Almqvist & Wiksell, 1951–67)

Chronicles of the Investiture Contest: Frutolf of Michelsberg and His Continuators, trans. T.J.H. McCarthy (Manchester: Manchester University Press, 2014)

Chronicles of the Reigns of Stephen, Henry II and Richard I, ed. Richard Howlett, 4 vols (London: Rolls Series, 1884–89)

The Church Historians of England, trans. Joseph Stevenson, 5 vols (London: Seeleys, 1853–58)

Eadmer of Canterbury, *Historia Novorum*, ed. Martin Rule (London: Rolls Series, 1884)

— *Eadmer's History of Recent Events in England*, trans. Geoffrey Bosanquet (London: Cresset, 1964)

Ekkehard of Aura, *Die Chronik des Ekkehard von Aura*, trans. W. Pflüger (Leipzig: Verlag der Dytschen Buchhandlung, 1893)

— *Chronica*, in *Frutolfi et Ekkehardi chronica necnon anonymi chronica imperatorum*, ed. Franz-Josef Schmale and Irene Schmale-Ott, *Ausgewählte Quellen zur deutschen Geschichte des Mittelalters*, 15 (Darmstadt: Wissenschaftliche Buchgesellschaft, 1972), pp. 124–209, 268–377

English Historical Documents, Vol. 2: 1042–1189, ed. D.C. Douglas and G.W. Greenaway, 2nd edn (London: Eyre Methuen, 1981; orig. 1953)

Florence of Worcester, *The Chronicle of Florence of Worcester*, ed. and trans. Thomas Forester (London: Henry Bohn, 1854)

Frutolf of Michelsberg, *Chronica*, in *Frutolfi et Ekkehardi chronica necnon anonymi chronica imperatorum*, ed. Franz-Josef Schmale and Irene Schmale-Ott, *Ausgewählte Quellen zur deutschen Geschichte des Mittelalters*, 15 (Darmstadt: Wissenschaftliche Buchgesellschaft, 1972), pp. 47–121

Geoffrey Gaimar, *L'Estoire des Engleis by Geffrei Gaimar*, ed. Alexander Bell (Oxford: Anglo-Norman Text Society, 1960)

Geoffrey of Monmouth, *The History of the Kings of Britain*, ed. Michael D. Reeve, trans. Neil Wright (Woodbridge: Boydell Press, 2007)

Gerald of Wales, *Opera*, ed. J.F. Dimock, 8 vols (London: Rolls Series, 1861–91)

Gervase of Canterbury, *The Historical Works of Gervase of Canterbury*, ed. W. Stubbs, 2 vols (London: Rolls Series, 1879–80)

Gesta Stephani, ed. and trans. K.R. Potter with notes and introduction by R.H.C. Davis, Oxford Medieval Texts (Oxford: Clarendon Press, 1976)

Gilbert Foliot, *The Letters and Charters of Gilbert Foliot*, ed. Adrian Morey and C.N.L. Brooke (Cambridge: Cambridge University Press, 1967)

Henry of Huntingdon, *The Chronicle of Henry of Huntingdon*, ed. and trans. Thomas Forester (London: Henry Bohn, 1853)

— *Historia Anglorum*, ed. and trans. Diana Greenway, Oxford Medieval Texts (Oxford: Clarendon Press, 1996)

— *The History of the English People 1000–1154*, trans. Diana Greenway, Oxford World's Classics (Oxford: Oxford University Press, 2002)

L'Histoire de Guillaume le Maréchal, ed. Paul Meyer, 3 vols (Paris: Renouard, 1891–1901)

History of William Marshal, ed. and trans. A.J. Holden, S. Gregory and D. Crouch, 3 vols (London: Anglo-Norman Text Society, 2002–06)

Jocelin of Brakelond, *Chronicle of the Abbey of Bury St Edmunds*, trans. Diana Greenway and Jane Sayers, Oxford World's Classics (Oxford: Oxford University Press, 1989)

John de Marmoutier, *Historia Gaufredi ducis Normannorum et comitis Andegavorum*, in *Chroniques des comtes d'Anjou et des seigneurs d'Amboise*, ed. Louis Halphen and René Poupardin (Paris: Picard, 1913), pp. 170–231

John of Salisbury, *Historia Pontificalis: Memoirs of the Papal Court*, ed. and trans. Marjorie Chibnall (Edinburgh and London: Thomas Nelson, 1956)

— *Policraticus*, ed. Cary J. Nederman (Cambridge: Cambridge University Press, 1990)

John of Worcester, *The Chronicle of John of Worcester 1118–1140*, ed. J.R.H. Weaver (Oxford: Clarendon Press, 1908)

— *Chronicle*, ed. Reginald R. Darlington and Patrick McGurk, trans. Patrick McGurk and Jennifer Bray, 3 vols, Oxford Medieval Texts (Oxford: Clarendon Press, 1995–98)

Kaiserchronik, in *Frutolfi et Ekkehardi chronica necnon anonymi chronica imperatorum*, ed. Franz-Josef Schmale and Irene Schmale-Ott, *Ausgewählte Quellen zur deutschen Geschichte des Mittelalters*, 15 (Darmstadt: Wissenschaftliche Buchgesellschaft, 1972), pp. 212–65

Der Keiser und der kunige buoch, oder die sogenannte Kaiserchronik, Gedicht des zwölften Jahrhunderts, ed. Hans F. Massman (Quedlingburg and Leipzig: Gottfried Basse, 1854)

Matthew Paris, *Matthei Parisiensis historia Anglorum*, ed. F. Maddern (London: Rolls Series, 1866–69)

— *Matthei Parisiensis, monachi Sanctii Albani, chronica majora*, ed. Henry R. Luard (London: Rolls Series, 1884–89)

— *Chronicles of Matthew Paris*, ed. and trans. Richard Vaughan (Stroud: Sutton, 1986)

Orderic Vitalis, *The Ecclesiastical History of England and Normandy*, ed. and trans. Thomas Forester (London: Henry Bohn, 1854)

— *The Ecclesiastical History of Orderic Vitalis*, ed. and trans. Marjorie Chibnall, 6 vols, Oxford Medieval Texts (Oxford: Clarendon Press, 1968–80)

Otto of Freising, *Der Chronik des Bischofs Otto von Freising*, trans. Horst Kohl (Leipzig: Verlag der Dytschen Buchhandlung, 1894)

— *The Two Cities: A Chronicle of Universal History to the Year 1146 AD by Otto, Bishop of Freising*, trans. Charles C. Mierow, foreword and notes by Karl Morrison (New York: Columbia University Press, 2002; orig. 1928)

The Peterborough Chronicle 1070–1154, ed. C. Clark (Oxford: Oxford University Press, 1958)

Ralph of Coggeshall, *Radulphi de Coggeshall chronicon Anglicanum*, ed. J. Stevenson (London: Rolls Series, 1875)

Ralph of Diss, *Radulphi de Diceto opera historica*, ed. William Stubbs (London: Rolls Series, 1876)

Regesta regum Anglo-Normannorum 1066–1154, Vol. III: Regesta Regis Stephani ac Matildis imperatricis ac Gaufridi et Henrici ducum Normannorum, 1135–1154, ed. H.A. Cronne and R.H.C. Davis (Oxford: Clarendon Press, 1968)

Robert de Torigni, *Chronique de Robert de Torigni*, ed. Leopold Delisle, 2 vols (Rouen: Société de l'Histoire de Normandie, 1872–73)

— *The Chronicles of Robert de Monte*, trans. Joseph Stevenson (London: Seeleys, 1855; facsimile repr. Felinfach: Llanerch, 1991)

— *Interpolations: Robert of Torigny's Interpolations in the Gesta Normannorum ducum*, ed. Jean Marx (Rouen: Société de l'Histoire de Normandie, 1914)

Roger of Howden, *Chronica Rogeri de Houedene*, ed. William Stubbs, 4 vols (London: Rolls Series, 1868–71)

— *The Annals of Roger of Hoveden*, trans. Henry T. Riley, 3 vols (London: Henry Bohn, 1853; facsimile repr. Felinfach: Llanerch, 1997)

Roger of Wendover, *Rogeri de Wendover liber qui dicitur flores historiarum*, ed. H.G. Hewlett (London: Rolls Series, 1886–87)

— *Roger of Wendover's Flowers of History*, trans. J.A. Giles, 2 vols (London: Henry G. Bohn, 1849; facsimile repr. Felinfach: Llanerch, 1995–96)

Simeon of Durham, *The Historical Works of Simeon of Durham*, trans. Joseph Stevenson (London: Seeleys, 1855)

— *Historical Works*, ed. Thomas Arnold, 2 vols (London: Rolls Series, 1882–85)

Stephen of Rouen, *Draco Normannicus*, in *Chronicles of the Reigns of Stephen, Henry II and Richard I*, ed. Richard Howlett (London: Rolls Series, 1884–89), vol. 2, pp. 589–762

Suger, *Vita Ludovici grossi regis*, ed. H. Waquet, *Les classiques de l'histoire de France au Moyen Âge*, 11 (Paris: H. Champion, 1929)

— *The Deeds of Louis the Fat*, trans. Richard Cusimano and John Moorhead (Washington, DC: Catholic University of America Press, 1992)

Wace, *Le Roman de Rou*, ed. A.J. Holden (Paris: Picard, 1970)

— *The History of the Norman People: Wace's Roman de Rou*, trans. Glyn S. Burgess (Woodbridge: Boydell Press, 2004)

Walter Map, *De nugis curialium: On Courtiers' Trifles*, ed. and trans. M.R. James, rev. by C.N.L. Brooke and Roger Mynors, Oxford Medieval Texts (Oxford: Clarendon Press, 1983)

William of Malmesbury, *William of Malmesbury's Chronicle of the Kings of England From the Earliest Period to the Reign of King Stephen*, ed. and trans. J.A. Giles (London: Henry Bohn, 1847)

— *Historia novella*, ed. Edmund King, trans. K.R. Potter, Oxford Medieval Texts (Oxford: Clarendon Press, 1998)

— *Gesta regum Anglorum: The History of the English Kings*, ed. and trans. R.B. Mynors, R.M. Thomson and M. Winterbottom, 2 vols, Oxford Medieval Texts (Oxford: Clarendon Press, 1998–99)

William of Newburgh, *The History of English Affairs*, ed. and trans. P.G. Walsh and M.J. Kennedy (Warminster: Aris & Phillips, 1988)

William of Tyre, *A History of Deeds Done Beyond the Sea*, trans. and annotated by Emily A. Babcock and August C. Krey, 2 vols, *Records of Civilization and Studies*, 35 (New York: Colombia University Press, 1943)

BIBLIOGRAPHY

Secondary sources

Abels, Richard, 'Cultural Representation and the Practice of War in the Middle Ages', *Journal of Medieval Military History*, 6 (2008), pp. 1–31

Abels, Richard P. and Bernard S. Bachrach (eds), *The Normans and Their Adversaries at War: Essays in Memory of C. Warren Hollister* (Woodbridge: Boydell Press, 2001)

Aird, William M., *Robert Curthose, Duke of Normandy, c. 1050–1134* (Woodbridge: Boydell Press, 2008)

Allmand, Christopher, 'War and the Non-Combatant in the Middle Ages', in *Medieval Warfare: A History*, ed. Maurice Keen (Oxford: Oxford University Press, 1999), pp. 253–72

— 'The Reporting of War in the Middle Ages', in *War and Society in Medieval and Early Modern Britain*, ed. Diana Dunn (Liverpool: Liverpool University Press, 2000), pp. 17–33

Alsop, J.D., 'The Act for the Queen's Regal Power, 1554', *Parliamentary History*, 13 (1994), pp. 261–76

Anderson, Carolyn B., 'Narrating Matilda, "Lady of the English", in the *Historia novella*, the *Gesta Stephani*, and Wace's *Roman de Rou*: The Desire for Land and Order', *Clio*, 29 (1999), pp. 47–67

Appleby, J.T., *The Troubled Reign of King Stephen* (New York: Barnes & Noble, 1970)

Arnold, Benjamin, *German Knighthood 1050–1300* (Oxford: Clarendon Press, 1985)

Asbridge, Thomas, *The Greatest Knight: The Remarkable Life of William Marshal, the Power Behind Five English Thrones* (London: Simon & Schuster, 2015)

Ayton, Andrew, *Knights and Warhorses* (Woodbridge: Boydell Press, 1994)

Bandel, Betty, 'The English Chroniclers' Attitude toward Women', *Journal of the History of Ideas*, 16 (1955), pp. 113–18

Barber, Richard, *Henry Plantagenet* (Woodbridge: Boydell Press, 2001; orig. 1964)

— *Henry II: A Prince among Princes* (London: Allen Lane, 2015)

Barlow, Frank, *The Feudal Kingdom of England 1042–1216*, 5th rev. edn (Harlow: Longman, 1999; orig. 1955)

Bartlett, Robert, *England under the Norman and Angevin Kings, 1075–1225* (Oxford: Oxford University Press, 2000)

— *Gerald of Wales: A Voice of the Middle Ages* (Stroud: The History Press, 2006)

Bates, David, *The Normans and Empire* (Oxford: Oxford University Press, 2013)

Bates, David and Anne Curry (eds), *England and Normandy in the Middle Ages* (London: Hambledon, 1994)

Bearman, Robert, 'Baldwin de Redvers: Some Aspects of a Baronial Career in the Reign of King Stephen', *Anglo-Norman Studies*, 18 (1996), pp. 19–46

Beeler, John, 'The Composition of Anglo-Norman Armies', *Speculum*, 40 (1965), pp. 389–414

— *Warfare in England, 1066–1189* (Ithaca, NY: Cornell University Press, 1966)

Beem, Charles, *The Lioness Roared: The Problem of Female Rule in English History* (New York: Palgrave Macmillan, 2006)

— '"Greater by Marriage": the Matrimonial Career of the Empress Matilda', in *Queens and Power in Medieval and Early Modern England*, ed. Carole Levin and Robert Bucholz (Lincoln, NB: University of Nebraska Press, 2009), pp. 1–15

Bennett, Judith, *Medieval Women in Modern Perspective* (Washington, DC: American Historical Association, 2000)

Bennett, Matthew (ed.), *The Hutchinson Dictionary of Ancient and Medieval Warfare* (Oxford: Helicon, 1998)

Bernau, Anke, 'Medieval Antifeminism', in *The History of British Women's Writing, 700–1500*, ed. Liz Herbert McAvoy and Diane Watt (Basingstoke: Palgrave Macmillan, 2015), pp. 72–82

Blackburn, Mark, 'Coinage and Currency', in *The Anarchy of King Stephen's Reign*, ed. Edmund King (Oxford: Oxford University Press, 1994), pp. 145–205

Bliese, John, 'The Just War as Concept and Motive in the Central Middle Ages', *Medievalia et Humanistica*, 17 (1991), pp. 1–26

Blumenthal, Ute-Renate, *The Investiture Controversy: Church and Monarchy from the Ninth to the Twelfth Century* (Philadelphia, PA: University of Pennsylvania Press, 1988)

Blythe, James M., 'Women in the Military: Scholastic Arguments and Medieval Images of Female Warriors', *History of Political Thought*, 22 (2001), pp. 242–69

Bournazel, Eric, *Louis VI le Gros* (Paris: Fayard, 2007)

Bradbury, Jim, 'Battles in England and Normandy, 1066–1154', *Anglo-Norman Studies*, 6 (1983), pp. 1–12

— 'The Early Years of the Reign of Stephen, 1135–39', in *England in the Twelfth Century*, ed. D. Williams (Woodbridge: Boydell Press, 1990)

— *The Medieval Siege* (Woodbridge: Boydell Press, 1992)

— *Stephen and Matilda: The Civil War of 1139–53* (Stroud: Sutton, 1996)

— *The Routledge Companion to Medieval Warfare* (London: Routledge, 2004)

Bräuer, Rolf (ed.), *Geschichte der deutschen Literatur: Mitte des 12. bis Mitte des 13. Jahrhunderts* (Berlin: Volk und Wissen, 1990)

Breisach, Ernst, *Historiography: Ancient, Medieval and Modern* (Chicago and London: University of Chicago Press, 1983)

Broughton, Bradford (ed.), *Dictionary of Medieval Knighthood and Chivalry* (London: Greenwood, 1986)

Bumke, Joachim, *Geschichte der deutschen Literatur im hohen Mittelalter* (Munich: dtv, 1990)

Butcher, W.H., 'Historical Sketch of the Castle of Devizes', *Journal of the British Archaeological Association*, 40 (1884), pp. 133–51

Cassagnes-Brouquet, Sophie, *Chevaleresses: Une chevalerie au féminin* (Paris: Perrin, 2013)

Castor, Helen, *She-Wolves: The Women Who Ruled England before Elizabeth* (London: Faber and Faber, 2010)

Chibnall, Marjorie, *The World of Orderic Vitalis* (Woodbridge: Boydell Press, 1984)

— *Anglo-Norman England, 1066–1166* (Oxford: Blackwell, 1986)

— 'The Empress Matilda and Church Reform', *Transactions of the Royal Historical Society*, 5th series, 38 (1988), pp. 107–33

— *The Empress Matilda: Queen Consort, Queen Mother and Lady of the English* (Oxford: Wiley-Blackwell, 1991)

— 'The Charters of Empress Matilda', in *Law and Government in Medieval England and Normandy: Essays in Honour of Sir James Holt*, ed. George Garnett and John Hudson (Cambridge: Cambridge University Press, 1994), pp. 276–98

— 'Empress Matilda and Her Sons', in *Medieval Mothering*, ed. John Carmi Parsons and Bonnie Wheeler (New York: Garland, 1996), pp. 279–94

Clanchy, M.T., *England and Its Rulers, 1066–1272* (London: Wiley-Blackwell, 1983)

— *From Memory to Written Record: England 1066–1307*, 2nd edn (Oxford: Blackwell, 1993; orig. 1979)

Coleman, Janet, *Ancient and Medieval Memories: Studies in the Reconstruction of the Past* (Cambridge: Cambridge University Press, 1992)

Contamine, Philippe, *La Guerre au Moyen Âge* (Paris: Presses Universitaires de France, 1992)

— *War in the Middle Ages*, trans. Michael Jones (Oxford: Blackwell, 1992)

Cormack, Margaret, 'Approaches to Childbirth in the Middle Ages', *Journal of the History of Sexuality*, 21 (2012), pp. 201–7

Coss, Peter, *The Knight in Medieval England 1000–1400* (Stroud: Sutton, 1993)

— *The Lady in Medieval England 1000–1500* (Stroud: Sutton, 1998)

Coulson, Charles, 'The Castles of the Anarchy', in *The Anarchy of King Stephen's Reign*, ed. Edmund King (Oxford: Oxford University Press, 1994), pp. 67–92

— *Castles in Medieval Society: Fortresses in England, France and Ireland in the Central Middle Ages* (Oxford: Oxford University Press, 2003)

Creighton, Oliver, *Castles and Landscapes: Power, Community and Fortification in Medieval England* (London: Equinox, 2005)

Creighton, Oliver H. and Duncan W. Wright, *The Anarchy: War and Status in 12th-Century Landscapes of Conflict* (Liverpool: Liverpool University Press, 2016)

Cronne, H.A., *The Reign of Stephen: Anarchy in England 1135–54* (London: Weidenfeld & Nicolson, 1970)

Crosland, Jessie, *Medieval French Literature* (Oxford: Blackwell, 1956)

Crouch, David, *The Beaumont Twins: The Roots and Branches of Power in the Twelfth Century* (Cambridge: Cambridge University Press, 1986)

— *William Marshal: Court, Career and Chivalry in the Angevin Empire 1147–1219* (Harlow: Longman, 1990)

— *The English Aristocracy 1070–1272: A Social Transformation* (New Haven, CT: Yale University Press, 2011)

— *The Reign of King Stephen: 1135–1154*, 2nd edn (Oxford: Routledge, 2013; orig. 2000)

Dalton, Paul, 'Allegiance and Intelligence in King Stephen's Reign', in *King Stephen's Reign, 1135–1154*, ed. Paul Dalton and Graeme White (Woodbridge: Boydell Press, 2008), pp. 80–97

Dark, Patricia, '"A Woman of Subtlety and a Man's Resolution": Matilda of Boulogne in the Power Struggle of the Anarchy', in *Aspects of Power and Authority in the Middle Ages*, ed. Brenda Bolton and Christine Meek (Turnhout: Brepols, 2007), pp. 147–64

David, Charles Wendell, *Robert Curthose, Duke of Normandy* (Cambridge, MA: Harvard University Press, 1920)

Davis, H.W.C., 'The Anarchy of Stephen's Reign', *English Historical Review*, 18 (1903), pp. 630–41

— 'Henry of Blois and Brian Fitzcount', *English Historical Review*, 25 (1910), pp. 297–303

Davis, R.H.C., 'What Happened in Stephen's Reign', *History*, 49 (1964), pp. 1–12

— *King Stephen*, 3rd edn (Harlow: Longman, 1990; orig. Berkeley: University of California Press, 1967)

Dendorfer, Jürgen, 'Heinrich V: König und Große am Ende der Salierzeit', in *Die Salier, das Reich und der Niederrhein*, ed. Tilman Struve (Cologne, Weimar and Vienna: Böhlau Verlag, 2008), pp. 115–70

— 'Das Wormser Konkordat', in *Das Lehnswesen im Mittelalter: Forschungskonstrukte – Quellenbefunde – Deutungsrelevanz*, ed. Jürgen Dendorfer and Roman Deutinger (Ostfildern: Thorbecke, 2010), pp. 299–328

DeVries, Kelly and Robert Douglas Smith, *Medieval Military Technology*, 2nd edn (Toronto: University of Toronto Press, 2012; orig. Peterborough, Ontario: Broadview, 1992)

Duby, Georges, *The Chivalrous Society*, trans. Cynthia Postan (London: Edward Arnold, 1977)

— *France in the Middle Ages 987–1460*, trans. Juliet Vale (Oxford: Blackwell, 1994)

— 'Women and Power', in *Cultures of Power: Lordship, Status and Process in Twelfth-Century Europe*, ed. Thomas N. Bisson (Philadelphia, PA: University of Pennsylvania Press, 1995), pp. 69–85

Duggan, Anne (ed.), *Queens and Queenship in Medieval Europe* (Woodbridge: Boydell Press, 1997)

Dutton, Kathryn, 'Geoffrey, Count of Anjou and Duke of Normandy, 1129–51', unpublished PhD thesis, University of Glasgow, 2011

Dyer, Christopher, *Making a Living in the Middle Ages: The People of Britain 850–1520* (New Haven, CT, and London: Yale University Press, 2009; orig. 2002)

Erler, Mary and Maryanne Kowaleski (eds), *Women and Power in the Middle Ages* (Athens, GA: University of Georgia Press, 1988)

Fenton, Kirsten A., *Gender, Nation and Conquest in the Works of William of Malmesbury* (Woodbridge: Boydell Press, 2008)

Fleischmann, Suzanne, 'On the Representation of History and Fiction in the Middle Ages', *History and Theory*, 22 (1983), pp. 278–310

Flori, Jean, *La Chevalerie en France au Moyen Âge* (Paris: Presses Universitaires de France, 1995)

— *Chevaliers et chevalerie au Moyen Âge* (Paris: Hachette, 1998)

France, John, *Western Warfare in the Age of the Crusades 1000–1300* (London: University College London Press, 1999)

Fraser, Antonia, *Boadicea's Chariot: The Warrior Queens* (London: Weidenfeld & Nicolson, 1988)

Fuhrmann, Horst, *Germany in the High Middle Ages c. 1050–1200*, trans. Timothy Reuter (Cambridge: Cambridge University Press, 1986)

Gaettens, R., 'Das Geburtsjahr Heinrichs V: 1081 oder 1086', *Zeitschrift für Rechtsgeschichte germanistische Abteilung*, 79 (1962), pp. 52–71

Galbraith, V.H., 'Good and Bad Kings in History', *History*, 30 (1945), pp. 119–32

— *Roger Wendover and Matthew Paris* (Glasgow: University of Glasgow Press, 1970; orig. 1944)

Geldner, Ferdinand, 'Kaiserin Mathilde, die deutsche Königswahl von 1125 und das Gegenkönigtum Konrads III', *Zeitschrift für bayerische Landesgeschichte*, 40 (1977), pp. 3–22

Gillingham, John, 'War and Chivalry in the *History of William the Marshal*', in *Thirteenth-Century England II: Proceedings of the Newcastle-upon-Tyne Conference 1985*, ed. P.R. Coss and S.D. Lloyd (Woodbridge: Boydell Press, 1986), pp. 1–13

— 'Love, Marriage and Politics in the Twelfth Century', *Forum for Modern Language Studies*, 25 (1989), pp. 292–303

— *The Angevin Empire*, 2nd edn (London: Bloomsbury, 2001; orig. 1984)

— 'Civilizing the English? The English Histories of William of Malmesbury and David Hume', *Historical Research*, 74 (2001), pp. 17–43

— 'At the Deathbeds of the Kings of England, 1066–1216', in *Herrscher- und Fürstentestamente im westeuropäischen Mittelalter*, ed. Brigitte Kasten (Cologne, Weimar and Vienna: Böhlau Verlag, 2008), pp. 509–30

— *William II: The Red King* (London: Allen Lane, 2015)

Given-Wilson, Chris, *Chronicles: The Writing of History in Medieval England* (London and New York: Hambledon and London, 2004)

Given-Wilson, Chris and Alice Curteis, *The Royal Bastards of Medieval England* (London: Routledge & Kegan Paul, 1984)

Goodall, John, *The English Castle* (London: Yale University Press, 2011)

Gransden, Antonia, *Historical Writing in England, Vol. I: C. 550–c. 1307* (London: Routledge & Kegan Paul, 1974)

Grant, Lindy, *Blanche of Castile: Queen of France* (London: Yale University Press, 2016)

Green, Judith A., *The Government of England under Henry I* (Cambridge: Cambridge University Press, 1986)

— *The Aristocracy of Norman England* (Cambridge: Cambridge University Press, 1997)

— 'Aristocratic Women in Early Twelfth-Century England', in *Anglo-Norman Political Culture in Early Twelfth-Century England*, ed. C. Warren Hollister (Woodbridge: Boydell Press, 1997), pp. 60–72

— 'Family Matters: Family and the Formation of the Empress's Party in South-West England', in *Family Trees and the Roots of Politics: The Prosopography of Britain and France from the 10th to the 12th Century*, ed. K.S.B. Keats-Rohan (Woodbridge: Boydell Press, 1997), pp. 147–64

— *Henry I: King of England and Duke of Normandy* (Cambridge: Cambridge University Press, 2009; orig. 2006)

— 'Duchesses of Normandy in the Eleventh and Twelfth Centuries', in *Normandy and Its Neighbours, 900–1250: Essays for David Bates*, ed. David Crouch and Kathleen Thompson (Turnhout: Brepols, 2011), pp. 43–60

Hamilton, B., 'Women in the Crusader States: The Queens of Jerusalem, 1100–1190', in *Medieval Women*, ed. D. Baker (Oxford: Studies in Church History, Subsidia I, 1978), pp. 143–74

Hanley, Catherine, *War and Combat 1150–1270: The Evidence from Old French Literature* (Woodbridge: D.S. Brewer, 2003)

Harris, Irene, 'Stephen of Rouen's *Draco Normannicus*: A Norman Epic', *Sydney Studies in Society and Culture*, 11 (1994), pp. 112–24

Hay, David, J., *The Military Leadership of Matilda of Canossa, 1046–1115* (Manchester: Manchester University Press, 2008)

Hicks, Sandy Burton, 'The Impact of William Clito upon the Continental Policies of Henry I of England', *Viator*, 10 (1979), pp. 1–21

Hill, J.W.F., *Medieval Lincoln* (Cambridge: Cambridge University Press, 1948)

Hill, Rosalind, 'The Battle of Stockbridge, 1141', in *Studies in Medieval History presented to R. Allen Brown*, ed. Christopher Harper-Bill, Christopher Holdsworth and Janet L. Nelson (Woodbridge: Boydell Press, 1989), pp. 173–77

Hollister, C. Warren, *The Military Organization of Norman England* (Oxford: Clarendon Press, 1965)

— 'The Anglo-Norman Succession Debate of 1126: Prelude to Stephen's Anarchy', *Journal of Medieval History*, 1 (1975), pp. 19–41

— 'The Magnates of Stephen's Reign: Reluctant Anarchists', *Haskins Society Journal*, 5 (1993), pp. 77–87

— *Henry I* (New Haven, CT, and London: Yale University Press, 2001)

Holt, J.C., '1153: The Treaty of Winchester', in *Colonial England, 1066–1215*, essays by J.C. Holt (London: Hambledon, 1997), pp. 271–90

Hosler, John D., 'Identifying King Stephen's Artillery', *Journal of Conflict Archaeology*, 10 (2015), pp. 192–203

Howard, Michael, *War in European History* (Oxford: Oxford University Press, 1977)

Huffman, Joseph P., *The Social Politics of Medieval Diplomacy: Anglo-German Relations 1066–1307* (Ann Arbor, MI: University of Michigan Press, 2000)

Huneycutt, Lois, 'Female Succession and the Language of Power in the Writings of Twelfth-Century Churchmen', in *Medieval Queenship*, ed. John Carmi Parsons (Stroud: Sutton, 1998; orig. 1994), pp. 189–202

— *Matilda of Scotland: A Study in Medieval Queenship* (Woodbridge: Boydell & Brewer, 2003)

Hyland, Anne, *The Horse in the Middle Ages* (Stroud: Sutton, 1999)

Isaac, Stephen, 'The Problem with Mercenaries', in *The Circle of War in the Middle Ages: Essays on Medieval Military and Naval History*, ed. Donald J. Kagay and L.J. Andrew Villalon (Woodbridge: Boydell Press, 1999), pp. 101–10

Jaeger Reynolds, Rosalind, '*Nobilissima Dux*: Matilda of Tuscany and the Construction of Female Authority', unpublished PhD thesis, University of California, Berkeley, 2005

Jeep, John M., *Medieval Germany: An Encyclopedia* (New York: Garland, 2001)

Johns, Susan M., *Noblewomen, Aristocracy and Power in the Twelfth-Century Anglo-Norman Realm* (Manchester: Manchester University Press, 2003)

Kaeuper, Richard, *Chivalry and Violence in Medieval Europe* (Oxford: Oxford University Press, 1999)

Kealey, Edward, *Roger of Salisbury, Viceroy of England* (Berkeley: University of California Press, 1972)

— 'King Stephen: Government and Anarchy', *Albion: A Quarterly Journal Concerned with British Studies*, 6 (1974), pp. 201–17

Keen, Maurice, *Chivalry* (New Haven, CT: Yale University Press, 1984)

Keene, D., 'Medieval London and Its Region', *London Journal*, 14 (1989), pp. 99–111

King, Edmund, 'Stephen of Blois, Count of Mortain and Boulogne', *English Historical Review*, 115 (2000), pp. 271–96

— 'The Memory of Brian FitzCount', *Haskins Society Journal*, 13 (2004), pp. 75–98

— 'The *Gesta Stephani*', in *Writing Medieval Biography, 750–1250: Essays in Honour of Professor Frank Barlow*, ed. David Bates, Julia Crick and Sarah Hamilton (Woodbridge: Boydell Press, 2006), pp. 195–206

— 'A Week in Politics: Oxford, late July 1141', in *King Stephen's Reign, 1135–1154*, ed. Paul Dalton and Graeme White (Woodbridge: Boydell Press, 2008), pp. 58–79

— *King Stephen* (New Haven, CT: Yale University Press, 2010)

King, Edmund (ed.), *The Anarchy of King Stephen's Reign* (Oxford: Oxford University Press, 1994)

Kuhl, Elizabeth, 'Time and Identity in Stephen of Rouen's *Draco Normannicus*', *Journal of Medieval History*, 40 (2014), pp. 421–38

Leedom, Joe, 'William of Malmesbury and Robert of Gloucester Reconsidered', *Albion: A Quarterly Journal Concerned with British Studies*, 6 (1974), pp. 251–65

Legge, M. Dominica, *Anglo-Norman Literature and Its Background* (Oxford: Clarendon, 1963)

Leyser, Henrietta, *Medieval Women: A Social History of Women in England 450–1500* (London: Weidenfeld & Nicolson, 1995)

Leyser, Karl, *Medieval Germany and Its Neighbours, 900–1250* (London: Hambledon, 1982)

— 'The Anglo-Norman Succession, 1120–5', *Anglo-Norman Studies*, 13 (1990), pp. 225–42

LoPrete, Kimberly, 'The Gender of Lordly Women: the Case of Adela of Blois', in *Studies on Medieval and Early Modern Women*, ed. Christine Meek and Catherine Lawless (Dublin: Four Courts Press, 2003), pp. 90–110

— *Adela of Blois: Countess and Lord (c. 1067–1137)* (Dublin: Four Courts Press, 2007)

Lyon, Ann, 'The Place of Women in European Royal Succession in the Middle Ages', *Liverpool Law Review*, 27 (2006), pp. 361–93

McGlynn, Sean, *By Sword and Fire: Cruelty and Atrocity in Medieval Warfare* (London: Weidenfeld & Nicolson, 2008)

McLaughlin, Megan, 'The Woman Warrior: Gender, Warfare and Society in Medieval Europe', *Women's Studies*, 17 (1990), pp. 193–209

Maschek, Hermann, *Deutsche Chroniken* (Leipzig: Reclam, 1936)

Meuleau, Maurice, *Histoire de la chevalerie* (Rennes: Éditions Ouest-France, 2014)

Meyer, Paul, '*L'Histoire de Guillaume le Maréchal, comte de Striguil et de Pembroke, régent d'Angleterre*: Poème français inconnu', *Romania*, 11 (1882), pp. 22–74

Mirov, Lev, '"Our Beloved Protectress": Lordly Women and Military Activity in the Anglo-Norman and Angevin World of the Twelfth Century', unpublished BA dissertation, Goddard College, 2011

Mollat, Michel, *The Poor in the Middle Ages*, trans. Arthur Goldhammer (New Haven, CT: Yale University Press, 1986)

Morillo, Stephen, *Warfare under the Anglo-Norman Kings 1066–1135* (Woodbridge: Boydell Press, 1994)

Nash, Penelope, *Empress Adelheid and Countess Matilda: Medieval Female Rulership and the Foundations of European Society* (New York: Palgrave Macmillan, 2017)

Newman, Charlotte, *The Anglo-Norman Nobility in the Reign of Henry I* (Philadelphia, PA: University of Pennsylvania Press, 1988)

Nicolle, David, *Medieval Warfare Source Book*, 2 vols (London: Brockhampton Press, 1998)

— *Arms and Armour of the Crusading Era, 1050–1350* (London: Greenhill, 1999; orig. 1988)

Nicolle, David (ed.), *A Companion to Medieval Arms and Armour* (Woodbridge: Boydell Press, 2002)

Norton, Elizabeth, *England's Queens: The Biography* (Stroud: Amberley, 2012)

Oksanen, Elijas, *Flanders and the Anglo-Norman World, 1066–1216* (Cambridge: Cambridge University Press, 2012)

Orme, Nicholas, *From Childhood to Chivalry: The Education of the English Kings and Aristocracy 1066–1530* (London: Methuen, 1984)

— *Medieval Children* (New Haven, CT, and London: Yale University Press, 2001)

Pain, Nesta, *Empress Matilda: Uncrowned Queen of England* (London: Weidenfeld & Nicolson, 1978)

Painter, Sidney, 'The Rout of Winchester', *Speculum*, 7 (1932), pp. 70–75

— *William Marshal: Knight Errant, Baron and Regent of England* (Baltimore, MD: Johns Hopkins University Press, 1933)

— *Medieval Society* (Ithaca, NY: Cornell University Press, 1951)

Papin, Yves D., *Chronologie du Moyen Âge* (Paris: Éditions Jean-Paul Gisserot, 2001)

Partner, Nancy, *Serious Entertainments: The Writing of History in Twelfth-Century England* (Chicago and London: University of Chicago Press, 1977)

Patterson, Robert, 'William of Malmesbury's Robert of Gloucester: A Re-evaluation of the *Historia novella*', *American Historical Review*, 70 (1965), pp. 983–97

— 'Anarchy in England, 1135–54: The Theory of the Constitution', *Albion: A Quarterly Journal Concerned with British Studies*, 6 (1974), pp. 189–200

Poole, A.L., 'Henry Plantagenet's Early Visits to England', *English Historical Review*, 47 (1932), pp. 447–50

Poulet, André, 'Capetian Women and the Regency: The Genesis of a Vocation', in *Medieval Queenship*, ed. John Carmi Parsons (Stroud: Sutton, 1998; orig. 1994), pp. 93–116

Power, Daniel, *The Norman Frontier in the Twelfth and Early Thirteenth Centuries* (Cambridge: Cambridge University Press, 2004)

Prestwich, J.O., 'The Military Household of the Norman Kings', *English Historical Review*, 96 (1981), pp. 1–37

— 'Military Intelligence under the Norman and Angevin Kings', in *Law and Government in Medieval England and Normandy*, ed. G. Garnett and J. Hudson (Cambridge: Cambridge University Press, 1994), pp. 1–30

— *The Place of War in English History 1066–1214* (Woodbridge: Boydell Press, 2004)

Prestwich, Michael, *Armies and Warfare in the Middle Ages: The English Experience* (London: Yale University Press, 1996)

— 'The Garrisoning of English Medieval Castles', in *The Normans and Their Adversaries at War*, ed. Richard Abels and Bernard S. Bachrach (Woodbridge: Boydell Press, 2001), pp. 185–200

Pryor, John H. (ed.), *The Logistics of Warfare in the Age of the Crusades* (Aldershot: Ashgate, 2006)

Reilly, Bernard F., *The Kingdom of León–Castilla under Queen Uracca* (Princeton, NJ: Princeton University Press, 1982)

Richardson, H.G., 'The Coronation in Medieval England: The Evolution of the Office and the Oath', *Traditio*, 16 (1960), pp. 111–202

Rogers, Clifford (ed.), *Oxford Encyclopaedia of Medieval Warfare and Military Technology*, 3 vols (New York: Oxford University Press, 2010)

Rössler, Oskar, *Kaiserin Mathilde* (Berlin: Ebering, 1897)

Russell, Frederick, *The Just War in the Middle Ages* (Cambridge: Cambridge University Press, 1975)

Sassier, Yves, *Louis VII* (Paris: Fayard, 1991)

Saul, Nigel, *A Companion to Medieval England 1066–1485*, 3rd edn (Stroud: Tempus, 2005; orig. 1983)

Saunders, Corinne, 'Women and Warfare in Medieval English Writing', in *Writing War: Medieval Literary Responses to Warfare*, ed. Corinne Saunders, Françoise le Saux and Neil Thomas (Cambridge: D.S. Brewer, 2004), pp. 187–212

Schmale-Ott, Irene, 'Untersuchungen zu Ekkehard von Aura und zur Kaiserchronik', *Zeitschrift für bayerische Landesgeschichte*, 34 (1971), pp. 403–61

Schnith, K., 'Zur Vorgeschichte der "Anarchie" in England, 1135–54', *Historisches Jahrbuch*, 95 (1975), pp. 68–87

— '*Regni et pacis inquietatrix*: Zur Rolle der Kaiserin Mathilde in der "Anarchie"', *Journal of Medieval History*, 2 (1976), pp. 135–58

Searle, E., 'Women and the Legitimization of Succession of the Norman Conquest', *Anglo-Norman Studies*, 3 (1980), pp. 159–70

Slitt, R., 'The Boundaries of Women's Power: Gender and the Discourse of Political Friendship in Twelfth-Century England', *Gender and History*, 24 (2012), pp. 1–17

Spiegel, Gabrielle, *The Past as Text: The Theory and Practice of Medieval Historiography* (London: Johns Hopkins University Press, 1997)

Stacy, N.E., 'Henry of Blois and the Lordship of Glastonbury', *English Historical Review*, 114 (1999), pp. 1–33

Stafford, Pauline, 'The Portrayal of Royal Women in England, Mid-Tenth to Mid-Twelfth Centuries', in *Medieval Queenship*, ed. John Carmi Parsons (Stroud: Sutton, 1998; orig. 1994), pp. 143–68

Staunton, Michael, *The Historians of Angevin England* (Oxford: Oxford University Press, 2017)

Strickland, Matthew, 'Against the Lord's Anointed: Aspects of Warfare and Baronial Rebellion in England and Normandy, 1075–1265', in *Law and Government in Medieval England and Normandy*, ed. George Garnett and John Hudson (Cambridge: Cambridge University Press, 1994), pp. 56–79
— *War and Chivalry* (Cambridge: Cambridge University Press, 1996)
— 'Henry I and the Battle of the Two Kings: Brémule, 1119', in *Normandy and Its Neighbours, 900–1250: Essays for David Bates*, ed. David Crouch and Kathleen Thompson (Turnhout: Brepols, 2011), pp. 77–116
Stringer, Keith, *The Reign of Stephen* (London: Routledge, 1993)
Thomas, Hugh M., 'Violent Disorder in King Stephen's England', in *King Stephen's Reign, 1135–1154*, ed. Paul Dalton and Graeme White (Woodbridge: Boydell Press, 2008), pp. 139–70
Thomson, Rodney M., *William of Malmesbury*, 2nd edn (Woodbridge: Boydell Press, 2003; orig. 1987)
Townsley, Linda, 'Twelfth-century English Queens: Charters and Authority', unpublished MPhil thesis, Trinity College Dublin, 2010
Truax, Jean A., 'Anglo-Norman Women at War: Valiant Soldiers, Prudent Strategists or Charismatic Leaders?', in *The Circle of War in the Middle Ages: Essays on Medieval Military and Naval History*, ed. Donald J. Kagay and L.J. Andrew Villalon (Woodbridge: Boydell Press, 1999), pp. 111–25
Turner, Edward, 'On the Leading Events in the History of the Empress Matilda, Arising out of Her Attempt to Establish Herself on the Throne of England', *Archaeological Journal*, 10 (1853), pp. 302–16
Turner, Ralph V., *Eleanor of Aquitaine: Queen of France, Queen of England* (New Haven, CT: Yale University Press, 2009)
Tyerman, Christopher, *Who's Who in Early Medieval England* (London: Shepheard-Walwyn, 1996)
Urbanski, Charity, *Writing History for the King: Henry II and the Politics of Vernacular Historiography* (Ithaca, NY: Cornell University Press, 2013)
Vale, Malcolm, *War and Chivalry* (London: Duckworth, 1981)
Verbruggen, J.F., *The Art of Warfare in Western Europe in the Middle Ages*, trans. Sumner Willard and S.C.M. Southern (Oxford: North-Holland, 1977)
— 'Women in Medieval Armies', *Journal of Medieval Military History*, 4 (2006), pp. 119–36
Warren, John, *The Past and Its Presenters* (London: Hodder & Stoughton, 1998)
Warren, W.L., *The Governance of Anglo-Norman and Angevin England, 1086–1272* (Stanford, CA: Stanford University Press, 1987)
Watkins, Carl, *Stephen: The Reign of Anarchy* (London: Allen Lane, 2015)
Weller, Tobias, *Die Heiratspolitik des deutschen Hochadels im 12. Jahrhundert* (Cologne: Böhlau Verlag, 2004)
White, Graeme, 'The End of Stephen's Reign', *History*, 75 (1990), pp. 3–22
— 'Earls and Earldoms during King Stephen's Reign', in *War and Society in Medieval and Early Modern Britain*, ed. Diana Dunn (Liverpool: Liverpool University Press, 2000), pp. 76–95
Williams, Alan, 'The Metallurgy of Medieval Arms and Armour', in *A Companion to Medieval Arms and Armour*, ed. David Nicolle (Woodbridge: Boydell Press, 2002), pp. 45–54
Wilson, Peter H., *The Holy Roman Empire: A Thousand Years of Europe's History* (London: Allen Lane, 2016)
Wolf, Armin, 'Reigning Queens in Medieval Europe: When, Where, and Why', in *Medieval Queenship*, ed. John Carmi Parsons (Stroud: Sutton, 1998; orig. 1994), pp. 169–88
Wood, Lynsey, 'Empress Matilda and the Anarchy: the Problem of Royal Succession in Medieval England', *History Studies: University of Limerick History Society Journal*, 11 (2010), pp. 26–37

BIBLIOGRAPHY

Online sources

Anglo-Saxon Chronicle, from Project Gutenberg, online at http://www.gutenberg.org/ebooks/657 (accessed 30 August 2018)

Anglo-Saxon Chronicle manuscript images, from the Luna website, online at http://bodley30.bodley.ox.ac.uk:8180/luna/servlet/view/all/what/MS.+Laud+Misc.+636 (accessed 30 August 2018)

Epistolae: Medieval Women's Letters, online at https://epistolae.ccnmtl.columbia.edu (accessed 16 August 2018)

Foundation for Medieval Genealogy, online at http://fmg.ac (accessed 16 August 2018)

Gallica (Bibliothèque nationale de France), online at http://gallica.bnf.fr (accessed 16 August 2018)

Internet Archive, online at https://archive.org (accessed 16 August 2018)

Monumenta Germaniae Historica, online at http://www.mgh.de (accessed 16 August 2018)

Oxford Dictionary of National Biography, online at http://www.oxforddnb.com (accessed 16 August 2018)

INDEX

All medieval individuals are listed by first name.